Stephen King and American History

This book surveys the labyrinthine relationship between Stephen King and American History. By depicting American History as a doomed cycle of greed and violence, King poses a number of important questions: who gets to make history, what gets left out, how one understands one's role within it, and how one might avoid repeating mistakes of the past. This volume examines King's relationship to American History through the illumination of metanarratives, adaptations, "queer" and alternative historical lenses, which confront the destructive patterns of our past as well as our capacity to imagine a different future. *Stephen King and American History* will present readers with an opportunity to place popular culture in conversation with the pressing issues of our day. If we hope to imagine a different path forward, we will need to come to terms with this enclosure—a task for which King's corpus is uniquely well-suited.

Tony Magistrale is Professor and former chair of the English Department at the University of Vermont where he has taught courses in writing, American literature, and Gothic Studies since 1983 when he returned to the United States after a Fulbright post-doctoral fellowship at the University of Milan, Italy. He has lectured at many universities in North and South America and Western Europe, including Pontificia Catholic University in Santiago, Chile and the Lehrstuhl für Amerikanistik Institute at Universität Augsburg, Germany. He obtained a Ph.D. at the University of Pittsburgh in 1981. He is the author of 23 books, several of them on Stephen King, and over 70 published articles.

Michael J. Blouin is Associate Professor of English and Humanities at Milligan University, where he co-founded and now co-directs the Honors Program. He recently finished a book entitled *Stephen King and American Politics*. His recent publications include "The Vietnamization of Stephen King" (co-authored with Tony Magistrale, *The Journal of American Culture*) and *Mass-Market Fiction and the Crisis of American Liberalism, 1972–2017* (2018). In addition, he served as guest editor for an issue of the *Journal of Popular Culture* entitled "Neoliberalism and Popular Culture" (2018).

Stephen King and American History

Tony Magistrale and Michael J. Blouin

NEW YORK AND LONDON

First published 2021
by Routledge
52 Vanderbilt Avenue, New York, NY 10017

and by Routledge
2 Park Square, Milton Park, Abingdon, Oxon OX14 4RN

Routledge is an imprint of the Taylor & Francis Group, an informa business

© 2021 Taylor & Francis

The right of Tony Magistrale and Michael J. Blouin to be identified as authors of this work has been asserted by them in accordance with sections 77 and 78 of the Copyright, Designs and Patents Act 1988.

All rights reserved. No part of this book may be reprinted or reproduced or utilised in any form or by any electronic, mechanical, or other means, now known or hereafter invented, including photocopying and recording, or in any information storage or retrieval system, without permission in writing from the publishers.

Trademark notice: Product or corporate names may be trademarks or registered trademarks, and are used only for identification and explanation without intent to infringe.

Library of Congress Cataloging-in-Publication Data
A catalog record for this title has been requested

ISBN: 978-0-367-49334-9 (hbk)
ISBN: 978-0-367-49330-1 (pbk)
ISBN: 978-1-003-04578-6 (ebk)

Typeset in Bembo
by Taylor & Francis Books

To our Students at the University of Vermont and Milligan University

Contents

List of figures   viii
Acknowledgements   ix

Introduction: Stephen King and the End of History   1

1   Stephen King and the Romance of American History   11
2   The Pasts of *Pet Sematary*   37
3   The Sutured Histories of *The Shining*   59
4   The Vietnamization of Stephen King   89
5   Outing Stephen King and the Queering of American History   110
6   The Events of 9/11 and Stephen King's Evolving Sense of History   133

Conclusion: The Inconstant Reader   148

Works Cited   159
Index   167

Figures

2.1 Rachel Creed hitches a ride onboard an Orinco truck—note the white 666 marking on the truck's undercarriage—from hell. 51
2.2 Jud Crandall and Louis Creed violate the concentric cairns of the Micmac cemetery in *Pet Sematary*. 52
3.1 The bloody handprint on the back of a ghost woman in Kubrick's *The Shining*. 64
3.2 Dick Hallorann's blood is spilled across a Native American floor mosaic in *The Shining*. 66
5.1 Former Nazi Kommandant Dussander is alone with his thoughts admiring his uniform in *Apt Pupil*. 114
5.2 Dussander's death stare at the conclusion of *Apt Pupil*. 130

Acknowledgements

In addition to our students, who over the years have taught us much about the films and novels of Stephen King, the authors recognize our debt to scholars and colleagues who read drafts of this book when it was in manuscript form and offered us critical help and shaping influence. Sarah Turner, Philip Baruth, Hubert Zapf, Dennis Mahoney, Huck Gutman, George Beahm, Ignacio Lopez-Vicuna, and Steven Bruhm made this book a better version than the authors could have by themselves. Michael's research assistant, Collin Hawley, did excellent work in preparing the film stills. At Routledge, Rhona Carroll was meticulous in her copy-editing work on this manuscript, and the authors are grateful. Any mistakes in the text of this book belong solely to the authors, not to her. Additionally, family and friends stayed the patient course with the authors as we spent many a weekend composing, polishing, and emailing ideas in this book. Our wives, Jennifer Magistrale and Kate Emmerich, in addition to our children, Christopher and Daniel, Willow and Emerson, provided us with the nurturance and child care necessary to write. Friends, Larry Bennett, Ken Wagner, Heather Hoover, Joseph Baker, and Lee Blackburn were constant allies in helping us to complete this project. The University of Vermont supplied Tony with a sabbatical year during which he wrote much of his contribution to this volume; his gratitude for this year is deathless.

We also owe thanks to Carl Sederholm, the editor of *The Journal of American Culture*, for initially publishing and providing valuable revisions to an abbreviated version of Chapter 4 that appeared first in the journal's issue 42:4 (2019): 287–301. This publication was unanimously selected as the winner of the Carl Bode Award for the journal's best article of the year from the Popular Culture Association (2019).

Introduction
Stephen King and the End of History

Perhaps unavoidably, King's account of American History ought to be considered within the broader conversations that have taken place over the course of his career. King's texts, for a variety of reasons, deconstruct the dominant stories that comprise American History, offering in their wake what he believes to be a more dynamic, genealogical, and truthful historical consciousness (history with a lower-case "h"). King, of course, is hardly alone in his challenge of established History. His literary and cinematic works reflect a growing cultural unrest regarding History with a capital "H"—oppressive national narratives that force the subject to behave in specific ways.[1] King's corpus echoes a set of ongoing questions concerning the nation's past: whether it is usable or disposable; whether it conveys a sense of indebtedness or release; whether it offers more hope than despair; and the extent to which violence propels events and/or traps individuals in cyclical patterns.

In King's multiverse, the gears of History seem to be greased always by violence. According to Paul Ricoeur, under a colonial as well as a Marxist mindset, "progress" demands bloodshed, a connection that is made evident in the recurring collapse of empires, the aggressive drive for prestige, and the ever-expansive ethos of empiricism with its thirst for domination. Violence remains "the very well spring of (H)istory." King understands this when he positions the gunslinger Roland in King's *Dark Tower* series within a mythological cycle, unable to escape from the bleak, bloodthirsty purpose that propels him. If History belongs to the most violent actors among us, Ricoeur wonders, what—if anything—is left to be done by non-violent participants? Are they condemned to the passive, marginal status of the yogi? If, in order to make History, one must indulge in one's sanguineous impulses, the only escape from such a state will involve a radically different approach. Like Ricoeur, King worries over the gory paths of American History that run through far-flung theaters of war and continue to linger in the fetid backwaters of small-town America. He expresses concern regarding the brutal concept of History as it has been conceptualized by Right and Left alike: from the Left, his fictional and filmic texts lament the gross human waste produced by the military-industrial apparatus; from the Right, these texts reject counter-hegemonic ideals of revolutionaries that claim to possess unique insight into how History unfolds. It appears as though all that remains for King is the "intermittent grace" of non-violent gestures, enacted by subjects that resign themselves to a world in which they cannot fathom how History's abstract machinations work—and, consequently, forfeit the intent to comprehend (Ricoeur 224, 232). In the end, Roland's saving grace stems from his unwillingness to think about History as a totality. "'It is not your nature,'" he is told, "'to think so far ahead'" (King *Dark Tower I* 293). King's characters thus endure what we will argue to be equally unpleasant fates: either a murderous metanarrative envelops the characters and compels them to kill others (for fuel), or they must learn to float "outside" of this murderous metanarrative (a delusional condition that does precious little to alter its homicidal trajectory).

In the twilight of the twentieth century, a variety of critics subject the latent logic of American History to intensified scrutiny. King's body of work most pointedly parallels the rise of New Historicism: a blurring of the object of historical accounts with its textual record. Generally speaking, New Historicism treats literature as well as history as "fictions in the sense of things made ... shaped by the imagination and by the available resources of narration" (Greenblatt 31). Rather than accept the constitution of History as colonial or Marxist, New Historicists like Catherine Gallagher "posit no fixed hierarchy of cause and effect as they trace the connections among texts" (37). King and the New Historicists tend to frame history as a text like any other, infused with the potentialities (and limitations) of the chosen medium. In a similar way, *The Shining* blurs the line that supposedly divides Jack's scrapbook from the events that color the Overlook's past by placing *how* Jack reads and interprets the story of the hotel very much at the core of King's novel (as well as Kubrick's film adaptation). That is, in both narratives, Torrance's understanding of History configures the legacy of the Overlook hotel into the larger post-war Histories of America to the point where Torrance yearns to be part of the composite dynamic that recreates itself in the simulacrum of the hotel. As it turns out, the Overlook's sense of past is colored by nostalgia and class differentiation to the point where Jack comes to identify with the fantasy reconstruction the hotel offers as a replacement for the mundane realities Jack must face, replete with wife, child, sobriety, and a banal middle-class lifestyle in the Eighties. By the close, Jack reveals himself as a warped New Historicist whose view of time is neither fixed nor objective. Yet, in point of fact, his understanding of History does not actually belong to Jack himself (a vital connection that intimates how King's presumed shift from engrossment in History to a world freed from History may prove illusory). Likewise, in King's *11/22/63*, Jake Epping struggles with writer's block as he concurrently struggles to re-write the past. Once he gives up his ambition to alter the Kennedy assassination, he becomes a better writer, crafting the manuscript that the reader now holds in her hands. With Jake, King at long last resolves Jack's writer's block and—in so doing—finally articulates a full answer that he has been cultivating for nearly fifty years to the stubborn spell of a malevolent American History. In King's corpus, History is not a pre-existing cause that triggers certain effects; instead, history (with a lower-case "h") is metatextual, poetic, and eternally malleable. Rather than remain beholden to a closed past (or future), King invites his reader to re-invigorate the potential fluidity of her own historical consciousness. In the opening lines of *The Tommyknockers*, King neatly sets up the competing visions: "It's either all an accident ... or all fate." The answer to King's binary comes swiftly, when Roberta Anderson stumbles, accidentally, into the discovery of an ancient saucer buried behind her home. Anderson misses the message that King forcefully declares to his reader: "That stumble was the root of the matter; all the rest was *nothing but (H)istory*" (11; emphasis ours). While Anderson goes on to be brainwashed into the pursuit of absolute mastery over History (she, and much of the rest of the town, seeks nothing less than immortality), the reader knows better because she has been trained from the very first page to respect the underlying pattern of history with a lower-case "h." From King's vantage point, a thunderous stumble is the root of it all. Accident compels genuine history—by ruptures, not by some overarching, barbarous determinism or conscious decision-making effort accompanied by bloodshed. Within a single paragraph at the start of *The Tommyknockers*, then, King reduces the delusion of a clear, linear History to rubble.

Once we acknowledge King's tacit alignment with New Historicism, we might consider how his works outline the contours of American History as a point of departure. King's works, at their most innovative, proactively point to "possibilities cut short, imaginings left unrealized, projects half formulated, ambitions squelched, doubts, dissatisfactions" (Greenblatt 74). For example, when read through a New Historicist lens, his multiple depictions of Vietnam—full, as they are, of gaps and omissions—reveal an erasure necessitated by the (aging) ideal of a singular American History. Specifically, the voices of the Vietnamese people as well as their point of view are glaringly absent amidst King's medley of post-war characters. Elsewhere, King's depictions of queerness also benefit greatly from a New Historicist reading: thanks to the generic demand of post-apocalyptic fiction for a Child to be born at the close (a phenomenon that Lee Edelman describes as "reproductive futurism"), King's audience witnesses the interrelated impediments to dominant fictional *and* historical projects. As forthcoming chapters consider, King shrouds in fog the supposed border between past events and their aesthetic renderings, thereby providing an opportunity for us to reconsider the manner in which we tend to make (or unmake) a shared history. If History (with a capital "H") provides a finished product to be imposed upon hapless dupes like Jack in *The Shining*, history (with a lower-case "h") invites an impish, open-ended work in progress to be enjoyed by unrepressed writers, such as Jake in *11/22/63*. Etymologically, although both names appear to stem from the Latin Jacobus, the name Jack derives from ordinariness, from the status of men as tools, while the more contemporary name Jake is slang for satisfaction. The final chapter argues that this "emancipatory" turn from Jack to Jake accelerates in the literary and filmic works released by King in the aftermath of the attacks on September 11, 2001.

But King's submission to the tenets of New Historicism also reveals underlying concerns. In the book's conclusion, we analyze how King's "floating" alternatives to History (unwittingly) augment alarming developments such as the rise of atomizing technologies, the drift into a post-truth society, and the rampant short-termism imposed by financial organizations run amuck.[2] For Elizabeth Fox-Genovese, the convergence of trendy post-structuralist thought—a diverse chorus to which King occasionally lends his influential voice—with historical analysis leads to profound misunderstandings. Fox-Genovese contends that to read history in a purely narrative fashion (as King does) requires losing sight of crucial qualifiers. For one, by its very definition, History is "the sum of reliable information about the past that historians have discovered and assembled." As a result, History is "inescapably structural," a stubborn fact that forces students to attend to tangible sources in order to grapple with real-world consequences. Although Fox-Genovese acknowledges the driving force behind the development of New Historicism, she worries over the state of the baby now suspended in mid-air and surrounded by unwanted bath water. Early on, she acknowledges, "Historians told the stories that legitimated and served the perpetuation of control of the powerful over the weak"; nevertheless, the subsequent backlash of New Historicism helped to open "the way to intellectual anarchism: to each his or her own history" (216–9). In other words, when King interprets American history with a lower-case "h" as pure narrative, an invitation to embrace a sort of hyper-libertarian spin on the subject, he obscures the structural underpinnings of History and buries archival principles that have long been practiced among dedicated Historians. As our book illustrates, in his rush to dismantle History as a tool manipulated by the powerful, *King sometimes empowers the ruling class that he apparently wishes to undermine.*

King's literary and cinematic output errs most egregiously on this front when it adopts the apolitical tenor of some New Historicists. In support of New Historicism, Gallagher contends that historical considerations do not, in all cases, require "political ignition" (46). Fox-Genovese picks up upon Gallagher's risky assertion and counters that human existence simply cannot be stripped of its Historical or political dimensions, insisting that these lenses depend upon one another for their coherence (Fox-Genovese 221). When Jake decides to forfeit his capacity to alter the past (and—concurrently—the future), he forfeits his political agency by throwing up his hands in defeat before what he presents to be the omnipotent, invisible hand of fate. Relearning a lesson that fell upon deaf ears in *The Tommyknockers*, Jake elevates an appreciation for capriciousness, of productive stumbles, while downplaying his initial efforts to plot the development of American society. Although King's distinctive brand of New Historicism appears to *enable* figures like Jake to write their own histories, to "float" above the dictates of bureaucracy (seen in foolish government officials that claim to know the future) or Marxism (seen in the humorless Lee Harvey Oswald and his vicious attempt to redirect History in favor of his fellow communists), in truth, King's revised version of American history actually *disenfranchises* the audience by forcing them to give up political power and accept the unwieldy state of affairs that is actually preferred by elites that persist—out of view—in writing their own History. In light of these circumstances, perhaps there exists a small fragment of merit in Jake's submission to a coherent History that warrants re-evaluation. Nonetheless, as Jack is dead and more and more people opt to float with Jake, "history surges on, but with no promise that past suffering will be redeemed, with no promise of eventual worldwide or even local emancipation, wellbeing, wisdom, or reduction of suffering. *Nihilistic* seems far too thin a term to describe such circumstances" (W. Brown 139; author's emphasis).

In short, even as King attempts to push past what he depicts as an older, oppressive view of History, his works cannot quite shake themselves free from the abject violence that acts as Its well-spring. In fact, in a cruel and ironic twist, King's vision for post-History reveals itself to be equally savage. In two of the early chapters in the book, we revisit *The Shining* and *Pet Sematary*, novels (and film adaptations) that condemn History as a perpetuation of the control of the weak by the powerful few. Jack and Louis Creed are victims of vast Historical forces; they serve as mere pawns in a game that they cannot hope to win. Yet the End of History that these texts faintly imagine—Jake's world, (somehow) liberated from this tyranny via "open roads" and playful counter-histories—fails to generate a model of history driven by a truly non-violent engine.[3] In contrast, King's "alternatives" circle back upon themselves, unconsciously conforming to the twists and turns of a bloody pathway from which they seemingly long to deviate. In response, Slavoj Žižek critiques "pseudo-liberals" like King for confusing subjective violence with structural violence: while King's texts freely attack the violence of "disciplined repressive apparatuses" or "fanatical crowds" (subjective), they are far less willing to acknowledge the "normal" violence that accompanies the status quo of late capitalism (systemic).[4] Said another way, when King pivots from Jack's closed History to Jake's open history, he obscures a continuation of systemic violence that has become quite indiscernible to the majority of his audience members (Žižek, *Violence* 3, 11). His costly move away from traditional modes of understanding History proves to be a pyrrhic victory because the American military machine has only *grown* in parallel with the cultural shift that King aids in advancing. Moreover, at the dawn of the Eighties, it comes as some surprise that the emerging modes of profit-extraction still demand the accumulation of corpses in the name of "progress." Built to encourage a more globalized economy, the modern roadway of *Pet Sematary* unconsciously facilitates the restive and murderous function of prehistoric energies, and in *The Shining*, the increasingly "updated" sensibility of Jack's son, Danny—a son that departs from rigid obedience to the father—exposes how "emancipated" bodies in a global economy are still coopted by an unseen gentry. Whether capitalized or not, whether singular or pluralized, H/history treats Jack as a naïve tool that is shockingly reified (his frozen visage at the close of Stanley Kubrick's film) or utterly atomized (his vaporous remains in the explosive finale of King's original text). Visible or not, these films and mass market paperbacks further secure violence as *the* foundation of American life. Even after things are "corrected" in the time of *11/22/63*, and the reader "satisfied" by her release from the vast force that overlooks American "progress," the violent march of History still comes to collect Jake into its ranks. Although it appears as though Jake emerges from his writer's block with a flourish, and Jack is never more than a typist, in fact the hero of *11/22/63* is simply *a typist of a new variety*: the contract writer that floats in the breeze, the kind of forsaken freelancer that characterizes this precarious new economy. King romanticizes Jake at our peril. We might reasonably conclude, then, that King's evolving sense of H/history has done precious little to modify the innate violence that underwrites it. More often than not, his enormously successful works merely repackage this barbarism into novel forms.

An Overview for the Book

The book before you grapples with several different kinds of histories particularly relevant to the fiction and film adaptations of Stephen King. In doing so, it includes original and detailed interpretations of what are by now considered principal texts in both his cinematic and narrative canons—*The Shining, Pet Sematary, Stand by Me, IT,* and *The Stand*. At the same time, we include close readings of work that has heretofore received little or no attention from the burgeoning field of King studies—including *Hearts in Atlantis, Dreamcatcher, Apt Pupil, Cell, 11/22/63, Lisey's Story, Mr. Mercedes, Under the Dome,* and *The Institute*. This book also refuses to privilege King's source work over film adaptations produced from it. We are convinced that in several instances—e.g., *Stand by Me, The Shawshank Redemption, The Dead Zone, Apt Pupil,* and *The Shining,* among others—the cinematic adaptations are worthy of the same scholarly seriousness that we apply to King's narrative texts, retaining the essence of the novelist's historical vision yet presenting it in a sometimes distilled and intensified form.[5]

Chapter 1 begins with connecting the King multiverse to the Historical sweep of nineteenth-century American literature. While our examination of this broad connection focuses specifically on intertextual links between Thoreau's *Walden* and the film *Stand by Me* and Melville's *Moby-Dick* and *IT*, the chapter also reads King's metageneric texts in light of the major tropes found in nineteenth-century American romanticism, particularly the major traditions associated with transcendentalism, pastoralism, and the gothic. King's main characters stand at an impasse between an ecstatic Oneness with the grand pantheon of History *and* an escape from its out-and-out totality (an individualism that can somehow move outside of this imposing metaphysical force). Indeed, this impasse remains a crux seen throughout King's body of work, and so it can be said to define his unsettled relationship to American History as a whole. This chapter compliments the book's overall thesis by demonstrating that King scholars need to pay attention to (literary) legacy even when it seems fashionable to unyoke ourselves from the oppressive demands of cause-and-effect.

Chapters 2 and 3 revisit two of the most important texts in the King film and narrative canons, *Pet Sematary* and *The Shining*, respectively. While both works have accumulated an enormous body of scholarly attention—Stanley Kubrick's *Shining*, for example, currently maintains a critical bibliography that is longer than film scholarship dedicated to all the cinematic adaptations of King combined—these two chapters are crucial for establishing the context of King's America. Approaches to *Pet Sematary* typically focus on the moral and familial transgressions of the two male characters. Our reading does as well, but in light of an economic capitalism that feeds a diabolical nexus that exists among an archaic Native American mythology, various kinds of white appropriation, the postmodern American penchant for violence and warfare, and a rural Maine highway that metaphorically connects all of these issues. Our analysis of these seminal texts suggests that History, one of modernity's most violent conceptual frameworks, is a prison from which no one—*not even King or Kubrick*—can easily escape.

Chapter 3 on *The Shining* may subvert its production chronology with that of *Pet Sematary*'s original novel and film, but it does so deliberately because we believe that the historical perspective King offers in *Pet Sematary* precedes what we find in King and Kubrick's specifically twentieth-century perspective on American capitalism. The chapter puts equal emphasis on King's novel and Kubrick's film adaptation. While there certainly exist substantial differences between the two works, we are interested in pursuing their similar arcs. Although Kubrick appears drawn to the post-World War I emergence of Modernism, while King references a more contemporary postmodern approach to America's past, film and novel explore the toxic allure of nostalgia and correspondent periods of unfettered capitalism. Both time frames end up consuming Jack Torrance—the modernist Twenties as well as the postmodern Eighties—and present a view of History that is remarkably consistent. Despite their temporal differences, then, Kubrick and King recognize Jack as a tragic figure, out of place and out of time, responding to a set of kindred forces.

King's attitude towards the American past is as complex as it is contradictory. In this book, Chapter 4 encounters the writer's fictionalization of the Vietnam experience, arguably the best illustration of this complexity.

The subject of Vietnam's influence on King, personally and professionally, has never before been addressed. This chapter suggests that Vietnam proved to be King's initiation into the full American experience with its emphasis on the theme of lost innocence. This loss became the archetype for the fiction that would emerge in the decades following the fall of Saigon: King's sensitivity to the potential that was squandered by the anti-war movement's dissolution as well as his realization that this historical moment was responsible for psychic wounds to the nation that have not yet healed. Even more specifically, from Vietnam's crucible emerged King's distrust of institutions, politicians and the military-industrial nexus certainly, but also his general indictment of adulthood as corrupt and duplicitous, willing to abuse and sacrifice its children in order to maintain a communal status quo. The Vietnam experience was the impetus for shaping central issues that found their way into the adult writer's political ideology and his critique of American priorities. In regards to the collective memory of the conflict in Vietnam, King's American History proves cannibalistic, regurgitating a familiar array of tropes while suppressing unsavory stories that remain mostly untold. Only when we turn to history with a lower-case "h," according to King, can we begin to see Vietnam through a plurality of perspectives.

Just as the impact of Vietnam has been overlooked by critics seeking to understand the historical disillusionment at the crux of King's critique of postmodern America, King scholars have not yet addressed the writer's treatment of homosexuality. Chapter 5 opines that, in contradiction to a Leftist and inclusive ideology found elsewhere in King's corpus, the monsters that populate his novels and film adaptations are often coded "queer" even when their sexualities remain indeterminate. Providing close alternative readings of *Apt Pupil, IT*, and Frank Darabont's screenplay adaptations of King's prison movies, this chapter oscillates between King's treatment of the monster as homosexual and the alternative reading of homophobia as monstrous. The chapter concludes in the bifurcated viewing of homosexuality as a stereotyped portrait of evil and, conversely, as a rejection of the heteronormative abuse typically found in King's fictional marriages. Here we find a brutal, heteronormative History that vilifies difference as well as (if we are willing to develop inventive acts of reclamation) a "queer" account of American history driven by something other than cultural assumptions tied to the logic of procreation.

The last chapter in this volume focuses upon King's most recent publications, those narratives that appeared after and oftentimes in response to 9/11. Chapter 6 interprets King's most recent work as offering possible alternatives to the cyclic destruction presented in his earlier narratives. Rather than viewing American History as a repetitive loop that dictates the lives of characters in *Pet Sematary, The Shining, Hearts in Atlantis, Dreamcatcher*, and *The Stand*, King's post-millennium novels sometimes offer an auxiliary paradigm, a blueprint for decamping from his earlier entropic cycles. In novels such as *Cell, 11/22/63, Mr. Mercedes*, and *Under the Dome*, for example, protagonists survive the cataclysm of 9/11 by recognizing and accepting the ambiguous status of their postmodern condition. These characters become "anti-Historians" who must adapt to uncertainty and randomness, accepting that they inhabit a broken, volatile world. A core protagonist in the King post-9/11 canon is the figure of the hard-boiled detective—most notably Bill Hodges—who becomes one such "anti-Historian," compelled by a bare instinct to survive as well as a refusal to surrender to the overwhelming forces of History that once consumed Jack and Louis.

Chapter 6 points the way to this book's conclusion insofar as it highlights the evolution of King's treatment of American History—from the dystopian enclosures featured in *The Shining* and *Pet Sematary*, to the more open and dynamic histories of *11/22/63* and *The Institute*. Without a doubt, the American record for genuine change, for forgiveness, for not repeating the mistakes of the past, is hardly auspicious. At the time of this writing, the Trump administration seems intent on provoking yet another war in the Middle East, this time with Iran. While recognizing the cadence of this grim march, King's fiction also offers his Constant Readers faith that the world and individuals might reshape themselves, break free of the degeneration that defines America's past (a History characterized by violence and selfishness) to something humbler and more in harmony with the sanctity of the individualism that King has long extolled. While his successes on this front deserve our attention, we must not lose sight of his failures. Stephen King's literary and cinematic corpus—with its inability to shake loose, in a substantial way, from the grip of a bestial History—has critical lessons to impart to an audience racing madly toward its own end.

Notes

1 On this point, King—however inadvertently—echoes the (problematic) thesis advanced by Francis Fukuyama that the collapse of communism in 1989 marks the End of History, which does not mean an end to "the occurrence of events … but History: that is, history understood as a single, coherent, evolutionary process" (Fukuyama xii). Because liberal democracy triumphs over all takers, Fukuyama contends, we need no longer rely upon a vast metaphysical force to make sense of where humanity has come from (or where it is headed next).
2 Wendy Brown notes, "The common instigators of the intellectual and political challenges to progress are certain concrete historical phenomena that include, *inter alia*, the contemporary character of capitalism" (W. Brown 8).
3 The absence of this alternative reflects a significant trend in American life. Thomas Merton discusses how, in America society, "an image of non-violence … is largely negative … an unhealthy kind of idealism … a serious and mysterious potential threat to the entire nation insofar as they bear witness to a radically different way of looking at life" (Merton 35).
4 Slavoj Žižek writes, "While they fight subjective violence, (pseudo-liberals) are the very agents of the structural violence which creates the conditions for the explosions of subjective violence. The same philanthropists who give millions for AIDS or education in tolerance have ruined the lives of thousands through

financial speculation and thus created the conditions for the rise of the very intolerance that is being fought" (Žižek, *Violence* 36–7).
5 In short, we do not wish to conflate the mediums of literature and film, and we remain well aware of their formal distinctions (King's film adaptations, for example, are certainly corporate efforts, not the direct products of a solitary writer). Instead, we endorse Simon Brown's description of Stephen King *as a brand*, one that has more or less retained an overall sense of coherence over the years. For an expanded discussion of this important classification, see Brown's excellent study *Screening Stephen King: Adaptation and the Horror Genre in Film and Television*.

1 Stephen King and the Romance of American History

While Stephen King's works attend at length to the disentangling of the individual from the ennui and destructive tendencies of "modern progress" (that most American of themes), like so many of his forbearers in American literature, his fiction also expresses sincere doubts about the ultimate success of such attempts. Nonetheless, it has become rather fashionable of late to contemplate the metageneric qualities of King's multiverse, a trend that often presumes a breakage with (or, at least, ironic distance from) American literary History. Given the polymorphic character of his prose, a number of critics contend that King practices Harold Bloom's poetic "swerve" to avoid the oppressive legacy of his literary ancestors.[1] While we do not question the merit of these analyses—indeed, King's historical moment is mired in this sort of metageneric work—we instead wish to consider King as the inheritor of a set of preoccupations from America's literary past. Specifically, the generic confusion at the heart of King's fiction reflects battle lines drawn nearly two hundred years ago around the tenets of American Romanticism. In this chapter we place King's fiction in conversation with figures less typically associated with it, such as Henry David Thoreau and his contemporary, Herman Melville. By so doing, we can better situate King's ongoing treatment of American History as a Romance.

For nearly half a century, King has been telling stories that are specifically about America.[2] In *The Stand, The Dark Tower*, and *The Mist* he has warned America about its dark fascination with the matrix of technology and militarism; in *Dolores Claiborne, Gerald's Game, Bag of Bones,* and *Rose Madder*, he has revealed uncomfortable truths about patriarchal abuse and the secret power of female friendships; in *Rita Hayworth and The Shawshank Redemption* and *The Green Mile* he has indicted America's antiquated and punitive prison system and its institutional web of internal corruption; and in *The Shining* and *Doctor Sleep* he has examined the inequities and contradictions inherent in capitalism, supplying fictional analogies that hinge on a tradeoff between success in America's corporate hierarchy and the sacrifice of family and personal ethics. In an interview twenty-six years ago, King expresses a conscious awareness of his canon's relevance to American institutions and society: "The work underlies again and again that I am not merely dealing with the surreal and the fantastic but, more important, using the surreal and the fantastic to examine the motivations of people and the society and institutions they create" (Magistrale, *Second Decade* 15). The King brand, in other words, remains heavily indebted to an American literary tradition, and so it behooves us to interrogate this debt further by placing King in dialogue with enduring narrative concerns, such as those considered in American Romanticism. If there is a narrative design that typifies the King story line, it centers upon *gothic disruption*: King characters regularly find themselves in a precarious situation that spirals out of control. In the specific context of the American pastoral, a place of beauty and harmony is threatened by the imposition of a reality (often some type of pollution) alien to the pastoral dream. Thus, the sweetness of the Territories in *The Talisman* are in danger of becoming as corrupt as the Blasted Lands, the placid lake atmosphere in *The Mist* is fractured by the results of military experimentation from the Arrowhead Project, and the serenity of small-town America is overwhelmed by supernatural intrusions bearing evil agendas in *'Salem's Lot, Needful Things, Storm of the Century* (and several other novels). King remains at home with this literary History as well as eager to evade its grasp.

The cinematic adaptations of King's fiction—at this point hovering over a hundred—address similar themes. These adaptations frequently manage to make money, and some of the films have now entered into Hollywood's pantheon of exceptional work. Rob Reiner's rendition of King's novella *The Body* (1982) into the film *Stand by Me* (1986) has long been recognized as a brilliant *Bildungsroman*, a coming of age narrative where four boys, like their larger nation, are portrayed on the cusp of great changes. Like the novella, Reiner's film portrays a turbulent American History—a Romantic force field through which many of the nation's cultural expressions must pass. Arthur W. Biddle may have been the first to interpret the narrative in mythic terms, arguing that the journey to view Ray Brower's dead body forces the film's main protagonist, Gordie Lachance, to "undergo a series of trials that bring him to selfhood, to an identity both as a young man and as a writer" (Biddle 83). Relying heavily on Joseph Campbell's archetypal rites of passage as detailed in *The Hero with a Thousand Faces* that define transitional elements from one life stage to another, Biddle traces the maturation process that Gordie undergoes during the last days of an adolescent summer. Most of the criticism that has followed Biddle likewise addresses the text as a coming-of-age story. Joeri Pacolet and Leonard G. Heldreth, for example, both view the novella as an autobiographical portrait of King's emergence as a writer of consequence: "To see Gordon Lachance as Stephen King is tempting ... that the search for and unification of identity should be a major theme of a writer as American as Stephen King is not surprising" (Heldreth 72–3). Mark Browning addresses the film adaptation as "a series of tests that the boys must overcome" in order to avoid becoming a parallel version of Ace Merrill and his gang, "literalizing what will happen to them if their lives do not change" (113). And Jeffrey A. Weinstock reads both film and novella as a confrontation with the reality of death: Gordie's obsession with viewing the corpse of Ray Brower forces him to confront the reality of his brother's death and then to "appreciate both the presence of death in life and the wondrousness of life amid mindless destruction" (48). What each of the critics who have written about either the novella or the film fails to supply, however, is a broader cultural context for interpreting their subject's decision to enter into the woods in the first place. While Gordie does not share Thoreau's confidence in going "to the woods because I wished to live deliberately, to front only the essential facts of life," he does recognize early on that "going to see a dead body maybe shouldn't be a party" and consequently learns "what [the woods] had to teach" (Thoreau 304). Gordie certainly follows an experiential learning curve, but it's important to note that its unfolding takes place within a specifically *American* experience.

Like Reiner's film, the novel *IT* (also 1986) chronicles a group of young people that come of age by wandering into the wild Barrens at the edge of Derry, Maine. These youths too must come to terms with the grotesque inheritance that they share as well as the unique singularities that empower them to transcend the corruption of their provincial hometown. In turn, both *IT* and the film *Stand by Me* recycle the concerns of nineteenth-century American Romantics by worrying over the confines of a world that grows smaller by the day while contemplating potential release from physical and psychic prisons. Just as Thoreau and Melville wrestle with a claustrophobic modernity (as well as the difficulties of overcoming such an oppressive climate), King contemplates an exit strategy from the gravitational pull of an American History that orients his own suffocating society. How, he asks us, can we preserve a vital sense of connection to a joint story—without, in the process, becoming mere pawns within a predetermined metanarrative? How can we maintain a moral consciousness beyond one imposed by state or industry—without, in the process, losing any semblance of common ground? Just as these themes surface repeatedly in the imaginary wildernesses of *Walden* (1854) and *Moby-Dick* (1851), they surface once more in King's neo-pastoral efforts, appearing in the liminal space of the Romance. It is in this ambivalence that individual and collective H/histories clash as well as converge. It is back to this liminal space that our book must voyage in order to comprehend King's tormented dialectic of History (with a capital "H") and history (with a lower-case "h").

In short, this shift in focus allows us to reconsider King's literary ancestry, which is to say, his link to the concerns of his forefathers (a reappraisal of King as an inheritor rather than as strictly as a postmodern iconoclast). More important still, this shift underscores King's uniquely Romantic vision of American History, defined by the impasse between a stifling History ("progress") and the illusion of decampment from that History "into the woods" (or "out to sea").[3] Like Thoreau and Melville before him, King never loses his interest in the murky middle: the pastoral vision and its disintegration; lyrical nature and its hidden horrors; the maturation of the individual and the individual's crushing loss of innocence. That is, although at times King calls into question the strangulating aspects of American History, his literary and subsequent cinematic preoccupations establish a vital sense of continuity with the giants on whose shoulders he stands.

Stand by Me and the American Pastoral Tradition

One of the elements responsible for the popularity of Reiner's *Stand by Me* is how the film adheres closely to themes and tropes that are recognizably American. A defining characteristic of American Romanticism as well as the later artworks that it spawned is the confrontation between boyhood and tragedy. The ensuing loss of innocence serves to temper and redefine masculinity as well as American nationhood. It is a personal *and* a public History, one that threatens to destroy the individual while simultaneously challenging him to develop and grow. There are several classic American narratives that bear close similarities to *Stand by Me*. The importance of Mark Twain's *Huck Finn*, for example, is difficult to deny, as both narratives grapple with children on death-haunted journeys forced to process overwhelming adult realities. As such, Twain, King, and Reiner highlight a gap that exists between the decency of an adolescent value system and the violence and hypocrisy associated with adults. Additionally, *Stand by Me* bears similarities with other classic texts from the American literary canon. Like so many of Hawthorne's stories—"Young Goodman Brown," "Roger Malvin's Burial," and "My Kinsman, Major Molineau" come to mind immediately—it is a narrative journey into the woods that confronts and challenges the naïveté of these respective young protagonists; the events they experience radically reshape their identities. *Stand by Me* also owes something to Hemingway's Nick Adams stories insofar as they are all evidence of males undergoing a loss of innocence via personal interactions with the nature of tragedy. America's pastoral imagination continually contrasts urban corruption with the promise of relief in untainted wilderness beyond the edge of the city. Indebted to figures as diverse as Hawthorne and Hemingway, King conducts his characters "into the woods" to confront internal struggles that stew just below the surface.

Within King's own oeuvre, *The Girl Who Loved Tom Gordon* provides another example of the pastoral themes that are so central to American literature. In keeping with that subset of the American narrative, *Girl* is a relentless and unmodulated portrait of the wilderness. Trisha McFarland is beset by every manner of wild thing that calls the woods home—from insects to a huge black bear—when she becomes lost in the Maine wilderness: "The woods were filled with everything you didn't like, everything you were afraid of and instinctively loathed." Like the adult male relationships in *Stand by Me*, the dark corners of the natural world essentially provide a mirror to Trish and the domestic situations in both texts—alcoholism, parental neglect, and self-absorbed brothers. The protagonists in these narratives are equally lost in their respective places; Trish even assumes the name that Gordie calls himself in *Stand by Me*, as she refers to herself as "The Invisible Girl" because she is ignored by a distracted family, which ultimately results in her wandering off to escape their fighting and becoming lost in the dense forest. (*Girl* 56, 22). As in those moments in *Stand by Me* when the boys find themselves terrified by the distant howls of wolves or immersed in the leech pool, Trish finds herself far removed from any pastoral idyll. And just as the boys must learn to rely on interpersonal substitutes in order to fill the void created by paternal and fraternal abuse and neglect, the mythologized title figure Tom Gordon serves as a surrogate father figure who replaces Trish's biological father and his self-pitying immersion into the throes of divorce and alcoholism, abandoning his daughter to nature's hostile grip. Both the boys in *Stand by Me* and Trish must find replacement figures to enable their mutual survival.

Yet the most provocative (and perhaps least obvious) connection that *Stand by Me* shares with the American Romance tradition may well be Thoreau's *Walden*. One explanation for why Reiner chose to relocate the movie to an Oregon setting rather than keep it in Maine, especially in light of fact that King's fictional Castle Rock is very definitely located in central Maine, was to heighten the pastoral beauty of the scenic backdrops, present particularly in the long helicopter shots when the boys cross an elevated train trestle. While central Maine retains its share of scenic beauty, its heavily forested areas feature a different kind of grandeur than the sweeping vistas Reiner's crew found in Oregon. This is an important consideration as the film makes a highly conscious effort to maintain a contrast between the lyricism of the boys' journey into nature—the sapphire blue Royal River, stunning lake views, and open expanses of forest and summer sky—and those moments where nature reveals its less attractive, darker side: the wolves howling at night, the forlorn loneliness of Brower's remains left entangled in a thicket of blueberries, and, of course, the slimy leech pool.[4] In these moments, the concept of American "progress" subsumes the (shrinking) individual, threatening to crush her where she stands. Thoreau references similar moments in nature, relishing the various beauties available in the woods and at the pond—indeed, *Walden* features the German word for forest (*Wald*) in its title—but these appreciations are tempered by the severity of *Walden*'s winter chapters and, even more tellingly, by the proximity of his cabin to the Fitchburg railroad. Readers are introduced to the railroad through Thoreau's loaded question, "who buil[t] the railroad?" His sobering answer is that human lives are constantly being sacrificed in exchange for the "advance" of American History: "Each one is a man, an Irishman, or a Yankee man. The rails are laid on them, and they are covered with sand, and the cars run smoothly over them … We do not ride upon the railroad; it rides upon us." Thoreau's conscious awareness of the locomotive's presence "penetrates my woods summer and winter, sounding like the scream of a hawk." The assault of the machine is not only audible, but visual and olfactory as well, since the train engine disrupts the solitude that Thoreau values so deeply: "The iron horse makes the hills echo with his snort like thunder, shaking the earth with his feet, and breathing fire and smoke from his nostrils" (306, 321–2). Leo Marx reminds us that "There is scarcely a chapter [in *Walden*] in which Thoreau does not mention seeing or hearing the engine or walking 'over the long causeway made for the railroad through the meadows'" (260). The Fitchburg railroad serves as an emblem, much to Thoreau's dismay, of the encroachment of the machine age, the globalization of commerce as it extends its reach into the isolated sanctity of Walden Pond, as the railroad's indifference towards the "pastoral life whirled past and away." What were once "unfrequented woods on the confines of towns, where once only the hunter penetrated by day," has been invaded with the relentless punctuality and pervasiveness of business, "shouting [its] warning to get off the track" (Thoreau 326). In parallel with the climactic scene aboard the locomotive in Hawthorne's *The House of the Seven Gables*, Thoreau reflects a preoccupation among American Romantics with the liminal area between "progress" and the serene (as well as stationary) natural world, against which such "progress" must be foregrounded. The story of the railway in Concord, then, reveals itself to be the story of American History itself: a dizzying spectacle that overwhelms us in tension with the desire to abscond, to retreat back into our idiosyncratic, individualized nests.

In *Stand by Me*, there are several visual images that are constructed to contrast the pastoral ideal with the machine age. Most obvious is the fact that Ray Brower is killed by a moving train at the exact moment he is in the woods picking blueberries. The contrast between an adolescent boy enjoying the last days of summer vacation and the steam engine that takes his life, and never bothers subsequently to stop and render any kind of aid to the child victim, or the mangled body that has been knocked out its Keds (knocked out of his childhood), could not be starker. The scene in which a solitary Gordie is pictured early in the morning reading a comic book while sitting on one of the train tracks likewise contains strong echoes of *Walden*. A doe appears to the boy's right and the two share a tranquil moment alone in the forest before the deer walks away from the encounter. Child and animal commune with one another; neither is afraid of the other (nor has any reason to be). And while Gordie fails to make mention of it— he informs the viewer that until this point he has never mentioned the bucolic moment to anyone else—their silent communication is, as Thoreau experiences on a daily basis, punctuated by the arrival of a train that disrupts the scene. In fact, the train's interposition separates Gordie from the doe just as it separates the viewer from Gordie's sleeping friends, who are situated on the other side of the tracks and are awakened by the train's arrival as it passes between them and the camera. The languid passage of time during Gordie's commune with nature sharply contrasts with the ever-punctual train (we might gesture ahead to the train that appears in King's novel *Pet Sematary*, busily dropping off dead soldiers from the war like so many warming bottles of milk).

Stand by Me comes closest to paralleling events that take place in *Walden* in the train trestle scene. For his part, Thoreau always feels compelled to "get off the track and let the cars go by" (326). He doesn't have to mention that his body would be placed in immediate physical jeopardy should he refuse to comply with the insistent rite of passage demanded by the railroad. In the film's trestle scene, Vern and Gordie find themselves literally trapped by the steam engine that has already killed one child who lingered too close to its tracks. Throughout the film, the train always comes from the direction of Castle Rock, as if it were sent from the town in pursuit of wayward boys trying to escape. Before the train is even visible in the trestle montage, we are made aware of its presence by the thick black plume of smoke that it emits from behind a clump of trees. This moment in the film takes the viewer immediately back to the smoke of the locomotive in *Walden*, which puts Thoreau's field in shade. As Leo Marx has traced the emergence of the machine as an alien force intruding on the American pastoral landscape, "More often than not in these episodes, the machine is made to appear with startling suddenness" (15). In both contexts, the locomotive is a metaphor of environmental degradation (its smoke lingers in the clean air long after it passes by in Teddy's earlier abortive train dodge scene) that helps to give birth, in King's lifetime, to Earth Day and the Green Party. As the engine bears down relentlessly on the surprised and terrified boys, they are left with the choice of jumping to their deaths off the narrow bridge, or else racing the train to the other side in time to avoid being hit. As in *Walden*, what was once a pastoral moment, in which the boys are pictured alone in the sanctuary of nature's solitude, turns suddenly horrific: the diegetic sound of a loon that opens the frantic scene is displaced by the screams of the boys and the all-encompassing metallic cacophony of the train itself. The imposition of machine technology into the landscape is a counterforce to the realization of the American pastoral design, creating an interruption in the pursuit of idyllic pastoralism. In fact, the engineer driving the train appears to find a sadistic delight in adding drama to an already dangerous situation: ringing the train's bell and whistle frantically as his machine takes direct aim and thunders down at the hapless boys in front of him, all the while refusing to make any effort to apply its brakes or slow down. And, to some degree, the spectator may share in this perverse delight, just as Clifford revels in undisciplined life upon the rails in Hawthorne's *House*, or Thoreau *needs* the exhilaration of modern life as a counterpoint to his pre-industrial fantasy. Clearly, Reiner and King view the train metaphorically, not only as a symbol of the Castle Rock universe the boys seek to escape, but also as the implacable pursuit of American industrial "progress" threatening a pristine landscape. American History rushes onward, utterly indifferent to the carnage that It creates.

Just as Thoreau recognizes that the train signals the dawning of the new industrial age in the nineteenth century, Reiner's film employs locomotives as well as automobiles as intrusions into a pastoral ideal found in the surrounding wilderness. The motion machine is an implacable force in *Stand by Me* that is aligned metaphorically with the hard-hearted value system in place in Castle Rock society. These hulking engines of destruction embody the machinelike personalities of the Castle Rock adults, who are always prepared to inflict damage with their fists. Ace behaves in a similar manner to the train itself: a relentless force that will not stop and appears to direct his fury at those who are most vulnerable. Evidence of the destructive nature of the machine age—indeed, the destructive nature of American History in its entirety—is paralleled with the intransience and oppression associated with Castle Rock. Biddle suggests, "On the surface, the sterility of Castle Rock is a result of the prolonged drought and extraordinary heat of the summer. But on a deeper level, it is the aridity of a community that cannot love" (86). The destructive nature of the patriarchy is present in all King's texts set in Castle Rock, but fathers are particularly pernicious in *Stand by Me*. Chris Chambers feels the weight of his family's infamous reputation bearing down on him, certain that he will never be able to rise above his caste and escape the destiny that threatens to trap him in Castle Rock. Gordie's father views his only remaining son as "invisible," just as the train refuses to recognize the presence of Gordie and Vern on the tracks directly in front of the engineer. And although Teddy worships his father as a war hero, the latter reciprocates by burning his son's left ear on a hot stove. Milo's junkyard, littered with the rusting hulks of discarded automobiles and pickup trucks, exists at the outermost edge of Castle Rock: the last outpost of civilization that also comes to represent the symbolic center of the town. It contains the detritus of small-town America—discarded machinery that no one wants. A befouled and hostile place, it is the equivalent of Norris's dump heaps in *McTeague* or Fitzgerald's ash-heaps in *The Great Gatsby*, embodying the values of the throw-away culture that produced it. Milo and his dog ("sic balls, Chopper") reign over it with an aggressive hostility reflective of the adults, particularly the fathers and older brothers present in this movie, and their general antipathy toward their own children and siblings. Milo claims to "know all your fathers, and they are all going to get a call" regarding their trespassing sons in the junkyard, except for Teddy's father, whom Milo labels a "looney." Milo serves as the town Cryer at the edge of town; he knows the History of paternal abuse in Castle Rock and seeks to extend it through his own threat of violence against Teddy, thus maintaining the power of the town's patriarchy. The fact that Mr. Duchamps currently resides in an insane asylum, most likely the result of PTSD from his experience of "storming the beach at Normandy," elicits only derision from Milo, who is incapable of recognizing that an asylum in Castle Rock is merely the endpoint of a persistently violent American History, a junkyard for broken human psyches.

This carnage of History resembles Walter Benjamin's poetic image of debris being blown backwards. The cars that are associated repetitively with Ace and his gang are destined for Milo's junkyard, but until then they are employed to terrorize working men hauling wood on the backroads, to plunder rural mailboxes, and to drag race in the middle of the afternoon. In the hands of Ace and his fellow delinquents, automobiles are treated recklessly and always accompanied by drivers consuming open bottles of beer. The most destructive example of testosterone-driven bravado is evinced in the scene where Ace and Vince play chicken against each other down the highway. The fact that neither male is willing to fall back when a truck hauling firewood appears on Ace's side of the road indicates both the level of stubborn stupidity at work in the behavior of these men-children as well as the destructiveness of their masculine competitive spirit. In other words, they are both victims of automotive terrors *and* their human equivalent. Aligned with the posturing of the American Romantics, they pilot an unyielding History that races wildly out of control as they position themselves (improbably) behind the figurative wheel, staking a claim to a sort of hyper-individualism that is imagined to be guiding their fate. Ace and his gang represent the default position for teenagers in Castle Rock. Teddy, who will spend time in prison and remain a lost boy as an adult, will likely soon become part of Ace's world. And even Chris cannot escape Castle Rock ultimately, as his death is caused by two men fighting who might well be members of Ace's gang. The automobiles in this film are used and misused, a fact that Gordie and his friends appear to recognize intuitively in their deliberate decision to hike the distance to Brower's body instead of driving. They appear to understand that the journey through the wilderness itself is a part of the reason for their undertaking it, and that employing a car to get there is "cheating." Further, access to the use of cars separates Ace's gang from the twelve-year-old boys who do not yet possess driving licenses. As such, *The Stand* highlights an essential schism that exists between children and adults (although the film makes it clear that this gap is narrowing quickly insofar as Gordie and his friends appear on the cusp of entering into the adult world with all its particular liabilities and complications). Like many nineteenth-century Romantics, King imagines American History to be an immoveable force fueled by bloodshed—a force that the boys channel as well as repudiate as they each "come of age."

While we certainly would not suggest that all the cinematic adaptations of King's work expose America's failings to the same degree and with consistent level of insightfulness, the best of his adaptations—including Reiner's *Stand by Me*—recognize that at the heart of King's fictional universe is a profound awareness of the most deep-seated American anxieties regarding their latent linkage to a national H/history. No less than Hawthorne and Thoreau more than a century earlier, King serves as a moralist for our era, concerned with telling cautionary tales about a nation on the verge of destroying itself from within—a History, that is to say, that pushes his audiences into one of two Romantic alternatives, both attractive to nineteenth-century American Romantics: to dive into the whirl of History's parade via the throngs of the city; or, to retreat inward into a personal history, into the tranquil pool of a transcendental Self. King has set up a moral universe in which the state, government, politicians, schools, law enforcement, bureaucrats, and the military are almost never portrayed as the good guys. Reiner certainly manages to capture this social dysfunction in his adaptation of *Stand by Me*, but he also recognizes that the King vision almost always includes elements of hope, not only for the individual but also for America itself. And our attention to this admixture of despair and hope, of History with a capital "H" and history with a lower-case "h," sets the stage for issues addressed in the chapters to come.

David Cronenberg's film version of *The Dead Zone* parallels *Stand by Me* insofar as it is a darkly pessimistic study of the loss of innocence for both its protagonist, John Smith, and the American body politic embodied in the corrupt candidate for Congress, Greg Stillson. Yet in spite of the film's foreboding sense of doom, it also features a hero who, by the end of his life, clearly understands his purpose, his prescient gift, and finally is confident in his choice of action. Unwilling to serve as a passive agent of American History, he opts to *control* his own fate. Although Smith understands that he "will never get away" with an attempt on the candidate's life, he willingly sacrifices himself to make sure that Stillson's career ends before he can produce the nuclear Armageddon Smith witnesses in an accidental vision. Smith makes sacrifices to help others all through the film, especially imperiled children, and his death occurs from this same impulse, but his final actions occur willfully, the consequence of an individual American who becomes suddenly politicized because of Stillson's imminent danger. This point is highlighted in John Smith's choice of gun to assassinate Stillson: not a handgun, or assault weapon, but a hunting rifle that he takes from his father's home. The type of gun available to him is important to note as it signifies Smith's link with earlier frontier Americans that would have stalked the grounds of Walden Pond, and that would have, ironically enough, grasped the true inspiration behind the Second Amendment: the right to bear arms in order to protect "the security of a free state." It is the security and freedom of this state that the right-wing Stillson increasingly jeopardizes over the course of the movie. It is also probable that Smith's rifle is the only weapon he and his family own, and that it has never before been aimed at another human being. Stillson's emergence, linked to Hitler and Ronald Reagan throughout the film, transforms Smith's small-town political naïveté into patriotic martyrdom. He moves from being a deer in the headlights of History to an individual with real agency (a tenuous transformation that highlights King's own precarious sense of Romantic historicity). When Smith reveals to Roger Stuart that he, Smith, is not even registered to vote, Stuart is the first to warn him that Stillson is a "dangerous turkey." Stuart, however, lacks the moral courage to confront the politician himself, retreating behind a position of political expediency, leaving Smith to deal with Stillson on his own. Already we can see how King, from very early on, prides himself upon pivoting from a violent History to the kinds of private histories that grow ever more intriguing to King as his career evolves.

King's attraction to complicated yet ordinary protagonists who stumble into the corruption of American institutions and the individuals who pervert its ethical codes of behavior is mitigated by the writer's strong faith in acts of individual courage that split these protagonists from the mainstream corruption surrounding them. American History may have lost its moral compass, but King has always believed in the sanctity of the individual's history, shaped by moral intuition and defined by its capacity to inspire alternative choices. Although sharply critical of small-town American collective group think, *Stand by Me* also posits a minority position that supports the ideal of the American dream as an opportunity to rise beyond the limitations of the social class into which an individual is born and a stultifying conformist agenda. In other words, it invites the audience to go out once more into the rejuvenating wilderness. After all, moral survival in the King universe is typically available only to the individual willing to buck the hegemonic order and strike out on his or her own "into the woods" (or "out to sea"). To endure, the King hero or heroine must eschew entrenched social institutions (and the conformity demanded by them) and pursue new social identities, value codes, and interpersonal relationships. For our purposes, we might frame this movement as gesturing at a lower-case "h" history, identifiable due to its utter singularity and flexibility. To survive and discover happiness in the face of an on-rushing History that threatens to mow them down, these characters must become border-crossers, like Andy and Red at the end of *The Shawshank Redemption*, willing to defy codes of behavior, class and racial demarcations, the restrictive laws issued by the state and societal traditions. The burden of choice is placed squarely on the individual both in King's works and their film adaptations. Said another way, when King's American History splits along familiar lines between the hegemonic and the counter-hegemonic, it reveals itself to be a Romance of the most enduring order.

The four boys in *Stand by Me* provide us with a comprehensive set of alternatives that typically confront King's protagonists. Vern and Teddy represent one reality, while Gordie and Chris quite another; both are reflective of the American experience, however much they stand in opposition to each other. At the conclusion of the climactic scene that determines the fate of Ray Brower's body in *Stand by Me*, Ace menacingly threatens, "We're gonna get you for this," before slinking away without the dead child. This line possesses haunting implications—that manage to extend beyond Ace's promise of an imminent beating—regarding the boys' futures (the "We" being Castle Rock and perhaps even the town's configuration of adulthood in general, which Ace unconsciously predicts will indeed "get" them). Both Gordie and Chris use education as a means to "get out" of Castle Rock and thereby escape the death-in-life social conformity that ends up trapping Vern and Teddy. The moment when Gordie stands up to Ace and threatens to shoot him shows that he has seized control of his own history, that he, like John Smith, can choose to be an active agent in the shaping of his own life, and that he does indeed "possess some of his brother's good sense." As an agent of history with a lower-case "h," he is unlike Vern, who follows the easiest path of least resistance to marriage, children, and a job driving a forklift in a lumber-yard; he is also unlike Teddy, the latter veering off into Ace-like delinquency and time spent in prison. On the other hand, Gordie is very much like Chris, who is driven by his desire to stand up and change the things he does not like about himself, his town, adults, and the world at large. Even so, despite attending college and becoming a lawyer as an adult, Chris eventually falls prey to the random violence that distinguishes American History (especially in Castle Rock). The American wilderness is lovely, dark, and deep—a place of refuge as well as a charnel house. For Romantics like Thoreau and King, American History tramples us into dust, even as It drives us outward into the pitiless frontier—without communal comfort—to locate a greater purpose as individuals. For Chris Chambers and two of the other protagonists in *Stand by Me*, Ace's last words prove tragically prescient. In the King multiverse, we cannot escape from community—*and yet I must*. This impasse marks a core ambivalence between Oneness-as-connection and Oneness-as-release: an ambivalence that defines American Romanticism as a whole. The train in *Walden* is, finally, not just an intrusion on the pastoral landscape; it is also an avatar for Concord society, an accelerating sense of "progress" that reaches out to intrude on Thoreau and, as a result, to sharpen the Romantic's sense of solitude and independence. To explore further how King confronts an analogous conundrum, we might turn to *IT*, a novel that was published in the same year that Reiner's film was released (1986).

The Clown and the Whale

Generally speaking, works by Melville and King share a similar pathos because they tend to oscillate between deep pessimism (Melville's *The Confidence Man* [1857] and the books written under King's pseudonym, Richard Bachman) as well as moments of transcendental exuberance. To further ground the discussion in concrete texts and contexts, in this section we focus upon two representative novels, Melville's *Moby-Dick* and King's *IT*. In addition to their like-minded epic resonance, these sprawling narratives grapple with ongoing debates concerning the legacy of transcendental values. That is, these books remain thoroughly unsettled through their presentation of an all-encompassing synergy (that emancipates as well as oppresses) in tension with their sense of being solitary (that liberates as well as alienates). The fact that neither epic resolves these tensions completely does not indicate formal imperfection on the part of the authors (a common critique voiced by John Sears when he labels *IT* as "symbolically confused" and a "major ideological failure"); instead, this imperfection recycles core concerns that can be traced back to the nation's nineteenth-century literary renaissance (183–4, 188). The complexity of these metaphysical texts speaks across generations to a set of concerns unique to the American experience. Like *Moby-Dick*, *IT* is on the cusp of a historical brink, wedged awkwardly between Romanticized visions of globalization and a strident, exclusionary nationalism. For contemporary readers, *Moby-Dick* and *IT* speak to one of the most lasting questions in American Romanticism: namely, what represents the crux of American History—the glorified (and destitute) individual, or the restorative (and oppressive) community? Time and time again in King's universe, we become either consumed by the nation's sprawling History, or we float like Ishmael atop our respective coffins, individuals in tension with the unyielding sea.

Given the scope of King's endeavor, Melville's *Moby-Dick* provides an ideal template for revisiting the text. Although *IT* only overtly references *Moby-Dick* in a throwaway line about one of its overweight protagonists, another one of King's novels, *The Tommyknockers* (written during the same stretch of time in the mid-1980s), draws upon more pronounced parallels, and suggests that King had Melville in mind when he was composing his epic.[5] Jim Gardener, the poet-protagonist of *The Tommyknockers*, at times echoes Melville's Ishmael, who "finishes his tale with a biblical reference that appears as a desperate cry ... 'I only am escaped alone to tell thee'." In addition, the spaceship unearthed in *The Tommyknockers* is compared to "the greatest white whale ever dreamed of" (687, 130, 371). Written more than a century prior, Melville's epic also captures the inner turmoil of what it means to be human by moving dialectically between oppositions. As such, *Moby-Dick* embodies the slipperiness of metaphysical novels from the nineteenth century, and reveals to us how "their structures, in defiance of the rules of unity, are usually divided ... [a] combination of positivist and visionary strains" (Eigner 5–7). For instance, Captain Ahab pursues his own transcendent potential—apprehension of that elusive white whale—yet, at the same time, he remains hobbled by his significant physical (and existential) lack. Melville's *mythos* shifts back and forth between exuberant heights, in which the Romantic chases the Spirit that connects him to eternity, and devastating valleys, in which the disenchanted individual must witness his own fallibility. Edgar Dryden observes, "[*Moby-Dick*] was born of a tension between the realm of romance and that of reality, and its history may be seen as an attempt to resolve the paradox that this tension implies" (3). In terms of America's literary past, Melville's epic demarcates the tension, and eventual breaking point, of Emersonian lyricism (produced by the Unitarian cohort centered in Concord) and the subsequent movement towards realism in the aftermath of the Civil War (accompanied by a virulent rejection of Emerson's ideas, famously put on display when the elder philosopher was booed while on a speaking tour late in his career). *Moby-Dick* thus encapsulates America's mixed reaction to, and ultimate rejection of, the Utopian ideals that characterized the transcendental-inspired work of the Renaissance. As Lawrence Buell posits, "The same ambivalence is to be found in all the major American Renaissance authors ... they are metaphysical writings before they are anything else." Although Melville's work shares certain traits with the Concord transcendentalists—his propensity for using "catalogue rhetoric," for one—it often departs from major preoccupations of the movement, such as Melville's refusal of "the traditional theocentric framework of New England culture" (Buell 103, 167, 53). By re-reading *Moby-Dick*, we can begin to visualize the contours of a debate surrounding American Romanticism that endows one of King's most enduring works with its (ever shifting) shape.

IT expresses its own ambiguity towards what passes as transcendental philosophy. On one hand, a poster in the all-important library (a focal point for events in the novel) cites noted transcendentalist Ralph Waldo Emerson: "One Idea Lights a Thousand Candles" (*IT* 172). This reference highlights the novel's metaphysical underpinnings by gesturing at an Emersonian ideal of spiritual Oneness, generated (paradoxically) through a heightened individualism. One Idea can stir the mind of thousands, and so the circulation of Ideas embodied by the Derry Library affirms a universal presence that unifies Derry's children in their fight against evil. At the same time, *IT*'s sequel of sorts, the novel *Dreamcatcher* (2001), addresses King's debt to transcendentalism: "We are a *species* living in the dreamcatcher. I hate the way that sounds, phony transcendentalism" (*Dreamcatcher* 878; author's emphasis). King's body of work, in particular *IT* and the narratives that co-exist elsewhere in the writer's multiverse, constantly returns to foundational issues raised by Emerson and his disciples. Like *Moby-Dick*, *IT* navigates between Utopian interdependence and the antithesis. King's epic therefore conveys a Romantic sense of American History that oscillates perpetually between ecstatic convergence and extreme isolation.

Although traditionalists will likely bristle at the comparison, given King's status as a "popular" writer and Melville's accolades as an ensconced figure in the American canon, King's epic actually shares a great deal with Melville's classic.[6] *IT* aspires to be much more than the sum of its parts. Broken into individual tales from different eras, the novel weaves separate accounts together with a cosmic adhesive, slowly building from a focus upon the local histories of a band of misfit children to a much grander panorama of humanity's "noble, yet melancholy" History. *IT* examines the dynamism of human existence in form as well as content by tracking the biological as well as spiritual maturation of children as they become adults (and vice versa). To be a child—and, in some sense, an adult—involves living in "one insular Tahiti, full of peace," because you forget the imperfection that defines being human. Children (and adults) live on proverbial islands, certain that they are simply *being* (when, in actuality, they are forever *becoming* something else). Yet *IT* also lingers with children (and adults) as they are "encompassed by ... the half-known life" (Melville 70, 225). Put differently, King's characters remain keenly aware of their own limitations even as they are oppressed by the many-guised authorities sent to keep them in check, which is to say, bound by dutiful custodians of American History, like Jack Torrance in *The Shining* or Louis Creed in *Pet Sematary*. To illuminate King's Melvillean dialectic, we can expand upon four key themes from each text: a tension between the individual and the community; Lockean empiricism versus Kantian idealism; the intersection of self-consciousness and the consciousness of the Other; and, finally, the metaphysical journey of an artist in search of self-discovery through her art. Beyond being only a "confused," or stylistically unwieldy, example from the postmodern mold, *IT* can be read as a meaningful contribution to ongoing debates surrounding American Romanticism. Like *Stand by Me* and many of the narratives King published before (and since), *IT* reminds us of seminal issues that for the past two hundred years have come to constitute the American experience.

First, *IT* and *Moby-Dick* both juxtapose the individual's history (with a lower-case "h") alongside the group History of his community (with a capital "H"). A.N. Kaul views *Moby-Dick* as "an exploration into the scope and limitation of transcendental individualism: the individual's dream of becoming an all-powerful demigod and the opposite possibility of his being reduced to the helpless position of an Ishmael. The idea of isolated Ishmaels and Ahabs was connected in its turn with an insight into the necessity of human community" (Kaul 258). Melville responds to this transcendentalist tendency to blur the line thought to divide the categories of individual and community. Concepts like Emerson's "transparent eyeball," for instance, can be understood as collectivist (we share in a singular, universal vision) as well as individualistic (e.g., my particular vision encompasses all other visions, subsuming them, and forcing others to see through an imperial "I"). The respective epics of Melville and King concern themselves with this inner conflict. While unable (or unwilling) to dismiss outright a Utopian sense of interdependency, they remain reluctant to buy into Emerson's unifying vision wholesale. In *Moby-Dick*, readers contrast moments of visceral unification—"let us squeeze ourselves universally," the novel commands, "into the very milk and sperm of kindness"—with keenly-felt moments of abject loneliness—as when Ahab, with his missing limb, wails over his fallen state, his "ugly gaping wound" (Melville, *Moby-Dick* 323, 339). American Romanticism habitually walks a tight rope between a grand sense of History and the breakage of historical singularities.

While Melville's epic occasionally achieves soaring rhetorical heights, dancing above specific details of the whale hunt, the novel just as often fragments into competing individual accounts: "I look, you look, he looks, we look, ye look, they look" (335). *IT* likewise considers this borderland (if, indeed, it even exists) by slipping between the all-seeing "I" and a blind, stranded narrator that has been left to float upon a modest coffin in the mighty ocean. Originally demarcated by their unique traumas—histories damaged by abusive parents and Henry Bowers—individual members of the Losers' Club are eventually brought together by their specific threats *and* by the much larger danger of American History (represented by Pennywise). Indeed, while King hints at a collusion among these various manifestations of evil, he makes it absolutely clear that survival of the individual members in the Losers' Club is dependent on maintaining the communal unity of the club itself. A Melvillian clash delineates individual from community; in *IT*, the Losers' Club must distinguish the universal pull that brings them together, despite their private desires for autonomy: "'How much of this are we thinking up ourselves, and how much is being thought up for us?'" (*IT* 709). Members of the Club find solace in the belief that their "group will" speaks for all, but they take comfort as well in the belief that they each control their own individual fates. Echoing *Moby-Dick*, *IT* champions local narratives while also genuflecting before metaphysical wholeness.

In terms of History as a metaphysical concept, nineteenth-century American Romanticism elevates as well as depresses the lone individual. Consider, for instance, the eruption of "group will" aboard the *Pequod*, a burst of collectivist energy: "Truth hath no confines ... the cry! Are they not one and all with Ahab." And yet Ahab—perhaps *the* quintessential "loner" in nineteenth-century American literature, a perfect embodiment of Melville's commentary upon Emerson's perverse brand of individualism—depends upon the ship's laborers to a degree that strikes him as burdensome: "Cursed be that mortal indebtedness." The body politic represented by Melville's vessel seems paradoxical because it desires *and* despises its own cohesion. The crew coalesces around their captain—"'All your oaths to hunt the White Whale are as binding as mine'"—all, that is, except for Starbuck and Ishmael. While they begin the novel in sympathy with Ahab's quest, they end the book as independent agents. Ahab's spirit hardens against nature; Ishmael's softens. What begins as the narrator's near-suicidal urgings to escape from his terrible isolation on shore, "involuntarily pausing before coffin warehouses, and bringing up the rear of every funeral I meet," ends with his survival at sea as the only member of the crew left to tell the tale of the *Pequod* (Melville 140, 360, 644, 93). To be a part of this group (and a part of American History) means losing sight of the particulars that endow life with freedom and self-definition; at the same time, to be apart from the group means lacking an essential sense of what it means to be committed to a purpose larger than the self (a full, enduring sense of a shared History). Melville's friend and mentor, Hawthorne, understood the value inherent in the "magnetic chain of humanity" that Ethan Brand violates, but Melville was perhaps less optimistic than Hawthorne and more prone to recognize those forces—social as well as metaphysical—that keep men isolated from one another (Hawthorne 436).

Indeed, in King's epic, the individual needs exclusivity: "If we're supposed to do this as a group, why do you want us to start alone?" The answer: "It started alone for each of us." For every episode of communal cruelty—the "civic pride" that results in the murder of a gay man; the town's ecstatic massacre of the Bradley gang and torching of the Black Spot; the tyranny of parents that treat their children "like pets"; Derry's invisible tyranny over its citizens—there is evidence of a positive sense of unity to wed disparate elements (502, 536). The Losers in *IT* manage to avoid the negative group think that is so predominant among King's corrupted social communities and institutions. For example, the difference that separates the Losers in *IT* from the imposition of a single community mindset remains imperative to recognizing the life-affirming distinction between *IT* and fictions such as *'Salem's Lot, The Stand, Needful Things, Storm of the Century, The Mist, Cell, Under the Dome, The Tommyknockers,* and *Rita Hayworth and the Shawshank Redemption*. Each of these texts features a central figure of evil—typically a demonic male—who seeks to assert his tyrannical will over the citizens of a small Maine township. Anyone who disagrees with the larger group think subsequently imposed is subject to censorship and typically a violent death. Here, once more, we discover the hegemonic cause of the resultant carnage of American History. The "social contract" that is at the heart of many King novels parallels some of the same issues we find in *Moby-Dick*. For the society of the *Pequod* to surrender its independence to the "clamped mortar of Ahab's iron soul" is to become "like machines, dumbly moving about on the deck" (674). Ahab can be recognized as the sea-faring prototype for many of the gothic tyrants who would rule their respective corners of the King multiverse: Pennywise, Flagg, Andre Linoge in *Storm of the Century*, Leland Gaunt in *Needful Things*, the Crimson King in *The Dark Tower*, Rose the Hat and the True Knot in *Doctor Sleep*. Although Ahab drives American History to the brink of self-destruction, his example also suggests a powerful alternative: a willful subject (like Ishmael or Gordie in *Stand by Me*) that emerges from the woods or sea "all grown up," somehow divorced from the clutches of a vast network that failed to impose its corrupted will, somehow set apart from the ever-swelling junk-yard of History.

What differentiates King's heroes and heroines is their refusal to remain silent, and their corresponding effort, either alone or in concert with a small group of rebels, to fight the entropy of institutionalization and conformity. In *IT*, the Losers must be viewed, after all, as distinct from the Derry adults, and even other children, such as Henry Bowers, who capitulate to Pennywise out of fear or blind allegiance, rather than a commitment to a group identity forged by selfless love. Like Jack Torrance, Michael Hanlon from *IT* must piece together the History of Derry, a horrifying task that enslaves him, certainly, but that eventually sets him free by helping to sharpen the outline of his increasingly coherent subjectivity. Abandoned by social bureaucracies and the nuclear family itself, King's non-traditional alliances, such as the Losers' Club, represent light in the darkness. The Ritual of Chüd embodies the magical power of the whole that enables the Losers to battle It; in their courage they are ultimately enlarging themselves, becoming less individualistic, creating a group psychic potency: "It had felt an ominous, upsetting growth in their power when they joined together, and It had wondered for the first time if It had perhaps made a mistake." King's heroes and heroines establish character unions that appear to meld child with adult, and in turn insulate these small group dynamics from the larger contaminated whole. Each of the protagonists in *IT* must address his or her Ahab-like independence, yet each of the protagonists must also suspend their attendant fears and anomie in the name of a fraternal bond that aids in their survival. *IT* is very much a novel centered on the remembrance of things past: to survive as adults, the Losers must reconnect with the power they once possessed as children. The very act that initially seals the group together is the building of a dam in the Barrens—a barrier that, by its design, keeps certain things out, but a design which also serves as a symbol to keep things in: "The almost unconscious knitting together" that concurrently makes the children feel as though they are "strapped to the nosecone of a guided missile" (1018, 495). In a word, *Moby-Dick* and *IT* each take up the vague demarcation between individual and community—a liminal space that occupies so very much of American Romanticism. King's Romantic view of American History, as the chapters to follow demonstrate, upholds this foundational tension.

In this impasse, the Kantian ideal of individualism runs up against a kind of stark Lockean empiricism.[7] In *IT*, free will is sometimes understood to be a delusion that covers up the "iron skeleton" of instinct. Beneath fanciful dreams of Utopia, King's reader discovers the unmoving solidity of scientific reality, a realism that manifests most directly in Stan's bird watching. Stan, the character least likely to subscribe events to a supernatural cause, clings to the empirical world in order to keep himself grounded: "A creature of habit and convention." For Stan, the classification of bird species gives him a "sense of place," and provides him with a sort of "shield" to protect himself from the unknown. Although Stan's empiricism brings him temporary comfort, it reveals itself to be made of the same exclusionary stuff of the idealists (Eddie's mother, for one, also invests in the "bird logic" to justify her own racist ideals—thus revealing how "science," too, depends upon a kind of belief). "Growing up" into secular disbelief *seems* like "progress" for the likes of Stan; on the other hand, such belief provides "security," and holds people together in the face of their own worst impulses (134–5, 402, 407, 856). Eigner describes this strain as a crucial component of "the metaphysical novel, an oxymoron, in which experience is presented first in purely materialistic or associational or positivistic terms, which are then contradicted from the idealist point of view so that experience is mystically transformed" (Eigner 9). In just these terms, *IT* re-endows adult life—secular, hyper-rational, individualistic—with a degree of idealism. To do so, the text first works through Stan's empiricism and considers the blind spots of faith-driven worldviews.

Moby-Dick similarly treats the friction between empiricism and idealism as an unresolvable quagmire. Ishmael sorts out his confused nature by fully pursuing and absolutely abandoning "both his transcendental and his scientific quests ... (in order to realize) his essentially mixed nature" (Eigner 10). The metaphysical heaviness of Melville's tome cedes regularly to an empirical account of things, perhaps most notably in Chapter 32, "Cetology"—a verbose dissection of the whale's anatomy. The novel scolds overly-idealistic Romantics by asking, "Do you try to 'enlarge' your mind? Subtilize it." While the text drifts at times into ruminations upon the whale as a profound symbol, it snaps back to attention when its Lockean voice insists that sometimes a whale is just a whale: "What has the whale to say?" (264, 291). Melville's empirical interjections raise important questions about what it means to be human, echoed nearly a century-and-a-half later in King's musings upon a sublime entity and its many local manifestations. In *IT*, the presence of metaphysical evil eludes empiricists because it is fundamentally boundless—a solitary clown named Pennywise, a spider, and so forth *as well as* a vast being without boundaries; a white whale that possesses a distinctive anatomy *as well as* divine, unfathomable size. Empiricism plays a vital role in urging readers to conceptualize (temporarily) what could only ever be an abstraction (e.g., the whale and the shape-changing clown). The empiricist role is fulfilled by the obsequious Historian who forces murky shapes to adopt a form to be more readily grasped. But a structured History only dissolves back into formlessness—and mercifully so, because it is this dissolution alone that preserves the hunt (Ahab's very purpose). With its long, violent History and its limitless power as a Hobbesian "leviathan," the abstract idea of Derry will not hold still to have its portrait taken, just as Pennywise will not hold still inside the Hanlon town photograph taken from 1945 in Chapter 14 (730–1). Melville appears to have anticipated the existence of spaces such as Derry, places "not down in any map; true places never are" (Melville 59). Yet Derry is comprised of distinctive locations in which its citizens create the comforts of home—the Black Spot; the clubhouse in the Barrens—and King's text takes great pains to chart these spaces empirically, surveying the town via canal, trolley, and train: "Take out your map and look at it. See what a real corner of the world it occupies" (*IT* 64). In sum, *Moby-Dick* and *IT* both recognize the importance of the particular as well as the universal, an approach that tempers the sweeping rhetoric of Romanticism without sacrificing the conviction that distinctive pieces of nineteenth-century American History will somehow fit together to form a coherent whole.

In Chapter 35, "The Mast-Head," Melville juxtaposes the dialectical strains of the American pastoral/Emersonian unity of design with a starkly alternate vision of a separatist nature that is never far from resurfacing. The human appears to hang suspended between both orientations. On a whale watch observing from atop the *Pequod*'s Crow's Nest, Ishmael finds himself nearly hypnotized as he contemplates the mysteries inspired by the mystic ocean, "at his feet that deep, blue, bottomless soul, pervading mankind and nature; and every strange, half-seen, gliding, beautiful thing." Deep in such thought, Ishmael resembles an Emersonian pantheist in total harmony with the universe. But no sooner does he experience this holy moment than he is reminded that "while this sleep, this dream is on ye, move your foot or hand an inch; slip your hold at all; and your identity comes back in horror." *Moby-Dick* aims to be large enough to contain a universe of contradictions: while we may be surrounded by an ocean filled with beauty and color, none of it is ever secure or permanent. Just beneath the surface blue of the sea, down a bit more, the colors melt and fade, and blackness is all. After moments of harmony within this universe, "with one half-throttled shriek you drop through that transparent air into the summer sea, no more to rise forever" (257). Even as America's History demands a scrapbook from Its hostages, this History remains sublime, which is to say, It remains so vast that no moribund custodian could ever hope to bring the monster completely into frame.

To grasp History as a Romance, Ishmael must face up to an alternative reality, one that speaks to the "internal interrelatedness of the antagonists of man and whale, culture and nature" (Zapf 207). In his ecocritical reading of *Moby-Dick*, Hubert Zapf suggests that nature occupies a bifurcated role in Melville's novel. When examined from Ahab's perspective, Ahab's biophobic demonization of the White Whale is a "symbol of the global economic expansion and technological mastery of man over nonhuman nature" (206). In place of the whale and the ocean in *Moby-Dick, IT* provides us with an underground world in the Barrens, the locale where nature is most visible in the novel, located southwest of Derry's epicenter and in proximity to the Kenduskeag River and the town dump. The Barrens is appropriately named, for in spite of the landscape's lush environment, it houses one of the central thresholds that It employs—a cement cylinder that connects with the maze of drainage and sewage pipes beneath the Derry streets. But like the role of the White Whale in *Moby-Dick*, how we interpret the Barrens in *IT* depends upon the point of view of the interpreter. In contrast to the sterile and mean streets of Derry, the Barrens is a secreted space of greenery and clean running water; in the summer, it offers a reprieve from the concrete and human intrusions that characterize downtown Derry. It is a place where Derry's adults never venture. While it serves to hide Pennywise in its lush undergrowth, the Barrens is also the place where the Losers find play and each other, often rendezvous, and gradually build a private and secure bond that nurtures their renegade relationship. Moreover, while Pennywise often hides in the Barrens, his home is technically man-made: within the labyrinth of the concrete and metal sewer pipes honeycombed beneath Derry itself. So, the whale and the Barrens occupy deliberately ambiguous and shifting definitions of the natural world, equal parts pastoral nature and polluted wilderness. Pennywise remains connected to human evil—symbolized in the bowel functions associated with above ground Derry. Ahab defines the whale, and by extension all of nature, as evil and would destroy it out of a motivation fueled by a matrix of revenge, cosmic anger, and human hubris. The Losers must learn to read the Barrens as more than a place that belongs to It (a cosmic History), to confront Pennywise in its lair, and thereby to free this natural habitat from It's exclusive domain. Similarly, Ishmael and Starbuck come to recognize that Ahab's perception of the whale is warped; their survival is dependent upon their willingness to repudiate and replace it with an alternative historical consciousness.

The members of the Losers' Club begin alone because they see Derry's History like children, overlooking a grand metanarrative from positions of unearned confidence. They have not yet considered the perspective of the Other. It is only when they start to see through each other's eyes that they can cultivate a broader, more dynamic historical vision. For example, Bev does not know that she is beautiful until Eddie recognizes it in her; meanwhile, Bill does not realize that he can stop stuttering until Richie witnesses it and brings it to his attention. In King's novel, intersubjectivity forges relational bonds and expands imaginative horizons. King at his best—and *IT* can certainly be categorized as one of his best works—offers a new sense of H/history, driven by an ethics of the Other. This divergent model salvages communal History without forfeiting the mutability of individual histories.

Mike Hanlon occupies a pivotal role in *IT*, as he has been the one member of the Losers' Club to use his journal entries in order to surveil It for the past twenty-seven years. It is Hanlon who recognizes when it is time to summon the others; it is Hanlon who, because of his role as a vigilant Historian of Derry—Bill understands that Mike has "kept the lighthouse," while the others have left town to make their fortunes elsewhere—occupying the position of authority when the Losers reconvene (512). Although Denbrough is the acknowledged leader, Hanlon's role as chief Historian of Derry is no less significant, especially in his capacity to record the town's interactive relationship with It for the past half century and to interpret the weird events that have occurred to each adult member of the Losers' Club as they make their way back into the living memory of present-day Derry. Hanlon serves as a kind of high priest-therapist, encouraging the others to trust their individual and collective memories of the past, and to believe that Pennywise can be vanquished a final time. Like his father, who maintains his own historical record of Derry, and is the only parent in the novel who demonstrates real love for his child, Mike's life is colored by his unflinching courage. Although not physically present in the battle against the spider/It, Mike has prepared and led his friends to the point at which Denbrough is able to overcome his initial difficulty in recapturing his youth and to take over as the group's titular leader (597, 607).

Establishing a singular universalism embraced by later American Romantics like King, *Moby-Dick* oscillates between the particular and the universal, slipping from the sublime to the mundane (and back again). Perhaps the most resonant example in the novel occurs when Pip falls overboard and, as a result, experiences "the intense concentration of self in the middle of such a heartless immensity." In this moment, the boy's perspective becomes twofold: he baths in the sublimity of the measureless sea and, at the same time, he encounters himself as though from on high, looking down upon his scrawny form: "Base little Pip" (321, 366). As a consequence of his sorry condition, Pip transcends his limitations *and* feels them all the more acutely. Ishmael too finds himself stranded at the close, clinging to his friend Queequeg's coffin following the sinking of the *Pequod*. Ishmael's idealist expanse contrasts with his sense of smallness just as, for Queequeg, the coffin symbolizes a bridge between eternity and mortality. Ishmael's journey of self-discovery forces him to realize that being human means a ceaseless tension between overheated consciousness and the chastening that comes through meeting with the consciousness of Others (including big Others: God, the Oversoul, even a White Whale).

For another example of this ceaseless tension, we might fast forward to the unfolding consciousness of Pennywise the Clown. Improbably, the concluding section of King's text is composed from the vantage point of It. Until It meets the Losers' Club, the metaphysical entity naïvely holds that It alone enjoys a transcendental state of being. It's consciousness recognizes no horizons. Yet as the entity's presumed universality crashes up against the consciousness of the group (as well as the consciousness of a Final Other, "the author of all there was"), It realizes this damning blind spot and actually starts to evolve: "If all things flowed from It ... how could any creature ... fool It or hurt It? [...] Suppose It had not been alone ... suppose there was Another?" For the first time, It can no longer "simply take what It wanted" (974). Its particular shape, the laws of which the entity must "abide," collides with a universal Shape that far exceeds It, a venerable restaging of Ahab and the whale. "Perhaps," It realizes, "It was not eternal after all—the unthinkable must finally be thought" (966, 1034). King's epic remains rooted in the unfolding consciousness of the cosmic Spirit (perhaps most obviously symbolized by the Turtle) that has taken up residence in Derry. It's eternal formlessness must be given form, and then dissolve once more in order to be re-discovered again (*ad infinitum*). By wrestling with the intricate complexity of this metaphysical vision, *Moby-Dick* and *IT* manage to sustain a vital restlessness that complicates the illusions of a transcendental ego: "Facts and fancy, half-way meeting, interpenetrate, and form one seamless whole." In a word, the process of becoming never ends. In *IT*, Eddie does not get to figure out "how to finish" before he dies; in *Moby-Dick*, Elijah cryptically announces that "'what's to be, will be; and then again, perhaps it won't be, after all'" (*IT* 492; Melville 64). The common complaint that King does not know how to write a "good ending"—played for laughs in the film adaptation *IT Chapter Two* (2019) with a cameo by King himself—entirely misses the point. At his best, King recognizes, like Melville, that there is no such thing as ending. And so, in their stubborn refusal to conclude, these kindred epics underscore a staple of America's literary lineage that has been on prominent display since the American Renaissance: the ambivalence of a cohesive society (with its grand History) that instigates the advance of unfettered individuals (with their plenitude of histories).

In some of their most insightful passages, *Moby-Dick* and *IT* interrogate the role of America's artists in articulating this core ambivalence. Many critics credit the profundity of *Moby-Dick* to Hawthorne's recommendation that Melville re-visit Shakespeare; as a result, in Shakespearean fashion, Melville's text looks "to dramatize the American writer's concern with the nature of the relationship between art and life … the nature of the creative task itself" (Dryden 18–9). Ishmael comes to understand the nature of himself through uneven attempts to turn the White Whale into a work of art. On one hand, the presence of the whale lures the potential artist on, providing inspiration for ever more words; on the other hand, the leviathan "must remain unpainted to the last." Ishmael (impossibly) quests "to label (the whale) for all time," yet he recognizes that this transcendental fever will invariably cool: "God keep me from ever completing anything" (Melville 217–8, 117, 125). The artist in Melville longs to give form to the Idea but fails to do so because *every solitary shape is ultimately inadequate*. The creativity of humans cannot cease because, if it were to do so, their purpose would reach its terminus, that is, the existential hunt would draw to a premature close. King seizes upon this issue through his portrayal of aspiring writers, including Mike (Derry's Historian) and Bill (a horror novelist and stand-in for King himself).[8] *IT* parallels cosmic creation with Bill's narrative talent, thereby establishing a direct link between the artist's self-identity and the creation of art. Mike, meanwhile, realizes over the course of the novel a truth that links him also to Gordie in *Stand by Me*: that to formulate stories—and to arrange them alongside the stories of Others—is to move closer to genuine self-consciousness. Hanlon finds his way to his "father's final story" and, in doing so, he comes to comprehend that there is never a finale to the act of storytelling: "One leads to the next, to the next, and to the next" (*IT* 431–2). This dialectic illuminates a H/history that is both constant and unsettled. What better example of this truth than the prolific careers of both Melville and King? In both *IT* and *Moby-Dick*, while the creation of art provides a (brief) respite, art remains wholly insufficient, a mere stop-gap in the unfurling of an infinite tapestry. Melville's narrative posits that the use of allegory is "intolerable" because allegory paralyzes the human spirit by claiming (falsely) that it fixes everything to the spot; instead of allegory, the text prefers to employ symbolism, as the symbol can be slippery, ever-changing. In truth, the White Whale works precisely because of its open-ended function as a symbol

(Melville 172). King's narrative likewise considers symbolism to be paramount: the identity of It is an eternally changing representation—of itself as an avatar of evil, but likewise as the specific and individualized composite of what terrifies each of the children (e.g., Bev's merging of her father and the witch from "Hansel and Gretel," Mike Hanlon and his father's recollected presence of the airborne Rodan during the explosion at the Kitchener Ironworks). These associations must be confronted and retold to the group even if the endeavor only defers the inevitable, allowing members to cope (for a time) and thus keeping the wheels of the cosmos spinning. Out on their own, the children in the Losers' Club are easily victimized by Pennywise as well as Henry Bowers and his crew. But together, working in support of one another, each child gains courage and power even to vanquish foes that are physically superior. Through their glimpse of shape-shifting figures that will not hold still—a gesture beyond the lone subject to Emerson's pantheism—readers learn that art is only ever a pale substitute for the thing-in-itself. Nonetheless, against the ebullience of starry-eyed transcendentalists, the placeholder of a clown or a whale offer indispensable footholds in the grander pursuit of what it means to be human. In his loftier moments, King follows Melville into this slippery terrain, and manages to glimpse a historical consciousness that incorporates the grandeur of History (capital "H") with the relational dynamics of history (lower-case "h"). He is, after all, one of the big innovators of American Romanticism as well as one of the most prominent writers to carry forth its legacy at the close of the twentieth century.

American literature incessantly returns to these moments of ambivalence—and King is no exception. His fiction and its film adaptations regularly grapple with the primary concerns of American Romanticism: namely, a delicate balancing act between individuals in the pastoral tradition that elevate themselves above the ennui of modern life, and individuals that recognize their smallness in a universal mosaic. For Thoreau, Melville, and their contemporaries, Oneness often means synthesis (an Oversoul) as well as singularity (the adult no longer in possession of his innocence). Indeed, the oscillation at the heart of the American Romance reveals something fundamental about King's constructions of American History, considered at length in the pages to follow. His texts routinely juxtapose the claustrophobia of a subject caught in metaphysical currents with the elation of a subject that purifies itself via escape. In closing, then, we might set aside (for a moment) our discussion of the many ways in which King deviates from his literary forbearers and focus upon the debt that his works owe to America's enduring fascination with its own chameleonic History.

Notes

1 As a representative example, see Heidi Strengell's *Dissecting Stephen King: From the Gothic to Literary Naturalism*.

2. The reasons why King continues to write tales that have appealed to massive audiences for the past half a century require a multifaceted answer. Some are drawn to King's world because it is a place where monsters abound and subsist in multiverses that never existed and never will. Other readers come to his fiction for altogether the opposite reason, as for them King is revealing something important about the time and place in which he lives; indeed, Stephen King takes his writing no less seriously than other writers who do not have reputations so intimately aligned with gothic extravagances. As Simon Brown argues, "The idea of placing horrors within the real world was a key theme in King's writing from the beginning, and one of the elements that contributed to his literary success" (S. Brown 102).

3. This tension also appears in the Romantic poetry of the nineteenth-century America. Henry Wadsworth Longfellow's "The Fire of Drift-wood," for instance, mourns the "vanished scene" of a bygone era while, at the same time, in poems like "Sand of the Desert in an Hour-Glass," he relishes the vastness of History, which explodes "narrow walls" to glimpse an "unimpeded sky." William Cullen Bryant similarly contemplates a History that overwhelms us—in "Thanatopsis," he writes of "the great tomb of man" —while celebrating a sense of History that endlessly thrills. In "Mutation," he orders us: "Weep not that the world changes" (Spengemann 58–9, 11, 14).

4. The leech scene in the film *Stand by Me*, ironically, occurs immediately after the boys playfully dunk each other in the bog, leading Teddy to luxuriate, "I'm acting my age. I'm in the prime of my youth, and I'll only be young once." The leeches interrupt this boyhood idyll and serve as a reminder of the true precariousness of Teddy's status, especially in light of Gordie's reaction to the blood-bloated leech he finds in his underpants. His fainting immediately afterwards links him symbolically to the dead adolescents elsewhere in the text, but also fills him with a serious resolve to complete the journey-quest to Brower's body and transition out of the nostalgic space where Teddy currently resides. All of nature appears to respond to Gordie's emergence into a reality alien to the pastoral dream: from this point on in the film the sky turns milky overcast and a heady wind picks up challenging what had been a lovely summer day; these conditions accompany the boys down the length of Harlow Road to Ray Brower's corpse.

5. Also written during this stretch (under the pseudonym Richard Bachman), King's novel *Thinner* (1984) points at *Moby-Dick* when it describes a wealthy character cut down by his own pride, found raving "like Ahab during the last days of the Pequod" (King, *Thinner* 97).

6. While this chapter remains focused on the relationship among King's fiction, his cinematic adaptations, and nineteenth-century American literature, several scholars have already addressed the specific connection between *IT* and other major American writers; King's book has been compared, for example, to seminal texts such as William Carlos Williams's *Patterson* and even Walt Whitman's *Song of Myself*. But the American writer to whom *IT* is most persuasively indebted is William Faulkner (see Reesman and Dickerson). In *IT*, King was clearly inspired by Faulkner's narratological experimentation and his "handling of how the past insinuates itself into the present and how the landscape reflects the corruption of human potential for love and renewal" (Dickerson 171).

7. Buell examines the difference between Locke's stress upon rational reflection (over intuition) and the Unitarian (post-Kantian) blend of higher mental faculty—"Reason"—with an underlying spiritual truth preferred by most of the Transcendentalists (Buell 4).

8. King's fiction often focuses upon the kind of self-creation made possible through works of art. See, for example, *Duma Key*, "1408" from *Everything's Eventual, Bag of Bones*, and *The Dark Half*. Perhaps the most potent illustration of this self-

fashioning process in found in *Misery*, where Paul Sheldon writes to literally save his life. In doing so, however, the famous novelist also reshapes his personality—giving birth to a newfound humility in place of arrogance, and a sense of grateful appreciation for the plethora of benefits afforded him as a result of his creation of Misery Chastain. The man who begins *Misery* as a prisoner (of so many things, in addition to the bipolar wrath of Annie Wilkes) is not the same man who discovers the power of art as a means for self-rescue.

2 The Pasts of *Pet Sematary*

"The past is never past; it is always present," one of Stephen King's favorite musicians, Bruce Springsteen, once said. *Pet Sematary* forcibly juxtaposes moments from distant and not-so-distant American pasts with the present. It is a narrative that exploits and fuses together the cultural gaps that separate contemporary civilization and a primitive past, Native American mythology and white appropriation, the American penchant for violence and warfare, and the gendered differences that distinguish access to information and the sustaining of secrets. Even the Orinco tanker trucks that play such an important role in the narrative's exposition are tied to the essential conflict between past and present that is played out in the town of Ludlow, specifically on property purchased recently by Dr. Louis Creed. The issue of "ownership" is important to the story: does true ownership reside within the legal definitions of property lines, or is it a more expansive concept that crosses over to include History and mythology? Are sins of the father limited only to genealogy, or can they likewise be transferred to strangers, thereby enlarging their scope? These issues press against this particular place in Maine, a microcosm that parallels a nearly identical set of dynamics connected to America's larger cultural and economic legacy. Even as King's text contrasts America's bloody past with its bloodless future, supplementing a historical consciousness uniquely suited to the demands of a heavily financialized economy, *Pet Sematary* underscores an entrenched propensity for violence that continues to fuel the grand narrative of American History.

The subtexts at work in *Pet Sematary* are at first only indirectly related to the Creed family and their efforts to adjust to new lives in Ludlow. The Creeds are in the unfortunate position of entering unwittingly into an active confluence that existed long before their decision to leave Chicago (Boston in the second *Pet Sematary* film adaptation) for a more relaxed and rustic, family-centered existence in Maine (although, given the extensive range of power centered in the Micmac burial ground, the novel casts the volition that motivates their relocation severely in doubt). The Creeds are trapped within a matrix of supernatural energies that have been dormant—albeit quietly seething—on state land abutting their own property and within the "polluted" psyche of their neighbor across the street, Jud Crandall.[1] *Pet Sematary* is another Stephen King initiation story wherein innocence is betrayed. The Wendigo spirit that has assumed control over the "polluted" Micmac site first shapes and then feeds on Creed's tragic suffering, forcing him to put his creed in the sour promise of immortality, which is to say, in the impossible rewards promised for obedience to the *modus operandi* of American History. Right away, we must acknowledge that this "pollution" is never truly the mythical essence of Native American peoples (although King's record of exoticizing racial Others is admittedly notorious); instead, this sour promise of immortality displaces the national sin of Manifest Destiny by projecting it outward, cruelly, onto its very victims. If the Native America spirit seems inherently violent in *Pet Sematary*, it is because the colonial agents of History made it so. The innate violence of American History instigates ever more bloodshed by forcing peoples in its path to conform to its savage logic or be left for dead in a ditch by the proverbial highway.

King's story demonstrates how dominant values associated with American History—prowess in battle; redemption through violence—appropriate cultural legacies that pulsate throughout human History. The Micmac site corresponds to the Indian belief in a cosmological system of regeneration. Something happened to the original use of the graveyard enabling the Wendigo to intrude and pollute the former Micmac faith in benevolent resurrections. Like the tradition of the vampire that bears close similarities to the Wendigo itself, the dead now return from this place as undead, imbued not with the communal life-force of the Indian tribe, but with the misanthropic energies of their mythic enemy. The Wendigo is a cannibal/form changer from Native American folklore that was believed to haunt the burial grounds of several Indian tribes in the Canadian northeast. Since its affiliation is primarily with cold weather tribes, it is likely that the Wendigo fits into Indian folklore as a warning meant to fend off cannibalistic urges during winter months when the tribe's food supply was compromised. Among some of the more likely parallels that connect the Wendigo myth to the *Pet Sematary* texts is the belief that once the spirit of the Wendigo has tasted human blood, its appetite turns insatiable and it wanders the woods in search of another meal. Many of the legends claim that the spirit of the Wendigo has the potential to appear in the dreams of human men and women. Once visited, the dreamer must, like Louis Creed after Pascow's nocturnal warning, choose to reject the temptations of the Wendigo's power, otherwise the victim will become the Wendigo's willing protégé (Colombo 128). Like so many of King's protagonists, Creed eventually surrenders his place in the present to serve an "ancient," malevolent force. In other words, he succumbs to a History both vast and entropic. What vanishes in the process is any hope for an alternative history (with a lower-case "h") to be narrated by the tribe—a history that might have been less violent than the History (with a capital "H") that envelops Creed. In *Pet Sematary*, there is no real Wendigo spirit at odds with an Anglo-militant spirit; rather, the Anglo-militant spirit subsumes everything like a cancer before turning back, angrily, upon itself (we will see further evidence of this self-cannibalism in King's novels about Vietnam, as we discuss in Chapter 4).

The Orinco trucks and Route 15, the roadway the company uses to transport their product, serve as metaphors that understate the most fundamental conflict at the center of the book and films: the (blood-soaked) glories of "progress" versus the gory costs of obedience to this metaphysical narrative. Literally, one of these trucks serves as the tool that fuses together the domesticated world the Creeds inhabit with the archaic power that lurks in the woods at the perimeter of their property. The Orinco company specializes in transporting petroleum products. No version of *Pet Sematary* provides much information about Orinco's operation beyond the fact that their trucks are part of a distribution network for fuels and chemical fertilizers that are piloted recklessly along Route 15 by young men driving to the intense beat of the Ramones. What is crucial, however, is this fact: the oil at the heart of the Orinco business originates in the ground; it is connected to America's geological past via the decomposition of organic life that resulted in the creation of fossil fuel. As such, the Orinco company shares something in common with the Micmac burial place: in both cases, an archaic past lies buried underground, and its potential energy is summoned for use in the present. In King's hands, the process of oil extraction becomes a metaphor for a violent American History. The very ground where the Orinco oil originated and the cemetery itself belonged first to the Indians, "those state lands, the ones the Indians want back," and that the new owners of the land—white people—appropriated these assets with neither permission to do so nor a conscious appreciation and understanding of the forces behind the creation of these natural resources. The reality that "the remains of the Micmac Indian tribe had laid claim to nearly eight thousand acres, and the complicated litigation, involving the federal government as well as that of the state, might stretch into the next century" is an indication of the importance of this ground to its original owners as well as the long stretch of temporal time associated with it (King, *Pet* 39, 16). These subtexts are not irrelevant to the core plots of the novel and its adaptations, as issues of legitimation, ownership, corporate money, responsibility, and lawfulness create a web that connects past to present and future, to differing racial communities displaced in order to establish a myth of American prominence. Residents of Ludlow need the oil the Orinco trucks provide for heating their homes and/or the operation of their machines; similarly, Jud and Louis seek the return of beloved pets and family members who have abruptly died. To do so, they are willing to appropriate Indian land and culture for their own purposes. In both instances, what is underground born out of the archaic past is summoned for reactivation in the present. And both these exploitative impulses are generated from a selfish need that slides easily into blind arrogance.

Yet even as *Pet Sematary* critiques contemporary commerce for failing to respect life's mysteries, the novel (unwittingly) affords proper respect to the so-called invisible hand of the market—a field of contingencies that do not conform to the schemes of oft-denigrated "social planners." In effect, as one reads King's full-throated indictment of a contaminated History, rendered filthy by its mode of extraction, it becomes increasingly difficult for the reader to distinguish gaps in knowledge that might counteract Creed's blind arrogance from gaps in knowledge required by the volatile financial markets that have come to control the rhythm of our lives. When his young son Gage is run over by a truck and tragically killed, Creed must come to terms with his own lack of control over life and death; in turn, the reader is led to overlook the violent *intentions* behind the design of the modern roadway and the behemoth machines that ride over it (their latent thirst for blood) in favor of a vague existential reflection upon Creed's broadly-defined delusions of mastery. And perhaps this sleight of hand should not surprise us. King responds to his unique historical moment (the late 1970s/early 1980s) in which the Reagan administration had begun to gut the "nanny state." As we discuss at much greater length in Chapter 4, King often rejects the military-industrial apparatus that drove thousands upon thousands of young men into theaters of war in Europe as well as the jungles of Vietnam. His reasonable critique of America's blood-soaked History—including the nation's devastation of Native American peoples and the planet—raises uncomfortable truths through subtextual inferences that manage to implicate contemporary readers into this claustrophobic sense of History. As we now recognize, to bow down before the capricious whims of the invisible hand of the market is not automatically more palatable than prostrating oneself before the dismal, fascist energies residing in the Micmac cemetery. In either case, *the flow of blood never ceases*.

Pet Sematary articulates a schism between the "natural" march of American commerce—"natural" because it echoes the authentic fragility of properly chastened individuals—and the "unnatural" cycles of war in which America seems to be caught. In one sense, then, King's novel marks a changing of the guard from a dialectical History—driven by world wars—to a "post-History" heralded by the ascent of an American economic model. (Although the concept of post-History gains greater currency at the closing of the Cold War in 1989, six years after the publication of *Pet Sematary*, it is expressed at least as early as 1948 by Alexandre Kojève.) To unpack King's metaphor further: the highway serves as an emblem of these capricious whims as it runs through the middle of King's novel (and its two film adaptations), representing the speed, mobility, as well as the uncertainty that apparently characterizes postmodern "progress." The text opens with Louis dreaming of an escape from his family, an escape made possible by America's mythological open road (I-95 southbound). It's not that King's preference for post-History lacks the forward propulsion of colonial conquest; rather, his account choreographs the anxiety-ridden leaps of faith required to cross congested thoroughfares. As King's ultimately ambivalent relationship to the open road demonstrates, the division between America's bloody History and a congenial story based upon post-History remains, in the end, the stuff of mere illusion. War and commerce are never wholly isolated aspects of American development. In turn, we must consider how *Pet Sematary* attempts to sever these twin narratives (and how it does not succeed in doing so). That is, this chapter explores how the joint stories that King presents—the "enlightened" story of commercialism as well as the "unenlightened" story of endless American warfare (tied, throughout the twentieth- and twenty-first centuries, to the nation's unquenchable thirst for oil) —have been used, in different but related ways, to legitimize the high body count of the world's deadliest century.[2] An unpalatable commonality lingers beneath the surface of *Pet Sematary*, reemergent only in the story's most macabre moments.

The Drive to War

Facing down its own End of History (in particular, through Creed's unhappy domestication), *Pet Sematary* recalls the nineteenth-century's *fin-de-siécle*, a point in time in which many men feared the closure of the frontier, the reawakening of occult and mystical phenomena, the collapse of their so-called warrior beliefs, and the weakening of the "masculine spirit." Late Anglo-militants such as Jud and Creed, respond to a similar set of anxieties by appropriating the cosmic powers of regeneration associated with the Wendigo in order to sustain an imaginary revitalization. In fact, Creed's self-doubts directly call to mind the popular musings of historian and U.S. president Teddy Roosevelt, who sought a cure for what he perceived to be the fading vigor of his "race." Richard Slotkin observes how Roosevelt envisioned an American History that could plunge ahead thanks to the ceaseless clashing of swords: "Any weakening of that fighting spirit ... would necessarily produce a reversal of the course of (H)istory." Roosevelt discovered in the (disappearing) American wilderness a sacred space in which to recover a lost vitality, a "dark, raging, and howling" landscape where "the white man's purification [is] bought with Indian blood" (Slotkin 634, 623). Although Creed does not *literally* do battle with the Wendigo (his encounters remain a form of psychological warfare waged against proxy surrogates), the haunted woods still lure Creed with the promise of regeneration, through contact with a long-buried *potenza* that has not yet been extinguished—a drive to engage in combat that has enslaved white Anglo-militants from the days of the early frontier to the Great War (and beyond). Like Roosevelt, Creed appears to be caught up in a perverse, zero-sum game. A war-driven History that once destroyed the Micmac tribe come, at last, to demand blood from the victors that falsely believed they had tamed the tides of History. In truth, as a self-cannibalizing entity (not unlike the entity in King's *The Langoliers*), this violent History will not be sated until every eligible combatant has been "used up."

Despite its prominence, *Pet Sematary*'s sustained commentary upon twentieth-century warfare remains its most under-analyzed theme. The protagonist's name alerts readers to the issue: because the name "Louis" is rooted in the terms war and warrior, we might translate his name as *a religious faith in war/warriors*. By incessantly remembering combat, its casualties as well as its ostensible inevitability, King's novel forces readers to confront a troubling link between military conflict and the (d)evolution of his main characters (of note, this subtext is not always available in the film adaptations). The novel's references to the unsavoriness of war are numerous. For instance, Louis remembers his college roommate who left school to become a drug addict in Vietnam. More often, *Pet Sematary* gestures at World War I, the "Great War," by conveying the abject fullness of life during that period in a way that resurrects Roosevelt's bald jingoism: "Violent lives, violent deaths" (50). Jud buries his first dog in 1914—the year that this particular war started—while Louis makes models of World War I airplanes as a child until, one day, he simply tires of the activity because he's "growing up." And then there is the name of the family cat, Winston Churchill, a title that clearly conjures associations with both the world wars and the stubborn defiance of an old warhorse. Through its countless gestures at twentieth-century warfare, then, *Pet Sematary* underlines how American society romanticizes military conflict as an expression of a lost masculinity to be mourned (and then reinstated through armed combat).

To convey these connections, *Pet Sematary* produces two abstract constellations: life/peace/emasculation versus death/war/masculinity. Creed's cat Churchill—the novel casts his namesake as *the* representative "man's-man" —embodies the reckless, obstinate combativeness that Louis fears may be fading within himself as he ages. The cat's "masculinity," his "go-to-hell" stare, signals something that Louis has been conditioned by American culture to treasure. When the family spays the cat, the doctor surgically alters his presumed masculine spirit and Church becomes an "it." The male feline goes from "gunslinger" to "convalescent," gaining weight as "it" adheres to a domestic routine meant to dissuade it from crossing the deadly Route 15. After the cat dies, and Louis brings "it" to the Micmac cemetery to return "it" to life, the cat recovers his "real nature." He once again engages in ruthless deeds, like dispatching neighborhood birds with cold efficiency. This "restored" Churchill, janky and unpleasantly aggressive, highlights a jingoism wrapped in pure machismo, a ploy used by American authorities to inspire poor young men into joining the war cause of the moment.[3] How will Louis—and the rest of us, for that matter—cope with an imminent End of History at the close of the twentieth century, with its drudgery and utter banality? Does America *need* the threat of war to stay alive (literally as well as figuratively)? King contrasts Louis's quiet desperation, as he watches himself systematically domesticated—husband, father, infirmary worker—with his rebellious urge to "floor the accelerator and drive away without so much as a look back" (22, 90, 120, 4). *Pet Sematary* articulates this (monstrous) condition by depicting twentieth-century History as caught within a death drive in which the notions of life and death are reversed—to be alive requires death; to die bestows new life. As it becomes obvious that Louis must transcend the ennui of his suburban existence by coming into much closer proximity with death, jingoism forms an entropic loop. Arising from beneath the soil, the fuel of rejuvenating conflict propels a self-perpetuating war machine.[4] King's story reminds us of how, in the World War I-era poetry of W.B. Yeats, the absence of a fallen soldier looms to such a degree that the difference between presence and absence dissolves. Or, more appropriate still, the novel conjures the dark underbelly of Rupert Brooke's patriotic poem, "Nineteen-Fourteen: The Soldier," a poem that valorizes death in combat as a cure-all: "There shall be / in that rich earth a richer dust concealed" (Brooke). King's attentive reader grows slowly aware of the siren song that led many young men into the world wars as Louis eagerly quaffs the restless air of Micmac History retained in this unhallowed ground in order to feel young again, to feel "viscerally alive" like the "company commanders in World War I" who boldly faced down their imminent demise (King, *Pet* 157).

On Creed's initiation journey to bury Church, Jud assures Louis that the only way to get up to the "stony soil" of the Micmacs is to "keep walking and don't look down," a metaphoric revelation for how both inherently militant men—these would-be warriors—surrender willingly their judgment skills and volition to preternatural forces greater than themselves. Indeed, *Pet Sematary* contains an unhealthy array of male secrets, as if buried deep in the soil itself: a series of past sins—the disenfranchisement of the Native American, the sacrifice of American youth as a consequence of the country's deathless wars, the willingness to confer upon oil companies a free pass to extract natural resources and conduct business in whatever manner that most benefits the corporation, the masculine compulsion to lie and mislead women—that remain, like the secret of the graveyard itself, unexamined and subject to cyclical repetition. The more involved Creed becomes with the cryptic agency governing the Micmac woods, the less connected he becomes to his own life. This process of alienation is most evident in his estrangement from his wife and family after the death of his son (daughter in the second film iteration). Having strayed from the "civilizing" influence represented by women and family, Creed and Crandall are reduced to their basest, most selfish selves, transformed into extensions of the Wendigo at its most misanthropic. The Micmac site itself belonged to Native American *male* warriors—presumably, only men were buried there—and as the novel and films delve deeper into the realm of a specifically masculine grief, the two white men reveal their connection to the supposedly masculine energy that centers inside the Micmac graveyard. What is there about the Micmac site that draws men to it? And why *only* men? (We explore the implicit "queerness" projected in King's version of American History in Chapter 5.) Women are excluded, except as experimental victims, from the secreted knowledge of the power residing there. They are first to recognize, however, the products that emerge from the resurrection process as "abominations." "'Women are supposed to be the ones good at keeping secrets,'" Jud proposes to Louis after they bury Church, "'but any woman who knows anything at all would tell you she's never really seen into any man's heart. The soil of a man's heart is stonier, Louis—like the soil up there in the old Micmac burying ground'" (155, 141). The men in Ludlow keep their postmortem experiments to themselves, just as Creed keeps the truth of the place from his wife and daughter. In *Pet Sematary*, the violent wreathe of History recapitulates a toxic machismo that (the story claims) predates America's founding.

Jud and Louis are drawn into a fallacy so common among American males that it is their responsibility to "fix every problem"—a desire that extends into the realm of resurrecting dead cats and children—an urge that is not nearly so prevalent among the story's women.[5] As a man of science trained in cause-and-effect logistics, Doctor Creed trusts that he will be able to harness the powers of the Micmac and employ them for his own purposes. In the Lambert adaptation, Crandall admits that he "has my reasons" for introducing Creed to the burial site, but certainly the main reason is because Jud is drunk with an intoxicating brew of power and corruption too alluring to resist. In the end, they both become "polluted" as husbands, fathers, friends, even as "civilized" humans under the spell of the Wendigo's sophistry. This bears a parallel relationship to the same unquestioned machismo that has fed the mistakes of modern American History—from capitalism's exploitation of resources that belong to everyone in order to benefit the ruling class, to a foreign policy that has relied too heavily on military intervention inside sovereign nation-states in order to secure and protect perceived American corporate interests. In spite of such historical realities, America claims an allegiance with the innocuous, pastoral innocence residing in the children's Pet Sematary, a place where tragedy is lightened by the collective nostalgia of selective memory. Successive American administrations have chastised foreign nations for their human rights violations, but America itself is reticent to assume ownership for its share of similar sins. In spite of its official protestations, the nation's History maintains a profound connection to the corrosive inner workings of the secret cemetery in the wilderness: the repressed realities of "soured" democratic ideals born out of colonialism, white nationalism, racism, misogyny, Citizen's United, and income inequality. Like Mary Shelley's *Frankenstein*, *Pet Sematary* offers a sobering reminder that males are severely punished when they abandon humility in favor of arrogant misadventures. (The trick, as we will see shortly, is that even attempts at escape from the prison of Reason—a kind of "freedom" readily linked to the openness of the modern highway—wind up resurrecting impulses long thought buried. To carry the text's political metaphor to completion, the Wendigo's warriors invariably return as the warriors of Wall Street.)

To illustrate this cannibalizing drift, it is worth noting that the abundance of spiral and circular images associated with the Wendigo's power are present, to greater or lesser degrees, in all three of the *Pet Sematary* texts, although most extensively in King's novel. Initially, these images appropriate the Native American belief of human life as a circular voyage; death does not complete this voyage, it serves as a transition to another state of being. Images of the spiral and circle have mystical significance in Native American lore: they are often employed by artists and shamans to suggest levels of supernatural power, deviousness, and the torturous. Although the Indians no longer make use of the site because its properties have become perverted, the white men of Ludlow mirror the cyclical nature of sin—the circle of mistakes in which Jud and later Creed are entrapped and forced to repeat in feeding dead bodies to the site: Baterman -> Church -> Gage -> Rachel (and the rest of the Creed family in the film's second cinematic incarceration). In other words, the novel and films suggest that the wrongdoings and fateful consequences of one man can, and soon enough will, be the evil undoing of the next man. History, like the restless hunger at work in the Micmac site, forges a chain with which the archaic past is juxtaposed with the present, linking the mythology of the American Indian with the inimitable needs of vulnerable Yankee men. America (writ large) fails to recognize, much less learn from, its own mistakes—to break the circle of its own repeated failings. The archaic past requires an active connection to the present in order to reanimate itself. The male inhabitants of this small town constitute a line of participants spiraling up through History to the abandoned Micmac site, passing its dark secret on to the next generation. In the 2019 film, Crandall and Creed note the presence of a spiral image carved into the trunk of a tree on their passage to the Micmac cemetery. They interpret it only as a "warning." But it is more than that: it is also reflective of an inclusionary power, the desire to possess and to be possessed by the virulent and interactive spirit that still resides there. In this sense, the highway is not the noisome intrusion of a commercial present into an idyllic past that it initially appears to be; rather, it is another layer in a vast palimpsest of violence and self-destruction that gives American soil its rocky constitution. It is difficult for readers to imagine a more depressing vision of the nation's History, or a more dispiriting vision of human History.

The connection between a buried past resurrected for use in the present is a constant theme in King's canon (in fact, throughout the Gothic), and it typically provides a vehicle for the unleashing and exposure of evil. Something from the past—long gone, long dead—is either dug up, exposed, or compelled to return to life in the present. In King's world, the past is vampiric: it only plays at being dead and actually lives on forever, even in a dormant state. For instance, in the "Smoke-Hole Ceremony" in *IT*, Richie and Mike witness the birth of It in an era that roughly corresponds to the age of prehistoric America. Mike speculates that "'It's *always* been here since the beginning of time ... since before there were men *anywhere* ... It was there then, sleeping, maybe, waiting for the people to come'" (*IT* 763). In the inanimate, malevolent centers in King's fiction—from Christine, to the Marston House, to the Overlook Hotel, to the spaceship in *The Tommyknockers*, to the Micmac cemetery—an intimate connection between a specific tainted place and the human world is necessary to animate malefic energies. The fall of the Micmac site is reminiscent of the Garden of Eden. Their ground going "sour" can be seen as a parallel to original sin in the American-Christian formulation, and as a consequence a "barrier" was erected around the grounds to exclude future human contact. When the warrior men of Ludlow chose to transgress the barrier and reentered this place, they forged their own nexus with the sin that was born when the land originally belonged to the Micmacs. Evil in the King universe exists as a theoretical construct without human beings, that is to say, evil only becomes real when humans enter into its realm and serve as hosts to an unresolved past that waits anxiously to be reawakened.

Pet Sematary dismays over Louis's (ill-advised) submission to the terms and conditions of this corrosive History by puncturing delusions of romanticized death in a manner that echoes the Naturalist tendencies of Erich Maria Remarque's novel *All Quiet on the Western Front* (1928). After being resurrected, Churchill drags his bloody kill to the front step to expose his owner to the ugliness of actual death, and Louis's enflamed libido quickly cools at the sight. In *Pet Sematary*, death is never as life-giving as it seems to be because the figures that return from the grave—like Church or Louis's son—are somehow wrong, physically resembling the originally interred, but once reanimated more vicious and less humane. Backed by the sounds of the counter-cultural Ramones, the symbol of the modern highway is thus cast in a different light than the death drive of an American History steered by politicians with incessant plans for war. The murderous highway offers a bitter antidote for this American History by reminding Creed of his innate fallibility. Like King, Karl Popper critiques earlier Historians for attempting "to understand the meaning of the play which is performed on the Historical Stage." Because humanity lacks prophetic abilities, Popper argues, it is foolish to "believe that (H)istory has a meaning that can be discovered in (I)t" (Popper, *Volume I* 8; *Volume II* 279). King's grim text aims to dismantle the war machine, and to satiate America's endless thirst for violence, by radically altering our perception of History with a capital "H." By alienating readers from the draw to jingoism and machismo that destroys Creed, King hopes to disenchant Americans of their incessant self-sabotage. To learn this painful lesson, however, his audiences must separate the highway from the cemeteries—an imaginary separation that raises a number of concerns for us.

Our reading of *Pet Sematary* thus departs in significant ways from previous interpretations. Heidi Strengell, for one, highlights how Creed mimics Mary Shelley's creation, Victor Frankenstein, through his willingness to interfere with the "natural" order as well as his overall "lack of humility."[6] According to the logic of this analysis, if Creed had opted for "piety and patience" instead of hubris, he could have survived his ordeal (Strengell 62). But to accept the tacit alternative of "natural" incertitude—offered up, very clearly, by the unpredictable Route 15—is akin to embracing the barbaric laws of the highway itself. Strengell's implicit solution to Creed's crisis (to retreat into a constant state of unknowing, likely at the feet of cultural totems of change like the Dow Jones Index) overlooks the attendant pitfalls of resigning oneself to behaviors required by the dominant political economy. Put a bit differently, if audiences too hastily align Dr. Creed with Dr. Frankenstein, they might ignore the contemporary context that aligns Creed with his moment in time, and the far from "natural," highway deaths he witnesses. In resigning himself to Gage's death, it can be argued that Creed (and the audience, by proxy) must symbolically resign himself to the inevitability of everything that the roadway represents.

We must remember that it is Louis's *refusal* of what King depicts as a "natural" shift into existential incertitude that exposes him to the story's most abject terrors. Perhaps if he had simply left well enough alone, if he had simply let the highway do its work unimpeded, none of the other consequential horrors would have befallen him. In the *Frankenstein* mold, *Pet Sematary* contends that violence erupts when short-sighted human beings attempt to change fate's timeline. This cautionary tale would formulaically reiterate Shelley's lesson *if not* for the fact that Creed's refusal of social planning, especially in the context of the mid-1980s, is a fraught decision, one that parallels the broad disaggregation of the state's caretaking functions during that period. Whereas the state commits wanton destruction in episodes like the Great War, King's novel implies that the economy embodied in the highway facilitates more "natural" forms of creative destruction. For further support of this interpretation, we might recall how the evil of King's *Christine* (1983) tries to reverse the odometer of America's industrial evolution. Whenever King's fiction focuses upon American automotive culture, it concurrently advocates obsequiousness to an economic order that means to harness "the epistemological incertitude of the postmodern project in service of its aims" (Blake and Monnet 1). In *From a Buick 8* (2002), a boy embraces what he cannot comprehend (his father's death) thanks to the post-Fordist frenzy of a haunted Buick.[7] Along these same lines, Louis reluctantly admits that only mortality—not social conflict (he repeats the idea to emphasize it)—can be accepted with any degree of certainty. Like King's other automotive texts, then, *Pet Sematary* contrasts the healthy maturation of teenage boys with a perverted sense of "progress" linked to modern warfare. King's doomed teens are either prematurely old or they refuse to grow up. To avoid the fate of boys like Arnie, Louis would need to resign himself to "natural" paths of aging defined, above all else, by the credence that he can never really know what comes next. Whereas nostalgia begets war, King argues that willful blindness preserves peace. Route 15, in turn, overtly depends upon "luck" rather than jingoism (23). By encapsulating the contingencies as well as vulnerabilities of the contemporary American highway with the harsh realities of an inherently fragile existence during America's earlier wars, *Pet Sematary* declares a more benevolent vision of history (with a lower case "h"): a proposed alternative that all-too-neatly dovetails with the freer flows of commerce unleashed in the 1980s. As Thomas Friedman (infamously and erroneously) declared during the era, the rise of financial markets render obsolete the engine of warfare, as no advanced capitalist countries could ever possibly come to blows under these conditions. In short, by isolating the deaths caused by the highway (like Gage's) from prior deaths upon the battlefield (like Timmy Baterman's), *Pet Sematary* tacitly argues that America's post-History will prove to be a less bloody affair.[8]

Driving on the Open Road

Although Route 15 seems to open up an alternative to the entropic cycle of History, the complications of this illusory break manifest in the subplot of Timmy Baterman. After being killed in the line of duty during the Great War, the War Department returns Timmy's body to his father in Ludlow. His father, devastated by the loss, elects to bury his son in the Micmac cemetery in order to restore him to life. Unfortunately, like Church, Timmy's subsequent restoration is marred by a dramatically altered disposition. When a merciless Timmy mocks his father and friends and performs acts of violence against them, his father kills him for a second time (before killing himself). In this subplot, *Pet Sematary* takes aim at a cyclical war machine that deceived a seventeen-year-old boy and his parental guardians through the false promises of hyper-masculinity and jingoism. At the same time, King's readers might consider the way in which Timmy's body arrives home: via a train that speeds through towns such as Ludlow, dropping off coffins "like a fugging milkman" (340). We can note similarities between the novel's image of a train desensitized to human misery and the films' image of the highway, where trucks tasked with delivering petrol commodities disregard human life in order to keep the economy moving along at advanced speeds. Tracing the emergence of the modern transportation system in the United States, Ginger Strand notes, "America became more violent and more mobile at the same time" (1). The rise of the highway not only led to horrific carnage through automotive accidents, it also fueled a spike in gory encounters between strangers, radically disrupting the close-knit communities that it literally and figuratively stream-rolled in the name of "progress." Against the text's active delineation of the two impulses driving History—its resignation to blind "progress" (biological and commercial) and its distaste for efforts to reverse-engineer a better society/family—*Pet Sematary* unconsciously exposes an overlap that has been lurking below the surface all along.

Whether hauling corpses around like any other disposable good, or "using them up" in the name of material advancement, *war and commerce share a mutual indifference to human bodies.* This mutual indifference finds an analog once again in the rocky soil of the Micmac site, where apparently all dead organisms are welcomed—cats, dogs, human children of both sexes, and men and women of all ages. Conveyed through representative systems of transportation (railways and highways), *Pet Sematary* unwittingly underscores how the twin narratives of American History—martial and economic—are propelled by uninterrupted flows of violence.

It's not just that the "mean road" of economic advancement has failed to abolish military conflict as Friedman promised (although it has certainly failed to do so); the modern roadway also "uses up" bodies in ways that, while perhaps less stark than sending them into combat overseas, remain nevertheless violent by nature. Christian Marazzi labels this phenomenon "biocapitalism." He writes: "The post-Fordist productive strategies in which one's entire life is put to work, when knowledges and cognitive competences of the workforce ... assume the role played by machines in the Fordist period, incarnated in living productive bodies of cooperation, in which language, affects, emotions and relational and communication capacities all contributed to the creation of value" (113). Route 15 disrupts the everyday life of anyone that lives near it. "That frigging road," Jud moans, "No peace from it." While precariously crossing Route 15 involves less conscious planning on the part of the brave individual—a crucial, romantic aspect that supposedly elevates chaotic commerce above warfare—the highway still thrives upon the bodies that it "uses up." The name of Creed's son, Gage, highlights this omnipresent biocapitalism. The name functions as a homonym for the word gauge—a connection that intimately links the boy's body to a truck's vital signs, and turns him into part and parcel of the machinations behind America's imagined mobility. The notion that Gage may have been always-already part of the very truck that destroyed him may be the most devastating suggestion made in King's story. Biocapitalism, like war itself, involves the cooptation and calloused disposal of bodies (a point that *Pet Sematary* never fully admits, but of which it also never loses sight). If this grim reality is accounted for, then the modern highway and its attendant machinery may not be the ideal vehicle for delivering King's Shelley-esque message of resignation to unpredictability.

Nonetheless, King's reader is meant to accept the road's fast-paced intrusions and ignore Jud's lamentations for days gone by (it is, after all, Jud's noxious nostalgia that paved the way for murderous zombies like Timmy Baterman). The novel, of course, does not hide that its paved emblem of "progress" remains one of its main purveyors of violence. King's highway churns up living bodies, like feed, in order to keep itself going, "using up" organisms in a way that recalls Walter Benjamin's debris being blown backwards. If the text presents the Great War as a perversion that led

50   *The Pasts of Pet Sematary*

men to their premature deaths, what are we to make of this other destructive entity that mows down innocent victims like Gage? What are we to make of a town that sanctions a proven killer (the highway) in order to service the economic interests of arguably Ludlow's most important employer and corporate entity? Is it possible that the profits of the Orinco company have come to supersede the dangers posed by Route 15? And, even more to the point, is it likewise plausible that the radiant power of the Micmac cemetery has formed an unwitting collusion with both Orinco and the town highway commission in order to keep the flow of commerce as well as the flow of dead bodies coming through a pipeline that carries so much more than simple petroleum? A cancerous American History returns to feed upon itself. To give this circular connection a striking visual, after Rachel's rental car breaks down in the 1990 film of *Pet Sematary*, she hitchhikes a ride back to Ludlow in the cab of an Orinco truck—the same company, possibly even the same truck, responsible for recently killing her toddler. The film's implication is that the truck has been sent to "rescue" her and speed her return home to confront the transformation of her dead son into a Wendigo vampire. The filmic text does more than merely suggest a supernatural collusion that places Gage and his kite just beyond the reach of Louis and in the center of Route 15 at the worst coincidental moment. When Rachel descends from the truck, as Pascow's ghost notes, "at the end of the line," just under the big red door of the truck on the passenger's side the number "666" is revealed clearly stenciled in white letters, the numerical sign of the Devil, another not-so-subtle affirmation of the link between the Orinco company and the malefic force that animates the Micmac burial ground.

The same infernal nexus that connects the energies buried in the Micmac site with the Orinco company again manifests itself when Rachel is deposited directly in front of Crandall's house where she will become Gage's second victim. Had the truck dropped her off at home instead of at Crandall's, she and her husband might potentially have presented a united front against the demonic Gage. But as it is, she remains isolated and manipulated prey, only the most recent sacrifice by Route 15 to the sinister Micmac-Orinco merger.

For decades the American petroleum industry has been involved in a highly organized and duplicitous process of denial: denial over its periodic and random price gouging of the American public, denial over its corporate tax loopholes, denial over its collusion to subvert public transportation efforts in favor of single unit automobiles, denial over the number of dead expended in wars fought to possess or influence the flow of black gold, denial over its role in compromising human and planetary health and well-being, and ultimately denial over its contribution to lethal climate change. The secretive world of the oil industry, whose disinformation clogs the arteries of public discourse and political oversight, strikes a subtle parallel with the secret evil that resides underground in the Micmac soil. If the

Figure 2.1 Rachel Creed hitches a ride onboard an Orinco truck—note the white 666 marking on the truck's undercarriage—from hell.

argument made by the novel and films holds, King's readers and film patrons should resign themselves to a manipulative fate dictated by the necessity of the modern roadway and the global petro-chemical cartel: a price we all must pay for "progress." But what if Gage's death wasn't just an "accident" meant to expose Doctor Creed's latent hubris? As a metonym for the increasingly volatile marketplace of the 1980s and beyond, King's highway promulgates neo-Calvinist doom that humans can neither forecast nor avoid. Audiences must therefore hesitate before writing off the haunted thoroughfare as just another Frankenstein rip-off.

The story of *Pet Sematary* is full of binaries that prove to be false. In the novel and in both movies, Victor Pascow, the first to tell Creed about the dangers inside the Micmac site, warns that "the barrier was not meant to be broken." The use of the word "barrier" here is both literal (the deadfall) and cultural (the white man's intrusion into Native American land and burial rites). In this liminal space, local Ludlow History absorbs the Indian understanding of circles and spirals as symbols of eternity, a return to mother earth as a womb that continues the circularity of deathless birthing and rebirthing, the continuation of life beyond death. The Indians also made their camps in the shapes of circles, looking inward and outward simultaneously. The Micmac site is mirrored below in the actual Pet Sematary the town's children use to bury their pets. Like the continual references to America's various wars, both graveyards center around a similar circular pattern.

However, as delineated visually in the films, the pet graveyard seems smaller, more neatly organized, and it is clear that the ground upon which it sits is a safe place, "a good place … where the pain stops and the good

Figure 2.2 Jud Crandall and Louis Creed violate the concentric cairns of the Micmac cemetery in *Pet Sematary*.

memories can begin," as Jud reassures Ellie, verdant green with grass and wildflowers (this faux contrast is especially emphasized in the cinematography of the first film adaptation). In contrast, the Micmac site lacks all vegetation, a remote and alien place carved out of alabaster granite and stone rocks. It takes Creed literally hours to dig holes large enough to inter Church and, later, his son. The trailhead that Jud and Louis use is the only place where there is a deadfall of trees, suggesting that this threshold on the trail has been deliberately constructed so as not to be crossed, and that perhaps nature itself has created the barrier to halt human traffic from entering into the terrible power of the Wendigo. The natural world presented beyond the verdant soil of the children's Pet Sematary—from the deadfall, to the complex root system identified with the trees growing along the sharply uphill trail, to the slabs of smooth-faced granite on the outskirts of the Micmac site—seems deliberately designed as obstacles to human concourse. The difference between the two sites couldn't be more obvious: the genuine spirit of childhood innocence and grief is found in the burial ground for pets, whereas the darkly restless and manipulative spirit of the Wendigo fuels the Micmac ground. Recalling the Romance of American History that we analyzed in Chapter 1, Louis faces a bifurcated reality that is at once pastoral *and* horrifying.

And yet there is no real split here, only an unnerving blend of violent forces. The Orinco trucks—the sound of their speeding by the Creed and Crandall houses is a constant soundtrack in the Lambert film—echo the restless and relentless energy animating the Micmac graveyard. As the dead Pascow warns Creed in a dreamscape, "'Remember this: there is more power here than you know. It is old and always restless'" (87). Neither of the film adaptations nor the novel itself attempts to explain what went wrong in the Micmac ground—either how or why it turned malevolent. In the end, the difference between these two places may turn out to be another sinister subterfuge wrought by the Wendigo itself, hiding behind the mask of innocence in the children's burial ground as a means for disguising the soured dynamism seething in the Indian cemetery above it. Pascow recognizes this exact duplicity when he tells Creed the children's burial ground is "'not the real cemetery'" (74). Just as the cutesy Sematary (marked by its adorable misspelling) shares a root system with the more overtly aggressive ground that it borders, *prima facie* differences between World War I era Ludlow and the "real time" globalized Ludlow prove in the end to be a mere façade, one that speaks to dangerous misdirection experienced by King's audiences today. In the militant march of American History, children become men as men become children (we remember Paul in Remarque's *All Quiet on the Western Front*, prematurely aged and reduced to infancy as a result of the terrors of war), while life becomes death and death becomes life. Important psychic and physical borders bleed away.

In the same vein, although the two houses that are central to events in all of these texts—the Crandall and Creed residences—stand opposite one another, bisected by Route 15, their over-determined difference mirrors the false separation of the two nearby cemeteries. The Creed house is a "big old New England colonial ... surrounded by a luxuriant sprawl of lawn, lushly green in even this August heat" and it elicits instant joy from the Creed women; Rachel pronounces it "beautiful" on first sight. The Creeds greet their new home with a rustic innocence as city-dwellers face-to-face with their own piece of rural Maine real estate. This response parallels Louis's reaction to the lower-level children's Pet Sematary when it is first introduced into the text: "The forested backdrop lent the place a crazy sort of profundity, a charm ... the commitment of love and grief seemed to him staggering ... too perfect for a work of nature" (16, 42–6). Readers (and viewers, especially of the Lambert film) are thus set up to view Crandall's old house in sharp distinction from the manicured Creed estate—and, of course, the pet cemetery itself. Lambert's film emphasizes the gothic qualities of Jud's dilapidated home, with its weather-beaten clapboards, single front copula, sloping roof, and a general haunted house ambiance. The documentary entitled *Unearthed and Untold: The Path to Pet Sematary* provides actual footage of how Lambert's crew refashioned the quaint saltbox home that exists in real time across the road from Creed's house into a ramshackle monstrosity replete with fireboard dry-wall under the decaying grey edifice in order to protect the original home from the film's final conflagration. The purpose of this extra effort was to create out of Jud's house a subtle connection to the primitive Micmac graveyard, its aged and haunted milieu—evidence of Crandall's long-time affiliation with the site—while Creed's neat, freshly-sided yellow house is linked to the lovingly-kept innocent "charm" of the children's Sematary. It is therefore no accident that zombie Gage and his feline ally Church select Jud's house as the location to confront both Louis and Rachel. Once they return from the dead they are appropriately drawn to Crandall's house rather than Creed's. After the resurrected Gage has killed Jud and Rachel, Creed is confronted with a phantasm of the house's interior turned into a swamp-like nightmare, a place that is emblematic of the spiritual space linked to the Wendigo itself. Zombie Gage prepares his father for their reintroduction by first transforming Jud's house into a surreal simulacrum of the Micmac wilderness (restaging Timmy Baterman's reunion with his father). It is as if the revenant has brought Little God swamp into Jud's living room, with green moss lining the stairwell and flowing mud over the furniture and walls. Appearances also prove to be deceiving as the murderous highway does not so much bifurcate the past from the present—the grotesque trench warfare of World War I from the promised bounty of global capitalism—as it (unwittingly) joins them together, giving a passageway to the deadly secrets that they share.

And yet, despite all of this common ground, while the "unnatural" Great War apparently entices men to their death under the specious lure of revitalization, King's story seems to suggest that the naturalized highway cannot be blamed for its senseless killings. The highway subsequently blends into the rural Maine landscape, an element as capricious as a lightning strike. Once more, King's novel reveals nostalgia to be a toxic sentiment by focusing upon Louis's unwillingness to let go of things that should be left for dead; his defiance of the laws of "nature" is what consigns him to his death. Much like *Christine*, a story about a spurned blue-collar worker that impedes progress by zealously clinging to his youth, *Pet Sematary* petitions that we must accept the inexorable motion of "progress" as well as blissful ignorance of a more dynamic history (with a lower-case "h"): "'Some things it don't pay to be curious about'" (212). This vision of history—moved by capitalist advancement—may be agonizing, but it still proves preferable to a History driven by never-ending battle. Perry Anderson describes King's underlying ideal: "A world in which all states (share) a common normative commitment to free markets and free elections would not be one that generated the classical range of military hostilities." According to Anderson, the transition from world wars to global markets—in which "war was an evil to be overcome, whose necessity is diminishing as states approach their rational norm"—supports a fantasy that the American economy of the late twentieth century no longer necessitates violence (334, 336). We have moved across the proverbial street and found peace on the other side. Such an illusory split encourages audiences to isolate the End of History from the "unnatural" conflicts that precede it and, in so doing, to ignore the continuities that run beneath the surface. A thoroughly chastened Louis Creed can no more be "saved" than can Victor Frankenstein because, for Creed, his eventual admission that he could control the future (had he lived to realize it) would need to be read as a rather perverse prostration before the runaway trucks that killed his only son. Unlike the entropic cycle that manifests in the burial grounds, King's story implies that the modern highway must be forgiven, perhaps even respected, for delivering to Creed a moral lesson that might have brought about his redemption. It goes without saying that this grotesque alternative history (with a lower-case "h") hardly provides peace of mind to King's audience.

Against the neat-and-tidy binaries of the story, the unsavory aspects of capitalism race to the fore with no sign of slowing. The Lambert film gestures at a critique of capitalist excess when, in one scene, we see Creed reading a book by E. Nesbit. An early twentieth-century writer, Nesbit's proclivities for cat-themed tales for children (tales that walk a line between harsh realism and fantasy) make her work an ideal fit for *Pet Sematary*. At a deeper level, this reference underscores the story's latent distaste for everything that the Orinco company emblematizes by gesturing at Nesbit's well-known role in co-founding the socialist Fabian Society. In another instance (this time from the novel), Creed remembers the "showroom" of his uncle, an undertaker: "No new cars there, no televisions with all the modern features, no dishwashers with glass fronts" (19, 31). In this pregnant moment, King's horrifying palimpsest blurs the line between an undertaker's "showroom," the shiny spectacles of American consumerism, and the ancient burial sites that are appropriated from Native American lore. Just as the image of the coffin overlays the image of the new car, or aligns with the antiquated (if pedestrian) delivery of milk to one's doorstep, the American Dream cannot be completely isolated from the death drive that undergirds conflicts like the Great War and continues to feed the supernatural hunger of an archaic place that exists to exploit tears born from America's dark past. The rapid cross-cutting of these images produces one of King's most depressing portraits to date: a nation that, in spite of its apparent "maturation," in spite of its presumed transition from a violent History driven by war to the peaceful post-History promised by globalization, takes U-turns—obsessively—back towards self-destruction. At the time of this writing, the martial parade appears to be looping back to the oil-rich Middle East (a theater that it has never truly left) in order to engage with Iran.

King's treatment of this death drive unconsciously exposes a subtext that has for centuries lingered throughout American life. Even Teddy Roosevelt knew that his doctrine of self-reliance would be regarded as "merciless" because it sparks Darwinian economics, what he recognized as "an impersonal and indirect sort of genocide." Roosevelt could never adequately extricate his blood-soaked vision of Darwinian selection from the so-called invisible hand of the marketplace. Rather, industrial capitalism converged quite nicely with his preferred frontier traditions, helping him to conceptualize a "military aristocracy" worthy of its standing. Although Roosevelt's jingoism wishes to offer readers "an alternative to commercialism," his vision remains "nonetheless (the) product" of a capitalist order

(Slotkin 618, 637). *Pet Sematary* likewise conflates America's storyline of "regeneration through violence" by augmenting a brutal commonality shared by the twin impulses of American History (martial as well as economic). Even as King's text limits its reader by resigning her to the rules of the post-History road, it also unwittingly alerts her to the growing fallacy of a bloodless American History. Time and time again, it has been presented as perfectly "natural" to "use up" human bodies in service to the nation's global missions. King's presumed pivot from bloody to bloodless accounts of American History, then, must on some level be recognized as fancy footwork that provides reassurance to a culture apparently unable to escape from an "ancient" call to violence (a call that, in truth, comes not from without, from the Micmac warriors, but from within, from America's collective *mythos*). In the end, King cannot earn forgiveness for the modern highway, and his story's inability to uphold the boundaries that it erects suggests a suspicion that American History may remain savage to the bitter end. Perhaps this latent despair explains why King himself nearly didn't publish *Pet Sematary* for fear that it was too defeatist.[9]

In closing, one of the many things that makes *Pet Sematary* such a revelatory text for tracking attitudes toward American History over the past fifty years is the transformation of Pascow's "barrier" into a permeable border, incapable of protecting the invasion of the present by the past. To some extent, the "problem" posed in *Pet Sematary* parallels the current migration situation at the American border, only in this instance the border happens to be north instead of south. Since the white men of Ludlow once invaded property that belonged to the Micmacs—appropriating the land, the oil located under it, and, later, the transformative potential of their gravesite—the restless spirit of that ancient place, in turn, gained license to cross into the present and interface boldly with the Maine families and communities of contemporary white America. Literal and figurative walls are meaningless because *all* ground in King's fictional world—not just the tainted terra of the Micmac cemetery—reveals itself to be haunted. Although the issue is seldom framed in this way by the media, the CIA, or politicians, American History has implicitly been viewed as a one-way street: throughout its existence, colonial powerbrokers in the United States have felt free to invade other countries in order to obtain resources, worker bodies, enact regime change, and serve the will of American corporations.[10] This is reflective of Crandall and Creed's imperialistic postures. Neither male feels much compunction about accessing the Micmac site, and the notion that they are trespassing on Indian ground and culture never occurs to them. But what has occurred in both the *Pet Sematary* texts, and the corresponding geopolitical sphere, is that an expected one-way street has become a two-way thoroughfare with which immigrants approach the American border, requesting everything from asylum to reparations, while ghosts of the Wendigo dictate what kind of being can cross back across the border. Because the Micmac cemetery was invaded by men bearing much in common with colonial interlopers, it became, in a way, part of the United States. The Wendigo spirit gained permission to enter into Ludlow because Ludlow entered into the sacred land of the Micmac. Throughout King's Gothic works, the evil done to others invariably comes home to roost, and so the ending of *Pet Sematary* posits that the breeching of Pascow's "barrier" has unbarred the border to open traffic between past and present, contemporary trespassers and an archaic supernatural agency antithetical not only to white male privilege, but to all things human. King's multiverse thus reveals that even the most earnest attempts to abscond from the confines of American History—attempts, by King as well as his characters, to hit the open road without the "hang-ups" of previous generations—end in frustration, as the gates are once more left yawning and blood unfailingly issues forth.

Notes

1   In conversation with Stephen King several years ago when *Pet Sematary* was first published, Tony asked him about the role Jud Crandall plays in precipitating the tragedy the Creed family undergoes. After all, at one point in the book Jud confesses to Louis that "'the place might have *made* Gage die because I introduced you to the power in the place. I am saying that I may have murdered your son with good intentions'." King's reaction was almost immediate, labelling Jud "polluted," a term that implies that the old man had been morally tainted or poisoned because of direct contact with the Micmac burial site. The term is especially provocative in the context of the Orinco company's role in purveying a product that "pollutes" air and water as well as a force manipulated by the will of the "soured" Micmac burial ground. Curiously, King's choice of word to describe Crandall is the same as Mina Harker's self-description in *Dracula*, "my *polluted* flesh," after the Count forces her to drink his blood in Chapter 21 and begins the process of transforming her into his "companion and helper." As in the vampire tradition, Louis Creed must choose to enter the realm of the vampire; Crandall can introduce him, tempt him with the secret knowledge he possesses, but Louis ultimately makes his own decision to go ahead and disregard Pascow's warning in burying his cat beyond the deadfall. That introduction serves as a nexus connecting the doctor and the vampire-like powers that reside in the cemetery. As Crandall informs him: "'*Once you've been up there, it's your place and you belong to it*'" (275, 259, 252, 178; author's emphasis).
2   Oil lubricates America's modern military machine. Had the Japanese elected to bomb the oil reservoirs also housed at Pearl Harbor instead of concentrating on the docked fleet (which would be rebuilt in less than a year), the war might well have taken a different turn. Fifty years later, Vice-President Dick Cheney predicted (incorrectly, it would turn out) that Iraqi oil would foot the bill for the very expensive American invasion of the Middle East.
3   The revivalist element associated with the Micmac site is dramatically illustrated in the Lambert film when Jud introduces the place to Creed as the ground to inter his dead cat. As Louis struggles to climb uphill and to manage the smooth-faced granite slabs located at the top of the mountain, Crandall, who is close to twice the age of the doctor and a chain-smoker, seemingly strides up the mountain while carrying a pick and shovel. It is very clear from both Crandall's body language and words of encouragement that nearing contact with the Micmac soil revivifies the old man. His enthusiasm to lead the way and to share this secret place with Louis reflects the regenerative properties present there. At

58 The Pasts of Pet Sematary

the same time, the film reveals in Jud's obvious excitement the degree to which he remains polluted by his own past contact with its sour spirits.

4 Again, this entropic sense of enclosure appears, at least in the Western literary tradition, to be long-standing. The confines of a violent History specifically remind us of stories from the medieval era: "Replacing fear with gritty endurance and courage or even converting it into steel-edged battle fury must be a prime goal of any successful warrior culture" (Kaeuper 165). It would be perhaps interesting, then, to place Creed's (ambivalent) battle song in conversation with the *chanson de geste*: chivalric training manuals that prod audiences, in distinctive ways, into greater prowess as well as renewed restraint. Further, one way of reading American History in the twentieth century is as a perpetual war machine fed by efforts to preserve and counter the advance of fascism and, later, Marxist communism in its various manifestations.

5 Note how Rachel still suffers from the childhood trauma of her sister's illness and death, while Louis supplies the means for diffusing his wife's guilt and terror via sedatives and by placing the blame on Rachel's parents for their irresponsible act in leaving a sick child alone in the care of her younger sibling.

6 Other influential readings that compare *Pet Sematary* to *Frankenstein* include works by Ray Browne, Gary Hoppenstand, and Mary Pharr.

7 For more on the post-Fordist dimension of King's automotive texts, see Michael Blouin's *Stephen King and American Politics* (forthcoming, University of Wales Press).

8 In *The Lexus and the Olive Tree* (1999), Thomas Friedman famously argues his (now defunct) thesis that countries do not go to war once they have a McDonald's.

9 King writes, in his introduction to the novel, "*Pet Sematary* is the one I put away in a drawer, thinking I had finally gone too far ... I was horrified by what I had written, and the conclusions I'd drawn" (King, *Pet* xi).

10 Consider, for starters, the historical narrative of the Chiquita Brand Fruit Company, headquartered in Fort Lauderdale, Florida, successor to the notorious United Fruit Company, with vast agricultural holdings in Costa Rico, Guatemala, Honduras, and Panama. Chiquita remains the leading grower and distributor of bananas in the United States and throughout the world. To protect this investment in 1928, Chiquita and U.S. officials undermined a strike by workers, leading the U.S. government to threaten Columbia with a Marine Corps invasion if the Columbian government failed to protect Chiquita's interests. As a result, as many as 3,000 workers and their families were massacred on December 6 in the town of Ciénaga, Columbia (Lauterwasser). Since then, Cuba, Guatemala, El Salvador, and Nicaragua have all been invaded by the United States, while the American CIA staged a coup in Chile in 1973 to replace the democratically-elected socialist government of Salvador Allende with a repressive military dictatorship.

3 The Sutured Histories of *The Shining*

The Shining circles around the bloody debris left in the wake of American History, from the genocide of Native Americans through the "dirty wars" of the late twentieth century. As such, King's novel treads on much of the same haunted terrain as *Pet Sematary*: specifically, *The Shining* considers a gory sense of History, driven by death and destruction, as well as the (faux) pivot into a sort of post-History, in which History's oppressive hold might be broken, the cyclic spell broken, and an alternative future—one with dramatically reduced bloodshed—made possible. This (faux) pivot adopts many forms, including generic ones (such as modernist v. postmodern). Beneath this superficial departure, however, *The Shining* (like *Pet Sematary*) never truly lifts itself out of the perpetual violence that continues to grip Americans like a fever dream.

The Overlook Hotel is literally built upon the misery of America's endless wars. In its deepest stratum, again like *Pet Sematary*, King's text locates residual conflicts with Native Americans. Jack Torrance mishears Danny's repeated phrase "Redrum" as "Red Drum"—a reference, he concludes, to the "Indian warpath." The land upon which the Overlook was originally built, like the Micmac ground in *Pet Sematary*, is disputed territory where violence continues to settle more claims than any courtroom. Anticipating Louis Creed, Jack longs to abandon his domestic responsibilities in favor of a so-called "warrior's creed," an unconscious *impulse to fight*—first with George Hatfield, then with the novel's authority figures, then with his family, and, finally, with himself. *The Shining* raises the crucial question with which our book concerns itself: why does American History depend upon the perverse urge to clash with others? With its multiple allusions to rebellious Native Americans, King's text and especially Kubrick's film adaptation (mistakenly) identifies this intemperate compulsion as an "ancient force," one that has purportedly been a part of American History since its very inception. "Great place, the Overlook's Presidential Suite. Wilson, Harding, Roosevelt, Nixon, and Vito the Chopper" (*Shining* 191, 269). The deathless bloodletting at the Overlook, of course, does not actually stem from the character of any flesh-and-blood Native American peoples; rather, these works reveal how figures reportedly resistant to Anglo-militant History—

from Native Americans to postmodern critics—are steadily absorbed into that History as they are forced to mimic, in desperation, the violence that has been enacted upon them. As Paul Ricoeur reminds us, when it comes to American History, it seems as though we must either subscribe to a drive for greater bloodshed or accept the impotence of the yogi.

King's *Shining* understands America's twentieth-century wars as only the latest iteration of a much older death drive. Delbert Grady, a former colleague of Jack, kills his family with a souvenir World War II pistol, a connection that reveals how much constructed memory of the world wars influences the jingoistic cravings of the present. Later, Dick Hallorann—on his way to save the Torrance family—runs into a woman who laments America's "'dirty little wars,'" arguing that "'it is the line soldier who ultimately pays'" (502). Upon parting ways with Hallorann, she flashes him the peace sign, a signal to him (and to King's readers) that the novel shares in her anti-war sentiments. "Good people," the story's logic goes, recognize an unhealthy yearning for conflict in America and seek in its stead a more holistic connection (a "shining") with fellow human beings. The History that binds us together in a self-destructive spiral could supposedly be salvaged as a History that emboldens our better angels. King articulates this sentiment in novels such as *Hearts in Atlantis* and *Dreamcatcher* (see Chapter 4). But the potential with which King tarries has never been fully realized. By the end of the novel, King's characters share a common defeat as bleary-eyed survivors of America's relentless thirst for war. Resembling the somber voice of Walt Whitman in *Drum-Taps*, King appears haunted by the memory of "having lived to behold man burst forth and warlike America rise" (Whitman 319). Wendy and Hallorann are likened to "nightmare survivors from a bombed hospital"; Jack seeks respite in the Overlook like "a man who has come home from a long and bitter war" (*Shining* 293, 516, 653, 503). In a word, *The Shining* expresses a desire to escape from the cyclical prison of American History (a desire that King will re-articulate many times, in a wide range of contexts).

Before the novel imagines how the next generation (Danny, in particular) will break free of American History as constant warfare, *The Shining* first reveals the nation's level of entrenchment. It imbricates Jack's troubled psyche with the troubled collective psyche of the United States, creating a palimpsest of hang-ups and neuroses in order to display how completely the drive to war and self-destruction has brainwashed the American populace. In reference to Jack's alcohol abuse and his physical abuse of Danny, Wendy notes that "the wheels of progress" always lead back to where they started, which is to say, Jack's compulsion to harm his son stems from issues that remain so thoroughly embedded within him that they will not be easily extricated. Even as a young man, Jack displays an attraction to violence, as if it were an illness or addiction: "He remembered perfectly well that he had spent almost every minute of every game in a state of high piss-off, taking every opposing block and tackle personally. He had not enjoyed football.

Every game was a grudge match" (491, 110). In spite of the psychological, and biographical, thrust of King's text, though, *The Shining* should not be read as a singularly private affair. What ails Jack spreads like a contagion that sucks other, much stronger men into the fray. When, upon his exit from the Overlook, Hallorann feels suddenly an inexplicable compulsion to murder Wendy and Danny, King's novel reveals how even Hallorann (a representative black man and therefore an "outsider" from the monied white hierarchy of the hotel) remains tethered to the seminal curse of American History. Unable to sustain the path of a yogi, Hallorann is forced by circumstances to replicate the maniacal behavior of his enemies. In turn, King forces us to ask: are Americans doomed to repeat forever the sins of their literal and symbolic forefathers? Poised at the time of this writing at the precipice of yet another endless war (now with Iran), it behooves us to interrogate the macabre self-sabotage that King's work reveals.

To begin this inquiry, let's attend to one of the novel's breaking points in History: the party on that "hot August night in 1945, the war won, the future stretching ahead so various and new." King's novel repeatedly returns to this party precisely because it demarcates the time of the world wars from the post-war world—a glimpse of America's "whole character," neatly bifurcated, of which *The Shining* will serve as an "index." In theory, this soiree declares America's supremacy by announcing the nation's newly-minted status as "the colossus of the world" (355, 281, 232). Like *Pet Sematary*, the text focuses extensively upon a sort of conceptual hinge: a unique moment that separates American History as a story of ceaseless war from a vague post-History, one that could presumably re-set the proverbial clock. Indeed, the Overlook's explosive gathering aligns with the two nuclear blasts that ended the Pacific War as the frozen clock in the lobby of the Overlook conjures images of the frozen clocks of Hiroshima, permanently stilled by the sudden rupture in the "normal" order of things. For many critical historians, that moment in August 1945 delineates Modernism from a postmodern era that was violently born out of it. That is, *The Shining* dwells upon a hinge that connects a metaphysical History, utilized by the hotel's gentry to summon young men like Jack to their graves, with what we now recognize as Karl Popper's anti-Historicism (postmodern stories of fragmentation as well as disillusionment that madden and/or emancipate readers from the all-too-easy flow of King's prose).

Over the course of the novel, Jack—like a line soldier, consumed by the grand story of American "progress"—adopts "fawning servility" before the mighty machinations of what he gradually comes to accept as "the white man's burden," embodied by the mammoth hotel. He subsequently (d)evolves from a Vermont private school English teacher and Vietnam protestor to a compliant agent of "the cause" (more specifically, what the Overlook stands for in terms of class privilege). Above all else, the hotel conditions Jack to serve as a faithful custodian of American History, the hotel's version of Manifest Destiny—which dovetails neatly with America's Manifest Destiny insofar as the hotel represents the successful epitome of white male domination over all other races and women. Enlisting him to caretake the metanarrative that understands the nation's endless wars as evidence of a much larger and consistent plot, Jack is compelled to imagine that the chronology of his own life synthesizes perfectly with the hotel's bloody marching orders, and that he and this metonymic building are, in fact, "simpatico" (584, 358, 378). In this way, *The Shining* intentionally critiques a structuralist account of American History prevalent in the immediate aftermath of the world wars. Jack's proposed neat-and-tidy chronicle of the hotel—dependent as it is upon the illusion of omnipotence, the bird's-eye view from History's "overlook," nestled in Colorado in the middle of the American landscape—is revealed to be part and parcel of a curse that has enthralled generations of American citizens. By presenting Jack as unable to relinquish his delusion of a cohesive American History, King's novel advocates the flight into New Historicism.[1] Like Danny, King eventually embraces a kind of free-form poetics, a postmodern revelry, that bears an uncomfortable similarity to the rhetoric employed by the Overlook's rebellious (and murderous) party-goers.

Things decidedly take a turn for the worse when the hotel pushes Jack into acting as caretaker for the Overlook's sordid History. Upon discovering boxes of documents in the basement, including a scrapbook with juicy moments from the hotel's past especially designed to intrigue a writer's imagination, he is absorbed into the structuralist method, into piecing together the hotel's History "like pieces in a jigsaw" (a moment, as we show in Chapter 5, echoed in Bryan Singer's film adaptation of *Apt Pupil*). Jack feels emboldened in his quest due to his sudden conviction that there must be a "mystic connection" that ties together the stray bits of information scattered in the belly of the building. In spite of the modern tendency for "things to fall apart," Jack maintains that there simply *must* be an undergirding coherence, just waiting to be found. Like W.B. Yeats, he attempts to paper over the spiraling fatalism that surrounds him with a last-ditch effort to plunge into a supernatural sense of synergy with his national History. He starts to invest in the notion that "luck, fate, providence" will rescue him from his meaningless existence as a failed writer, unemployed teacher, and mediocre husband and father (322, 332, 419). American History manifests as grotesque in both deed and as a matter of public record. In *The Shining*, then, Jack's impulse to organize, to make meaning out of such gory madness, is itself a crucial component of the violent acts that he chronicles. Caretakers like Jack (or Creed) practice abject servility to the mighty tide of American History and, in turn, find themselves consumed by its relentless, cannibalizing force. For Jack, to seek to be "one of them and live forever"—in Yeats's terms, a stone amidst the rushing stream—means being transformed into mere fuel: a "line soldier" in the service of a march towards "progress" that eventually bears more in common with resurrected revenants from the Micmac cemetery than the independent agents of history (with a lower-case "h") that King later lionizes.

The Pivot into Post-History: From Watson to Ullman

To support the novel's claim that warfare drives American History, in his treatment of Kubrick's films, Geoffrey Cocks's *The Wolf at the Door* views *The Shining* as the apotheosis of Kubrick's obsession with all things Germanic; that the "Holocaust lies at the dark heart of *The Shining*, and it is therefore the Nazi devil that dwells in the details of the film." Summoning an array of objects that appear in the movie—the Torrance Volkswagen, Jack's German-made typewriter, the potential connections between Hitler's *Berghof* and the Overlook hotel, Grady's twins and the experiments of Mengele, the proliferation of bathrooms and gas chambers—Cocks raises a fascinating, if ultimately unconvincing, thesis (his argument is weakened by various far-fetched references to wolves and the symbolic mind-numbing multiples of seven that purportedly link the film to the Nazi occupation of Europe in the 1940s). While he does recognize that Kubrick's film "crystallizes most significantly into an elliptical comparison of Nazi genocide with the cultural genocide of Native Americans," Cocks centers his comparison on European History instead of American: "In Kubrick's telling it is not the ghosts of 'Indians' who haunt the Overlook but those of the European perpetrators" (219, 212). If we are committed to making critical judgments based upon the most persuasive and convincing evidence, however, the truest holocaust at work in Kubrick's film has far less to do with the Nazis and much more to do with the genocide of the American Indian. The famous river of blood flowing from the elevator shafts into the corridor of the Overlook forms a more direct connection to the History of the Overlook itself and the brutalization of the American Indian, the latter requiring extermination so that places such as the hotel could be built upon their usurped land. The other thing that the viewer encounters is the pervasiveness of Indian artifacts throughout the hotel. In comparison, it is understandable that we might overlook that Jack employs a German typewriter. The characters in this film live among a pronounced Native American presence, mostly Navajo and Apache motifs: the statue of a warrior on horseback in the center of the hotel's lounge, the "sand painting" on the wall at which Jack directs his tennis ball, and a buffalo's trophy head just to the right of the sand people illustrate the omnipresence of the motif. Even when Wendy is perusing Jack's typed "manuscript," Kubrick's camera films her from below so that viewers are supplied with an angled background fragment of the multicolored Navajo-inspired border along the edge of the ceiling behind Wendy's head. The many-limbed parade of American History leaves bloody handprints on nearly every frame of Kubrick's film, sometimes literally, as in the subliminal image of a large blood-red handprint that appears on the left buttocks of a 1920s flapper ghost wearing a sparkly champagne-colored dress who saunters by Jack in the Gold Room.

Figure 3.1 The bloody handprint on the back of a ghost woman in Kubrick's *The Shining*.

While unacknowledged by the majority of critics and viewers of the movie, that bloody handprint represents essential elements at work in the Overlook's patriarchal History: violence mixed with a blatant misogyny so commonplace as to be nearly imperceptible.

Pet Sematary is therefore hardly the only occasion when King appropriates Native American burial sites as intricate parts of his plot. It is interesting to speculate upon why both the novelist and director were drawn to such violations, especially in light of how different their priorities were in creating their respective *Shining*s. The appropriation of Indian land and culture may have carried a certain level of mystery for artists seeking to produce horror texts, giving birth to a supernatural agency that appealed to King and Kubrick's desires to tap into a distinctly *American* monster lore. Like Yeats and his obsession with Asian myth, Jack falls prey to a nationalist strain that problematically exoticizes the Other. The story's Native American references are associated with a mythic violation, a national sin that is like slavery insofar as it continues to fester in light of white America's consistent unwillingness to recognize and accept responsibility. The awakening of malefic supernatural energies associated with Indian legend in both *The Shining* and *Pet Sematary* can be interpreted, then, as a kind of guilt complex involving cultural retribution: the land itself reacts against violence performed by white males who imposed their collective and individual wills upon Native American territory and myth, usurping primitive power for their own selfish agendas. Just as *Pet Sematary* focuses on white male appropriation of sacred Indian ground, *The Shining*, especially Kubrick's film adaptation, puts particular emphasis on the exploitation of Indian artifacts and property by the men who built the Overlook. As we detail later in this chapter, these cosmopolitan men are representative of a ruling elite associated with both the 1920s and the Reagan era. This gentry built its hotel atop an ancient Indian burial ground where workers were forced to repel Indian attacks during construction. In this way (and a host of others), *The Shining* offers a dark portrait of the carnage littered throughout the wake of American History.

Other commentators on Kubrick's movie have addressed in detail evidence that the entire film is a metaphor for Native American genocide (see Blackmore and Whittington). Patrick Webster argues that Kubrick provided the audience with "signs of Native America in almost every frame of the film, but suggest[s] that we never really see them," a metaphor (similar to the subliminal bloody handprint) for the way in which the Native American has been "overlooked and written out of American (H)istory" (112). However, no *Shining* scholar has noticed the significance of where and how Hallorann is killed in Kubrick's film. When Jack murders him with an axe—symbol of the instrument used to "civilize" the western forests for white colonization—Hallorann's prone body sheds its blood directly atop a circular Navajo floor mosaic.

The various floor mosaics that appear in the Overlook's lobby are based on basket patterns associated with Californian Indian tribes. Thus, the image of a black man sacrificed atop an Indian design juxtaposes not by accident two of the greatest American atrocities: slavery and Native American genocide. It is a truly disturbing final *mise-en-scéne* for Dick Hallorann, made especially egregious given that his murder occurs at the hands of a deranged white man acting on behalf of the patriarchal hegemony that continues to operate at the Overlook. The unholy, albeit highly metaphoric, presence of Indian violations in both *The Shining* and *Pet Sematary* adds a layer of resonance to actions occurring in the present. Thus, both Jack and Louis Creed find themselves trapped between layers of History. They are doomed because their symbolic relationship to violent national transgressions remains unexculpated.

Meanwhile, King's Jack—Boswell to the Overlook's Johnson—succumbs to the hotel's structuralist urge to chronicle every minute detail of the building's History: "'You're a true scholar ... pursue the topic to the end'" (425, 535). Dragged into lockstep with this "'white man's burden,'" Jack forgets his own anti-authoritarian tendencies, initially displayed in his loathing of the hotel's manager, an "officious little prick," and his initial reaction to the dreadful History he finds contained in the hotel's scrapbook. By the novel's close, Jack is a (mad) scholar, entirely too willing to transpose a "senseless and pattern-less" narrative into a "stark black-and-white

Figure 3.2 Dick Hallorann's blood is spilled across a Native American floor mosaic in *The Shining*.

etching" (7, 421–2). This is the brilliance of Kubrick's decision to present Jack's madness—to both Wendy and the viewer—as a typed word labyrinth: a circular and entropic generic pastiche of the same phrase, devoid of meaning. Through Jack's transformation, the text argues that the compulsions of the Historian—the (perverse) need to know everything, to expose all of life's secrets—reveal the discipline of History to be *never far removed from the atrocities to which Historians attend*. Jack longs to "pull apart" the Overlook's History, ripping its unsightly innards out for inspection like a "dissected crayfish," and so Jack-as-Historian unveils the brutish (d)evolution of Western thought through the ever-tighter grip of Reason upon his neck (and the necks of the figures that he memorializes). In truth, absolute madness seems somehow preferable to the phony academic tenor behind his self-aggrandizement, as he supposedly converts his own madness into a "neutral prize" of passing "academic interest" and the possibility of writing a book that chronicles the Overlook's unsavory History (286, 172). In the end, Jack's interest in his book project quickly wans when presented with the alternative of *living* history rather than merely Historicizing it. Against an otherwise bloodless decorum, the lead Historian of *The Shining* becomes, as a result of his relentless, costly interrogation of the hotel's past, a blind participant in the very blood-soaked History that he imagines himself to be "overlooking" from a place of critical detachment. Jack's learned need for chronology as well as cohesion proves to be intimately wed to America's drive to colonize and control Others. As a result, a deterministic account of History is soundly rejected by King's novel: "This inhuman place," Jack's unconscious tells him, "makes human monsters." King employs Jack's infrequent anti-authoritarian sentiments to critique the grand narratives of History that compel him to act a certain way, turning him into a "puppet" to be manipulated by monied interests. Prior to his trial beneath the oppressive weight of American History (and a western American winter), Jack manages to resist the clinical indifference—itself a distinct form of aggression—demanded by the hotel's chroniclers. Before he was swept up in this story, in other words, Jack opted to write tales without the "cloak of the moralist"; now, as a result of his immersion into the role of Historian, he cannot stop judging his characters (213, 19, 389). Roland Barthes describes Jack's predicament as "the sanction of historical 'science', placed under the imperious warrant of the 'real', justified by principles of 'rational' exposition" (127). Jack obsessively imposes an organized plot onto his telling of the hotel (a choice that he would have previously avoided in favor of ambivalence). *The Shining* stresses how war-driven American History coopts Historians into its twisted internal machinations by forcing figures like Jack to obey its rigid logic. By way of a response, the novel invites us to extol the value of an alternative reading of American history (with a lower-case "h"), in which we can celebrate the merits of deconstructing Jack's misguided attempts at mastery. (While *The Shining* gestures obliquely at this alternative, King's contemporary works articulate it with much greater emphasis—a topic that we consider in Chapter 6.)

As the vicious version of American History succeeds in cannibalizing Jack, King's novel tacitly endorses a divergent approach to the nation's past: the breakdown of any singular recording of America's youth. For every effort to finish the jigsaw puzzle, King offers his stern reminder: "Curiosity killed the cat." *The Shining* pivots into a distinctive consciousness, closely aligned with Popper and anti-Historicism, when the text laughs at the Overlook's pompous maestros that, in reality, "didn't know everything after all." Through its perpetual laughter at the expense of these maestros, *The Shining* offers a story about how the imagined metaphysical bond between father and son—here a symbolic extension of the nation's power over its citizens—slips into a *genealogical* history in which unexpected ruptures realign characters and events in wholly unpredictable ways. Whereas the psychic DNA of the Overlook's History seems at first too monolithic, incestuous even, King begins to rethink the nature of DNA—full, as it is, of holes, of gaps, of sudden mutations. Hence the importance of King's ending (although regularly maligned by critics as sentimental as well as serving no appreciable purpose): when Danny ends up with Hallorann as a surrogate father-figure, the text illustrates how history's actors (with a lower-case "h") are *mercifully not pre-determined*. National history mirrors the Torrance's family history as a chaotic hodge-podge of random mutations and selective breeding. Notably, even when he has assumed the role of surrogate father, Hallorann does not command Danny; rather, in one of the novel's last lines, he tells the boy that he is "'doin' fine'" all by himself (323, 113, 683). In effect, the novel's final scene lifts the weight of the Overlook's History off of Danny's shoulders and supplants the "white man's burden" with a capricious field of contingencies. But even as Hallorann envisions an alternative to Jack-the-Historian, the black chef articulates a deterministic fear that Danny might well inherit both Jack's alcoholism and tendency towards self-pity—the exact issues that beset the adult Daniel Torrance in the first half of *Doctor Sleep*. Hallorann's prescient warning is the equivalent of King's take on American History, mired in the repetitive drama of violence and self-destruction. The novel thus closes with a range of open-ended possibilities. Unlike Kubrick's perilous escape by mother and child in the middle of a blizzard, King's novel concludes in the summertime, replacing the dysfunctional nuclear family in the Overlook with a reconstituted family that fishes from a dock at the edge of a placid lake. (King's emphasis upon familial mutability supports the reading of a possibly redemptive "queerness" at the margins of his multiverse, discussed in Chapter 5.)

Given the tenor of the era in question (the late 1970s), in which Fordist-Keynesian coordination is steadily replaced by more mercurial designs, Hallorann's shift into history with a lower-case "h" would appear appropriate. After all, "The more flexible motion of capital emphasizes the new, the fleeting, the ephemeral, the fugitive, and the contingent in modern life" (Harvey 171). Kubrick's film knits this thread into itself: whereas Jack drudges haphazardly along the logical path of the hedge maze until he dies, Danny innovates his father's *techne* by walking backwards through Jack's tracks in the snow and erasing the scent being followed by his murderous father. *The boy is finally free to adapt*. Although there are certainly no guarantees when the subject plunges onto a modern highway, or follows her gut in charting a different path down the mountain, the new kind of historians released from the demands of History (with a capital "H") argue that the lack of guarantees for characters such as *Pet Sematary*'s Creed or *The Shining*'s Hallorann is exactly what makes their survival possible in the first place. As Jack languishes in a rigid order established by the hotel's elites, King's reluctant heroes find ways to improvise, to be emancipated, at long last, from the confounding labyrinth of America's violent History.

The novel's survivors—Wendy, Danny, and Hallorann—embody the (supposed) virtues of a post-structuralist approach to American history. Wendy, for one, saves herself by clinging to instinct rather than rationality. She expresses a counter-point to Jack's moribund status in relation to a sanguineous History when, after he has engaged in a rather lengthy tangent, she reassures him: "'I like to hear you ramble'" (389). For his part, Danny learns to defy his father's mode of obedience when he recognizes that the Overlook presents a "false face," one that is "not real"—an acknowledgment that proves to be crucial for *The Shining*'s nascent historical consciousness. Finally, Hallorann offers the most fully-realized example of these sentiments, as his arduous journey to rescue the Torrance clan depends upon his resistance to the hyper-structural impulses at work in the hotel that drive its occupants to compile an exhaustive account of the building's History. While Jack buys into the Overlook's immortality (and, in turn, the endless open frontiers of American History that, ironically enough, turn out to be closed well in advance of Jack's journey westward), Hallorann accepts that to die is a vital part of life, and a part to which one must return "to be a whole person." He admits that death may be impossible to understand, but it need not be impossible to accept (398, 644, 472). Put differently, the lure of History—America's and the Overlook's—poses little sustained temptation for Hallorann because, in the end, he rescues Wendy and Danny in defiance of everything that the hotel represents, choosing to risk his own life in defense of theirs. Unlike Kubrick, who dispatches Hallorann merely as a means to the end of providing the snow cat necessary for rescuing Wendy and Danny, King's character recognizes that he has more in common with the oppressed mother and child than he does with the authoritarian males at the Overlook who refer to him as a "Nigger cook" or seek to goad the black man into completing their murderous design by killing Wendy and Danny once Jack becomes incapacitated. The black chef's embrace of personal limits remains crucial to King's critique of the Overlook's demonic blueprint for History. It diverges from the existential crises of Creed (in the midst of his suburban ennui) as well as Jack (in the conflation of his writing prowess with his sense of being absorbed into the metanarrative of America's biography). Only the "outsider" Hallorann fully comprehends history as genealogical, which is to say, as a capricious storyline that requires luck instead of heavy-footed plotting (486, 511). His status in the margins—a black man working in the kitchens of the wealthy—cements his ability to revise Jack's fatalistic relationship to History. Whereas Jack errs in his obsequious efforts to ingratiate himself with the ghosts, Hallorann is in possession of a healthy skepticism, he peers at events from below or from the side; he gazes out from blind spots that the hotel overlooks. His kitchen is a sanctuary, specifically for Wendy, and it stands in as a well-lit alternative to the dark and boozy places in the hotel where Jack takes up residence. Hallorann offers the text's most direct assertion of King's proposed deconstruction of American History when he describes his life as a "sunny plateau" of the here-and-now: a triumph of living exclusively in the present, in distinction from the "topography" of History's many "ups and downs" (480). At the novel's close, then, Hallorann departs from the barbarism of America's dismal History by ascribing to a set of values that run counter to Jack's zealous belief in the Overlook's white mythic superiority.

The Shining thus reflects King's postmodern turn in relationship to the discipline of history. Summarizing this position, Hayden White writes: "A failure of historical consciousness occurs when one forgets that history, in the sense of both events and accounts of events, does not just happen but is made" (13). Such an omission, in fact, isolates Jack from his progeny. Jack the father forgets what his son mercifully remembers. Jack's "false face," a symptom of the Overlook's multi-layered History, reminds Danny that the underlying History is not real (or, at least, not capable of being neatly sanitized). To reinforce this revelation from another vantage point, *The Shining* repeatedly recycles the command "Unmask!" from E.A. Poe's "The Masque of the Red Death" (1842). From Jack's perspective, "unmasking" the Overlook involves the exposure of its gory interior, as if its History could be laid bare on the dissection table (an inherently violent means of surgical exposure that unconsciously duplicates the hotel's brutish mode of achieving its "progress"). Danny, on the other hand, recognizes intuitively what White, Barthes, and others (including Poe) recognize: when the mighty avatar is finally "unmasked," and the crowd at last sees what lies beneath, or what sits perched upon that dignified bust, *there is nothing*. While "in the historical discourse of our civilization, the process of signification always aims at 'filling' the meaning of History ... to fill the void," Danny suddenly grasps that "historical discourse does not follow the real, it merely signifies it" (Barthes 137–9). Historical fact, Barthes insists, is only ever language, and the language of History is only ever just a copy of original events (or a copy of a copy, and so on *ad infinitum*). At the close of the novel, Danny recognizes the hotel's unhinged signification—its disparate phantoms from across the generations—as nothing more or less than faces in a picture book. Concomitantly, Jack gets lost in the hotel's story and surrenders his role as the writer. A point that Jack fails to convey to his patron Al Shockley, the well-networked man that gave Jack his job, *the hotel's history belongs to him*. Jack already holds the pen and the power, as both Shockley and Ullman recognize with corresponding degrees of terror when Jack threatens to write an exposé of their hotel. Thankfully, the boy need not follow his father's tracks in the snow; he can improvise by walking backwards, or erasing the tracks altogether. Jack, however, remains stuck in place until it is too late to save himself—a puppet to the hotel's grand metaphysical narrative that rushes to fill a void that could never be filled. It turns out that the "truth" behind American History has been "senseless and pattern-less" all along. When unmasked, the hotel exposes to Danny that "all times were one," undermining a chronological illusion that tethers his father to some semblance of "sanity" (460). In other words, the revelations of New Historicism are equal parts terrifying and emancipatory for a boy rushing headlong into the age of post-History. As we discuss later in this chapter, Kubrick's film extends this breakdown through a gradual erosion of the Overlook's temporal markers: from the movie's orderly narrative ("Interview Day") to a contextually abstract plot point ("4 pm"). Both the novel and film versions of *The Shining* intend to deconstruct the death drive of American History as well as Historians.

The text alludes to this postmodern deconstruction in its content as well as its form. Exposing the Overlook's History to be only so much text, Jack's face becomes "a strange, shifting composite, many faces mixed imperfectly." Gone is the polish, the glossy iconography of imagined decades, such as the Roaring Twenties or the post-war Forties; in their place, King's novel presents a slippery composite. In whispers that everyone but Jack can hear, the story routinely calls into question the reader's ability to conceptualize History as a unified whole: "The smooth sounds of some postwar band—but which war? *Can you be certain?*" The reader's grasp of History becomes increasingly tenuous as the dreams of King's characters are decoupled from imaginary sites of origin (their unconscious). Danny, in particular, receives dreams with "no meaning or reference for him" (654, 527, 458; emphasis ours). If Jack's take on History depends upon an impression of cause-and-effect, post-History no longer sustains this deadly fantasy. King's novel reveals that the foundation of ongoing war is no longer situated in tales of national struggle, evincing a jumble of sensations in lieu of "rational exposition." Importantly, King's prose—and Kubrick's filmmaking style—frequently follow suit. Random inner thoughts interrupt the order of things in the form of parenthetical injections. These gaping holes disrupt the flow of the narrative with periodic reminders of its many "senseless and patternless" subterranean tunnels. And yet we must ask: are King and Kubrick creatively doubling down on the deconstructions of Danny—or, in actuality, do they unconsciously follow Jack's lead and prove obedient to the grotesque expectations of their environment?

The concerns of *The Shining* (for King and Kubrick alike) echo Jean-François Lyotard's dismissal of the "grand narratives" that define the world prior to World War II. Readers as well as viewers sample the flavors of a burgeoning postmodern aesthetic. However, beyond the pages and pixels, post-History remains a rather violent affair, extending (rather than refusing) the bloody pathways that precede it. Like Creed in *Pet Sematary*, Jack is not quite Victor Frankenstein because the deflation of his hubris leads to even more death and destruction. The hotel's capriciousness proves as bloody as its earlier fascism. Given this inconvenient truth, we must place *The Shining* in its proper context by seeing the slippery character of the novel as well as its film adaptation as a symptom of the era rather than as a form of autonomous critique from an artist on high (Callinicos 6). By historicizing *The Shining* in this way, we recognize why the story's (faux) pivot has done little to nothing to re-direct the barbarous undercurrents of American History.

This failed pivot occurs at a definitive moment in *The Shining*: Watson, the regular caretaker and the text's embodiment of the so-called frontier spirit, leaves the hotel to vanish over the horizon. For onlookers, he epitomizes "what the West was supposed to be all about"—he is unpolished, bigoted, and he wears a pair of cowboy boots. He eschews political correctness in favor of the blunt, "authentic" talk of a gunslinger that promises ever more violence. King's novel augments the significance of Watson's departure with "brittle yellow aspen leaves," artifacts that, in Celtic mythology, symbolize the tenuous meeting of two worlds. Hovering at the threshold, Watson—"as mean as a snake with shingles"—stands in for a war-driven American History thanks to his inherently antagonistic personality. He leaves the hotel in the hands of its "bloodless" manager, Ullman (a symptom of a profiteering future directly linked to customers that demand to use their American Express credit cards as well as the hotel's old-fashioned cash registers, covered of late in credit card decals). Watson grows "smaller" as the text shifts from one historical consciousness to the next, a passing of the torch so profound that it holds the Torrance family in a "spell of silence" (145–6). While the figurative shrinking of Watson may initially suggest a nostalgia for the imaginary, anti-authoritarian Wild West, the hinge that connects Watson and Ullman does not actually signal a major breakage. In reality, *The Shining* reflects how Watson's violent legacy never genuinely leaves the hotel; it is diverted into alternative channels. The blood may exit the elevator on a different floor, but it comes nonetheless.

Skeptics of this postmodern pivot dismiss as premature the claims that an End of History will usher in a fundamentally different social order. For Alex Callinicos, the so-called postmodern turn—part and parcel of Danny's revelations about the Overlook—silences the kind of organization required to combat real-world atrocities. For figures like Barthes, Callinicos asserts, "the resistance to apartheid (in South Africa) must remain inarticulate, must not seek to formulate a political programme and strategy... the stuff of any real liberation struggle" (Callinicos 78). That is, the declared resistance to "grand narratives" in King and Kubrick's versions of *The Shining* can be read as inadvertently perpetuating the violence of Watson's war-torn era by undermining efforts to form new alliances, or efforts to write policies that could curb the ongoing bloodshed.[2] It is crucial to remember that, despite the broad appeal of these chameleonic haunts, it is excessive wealth—and the excessive leisure that such wealth brings—that renders it possible for *The Shining* to articulate the appealing idea of the Overlook as a kaleidoscope of horrors, and that this cultural and economic surplus can be traced directly back to the spoils of war. We must not forget that the Overlook's owner Horace Derwent made his fortune as a result of the conflicts in question. Derwent emerges as the archetypical American self-made capitalist-entrepreneur: a combination of real-life figures such as Ben Franklin and Howard Hughes. While Derwent is a scientist-inventor-financier, who invents items such as invisible bra straps for a Hollywood starlet, his most profitable inventions and investments are connected to the machinery of war. Because Derwent makes a clean break from nationalist struggle through his efforts to privatize weapons manufacturing, it may be tempting to read his character as "departing" from the norms associated with the military-industrial apparatus. In truth, Derwent supplements a mission that he shares with the preceding generations: although he dabbles in the hospitality industry, a service sector that characterizes the post-Fordist economy to come, Derwent is a purveyor of death who stimulates the American war machine. He continues to accrue "many patents" in the munitions market by developing potent weapons like a machine gun that cools itself with alcohol and a "bomb carriage used on the Flying Fortresses that had rained fire on Hamburg and Dresden and Berlin" (159). While he appears to be focused on impersonal profit and divorced from the dated logic of colonial conquest—indeed, he possesses the face of an accountant—Derwent's eyes reveal that "something else" drives him. His (d)evolution from soldier to entrepreneur to hotel magnate and organizer of a "key club" that makes corruption and murder its primary business does not signal a move away from the Overlook's initial bloody History (inspired by imperial aggression) to a bloodless post-History (moved by the tailwinds of globalization that carried Ullman into power). Derwent's (d)evolution illuminates how the index of the post-war American character is not all that dissimilar from the character of a society that hit pay dirt in two world wars. Just as America emerged from the Second World War as the only "colossus" left standing, Derwent should be viewed as a representative figure of the epoch: a capitalist who helped America win the war while making a fortune for himself, and an owner in possession of the appropriate stature capable of resurrecting and guiding the Overlook. His compulsion to violence reveals a common denominator between the likes of Watson and Ullman that mire the Overlook in perpetual gore.

As with the highway in *Pet Sematary*, an entity that churns up bodies and "uses them" as fuel, the Overlook's parties reveal themselves to be another example of biocapitalism. The unsavory narrative of American History threatens to swallow Jack's body, but he is in fact consumed by the Overlook *after* it has been "unmasked." That is to say, it is the postmodern side of the hotel—not its fascist ancestry—that finally succeeds in transforming Jack into the "strange, shifting composite" that keeps its machinery running. Jeffrey Nealon writes: "It's becoming increasingly unhelpful to replay the drama that posits a repressive, normative 'stasis or essentialism' that can be outflanked only by some form of more or less liberating, socially constructed 'fluid openness'. At this point, we'd have to admit that privatized finance capital has all but obliterated the usefulness of this distinction" (20–1). The "fluid openness" seen behind the façade of the hotel, as well as behind the façade of King's literary and Kubrick's filmic chronicles, does not offer a genuine escape from the heavy weight of the Overlook; instead, this presumed fluidity evokes a "constant reconstitution of value" that cannot, at the dawn of the 1980s, be described as truly counter-cultural. Quite the opposite. Danny warns Jack, "'When (the hotel's) done with you, you won't be anything at all'" (650). To take another step down that road, when the hotel is done with Jack, he has been "used up" in ways that exclusively befit a financialized

American economy. Because his composite body mirrors the wasp's nest, "constructed from the chewings and saliva of so many alien creatures," he becomes a site of endless deconstruction at the hands of an increasingly frenzied and financialized multiverse (179). In the endings of the novel as well as the film, Jack functions as fodder, to be burned up (novel) or frozen (film), disassembled for vulture capitalists or reified in the service of blind consumers. Like Creed, Jack provides free-floating human capital in service of an ever-shifting postmodern economy. Due to the fact that King and Kubrick seem condemned to capitalize upon their hapless custodian, the imagined pivot from History (capital "H") to history (lowercase "h") strikes us as little more than window-dressing for a violent status quo—a realization that may explain, in part, why the deep pessimism of Kubrick's film has generally spoken more effectively to its audiences than the maudlin coda of King's novel.

In sum, the culpability of King and Kubrick in Jack's abuse raises important inquiries regarding the postmodern posture of these figures. Although the work of the two artists is often compared because they tell the same story in different ways, we would argue that a common impulse runs through both iterations: namely, King and Kubrick each reject the "grand narrative" of History and, in so doing, they gloss over unpleasant continuities that carry over into their preferred models of post-History. Fredric Jameson worries that Kubrick's emphasis upon metacommentary, his "meta-generic solutions," will do little to address the underlying cultural crises (Jameson 98). Do gestures at post-History by King and Kubrick thereby serve as mere distractions from the nation's ongoing sadism? Or, worse still, do these works covertly assist in the relentless exploitation of bodies for the sake of American "progress"? (We will take up King's relative inability to imagine alternatives in this book's Conclusion.) Terry Eagleton criticizes Lyotard's jubilant destruction of "grand narratives" on just these grounds. Nazi death camps, Eagleton comments, reflect a "barbarous irrationalism which, *like some aspects of postmodernism itself,* junked [H]istory, refused argumentation, aestheticizes politics and staked all on the charisma of those who told the story" (Eagleton 194; emphasis ours). Whether he burns or freezes, Jack aids King/Kubrick in their respective efforts to negate an oppressive sense of History. But, as a result of his torching, his "creative destruction" at their hands, what is left of Jack besides debris? Whether interpreted as a "warrior" from the frontier (History), or as a trope to be employed in the name of metacommentary (post-History), one way or the other, King and Kubrick reduce Jack to a means to an end. In his story as well as its textual rendering, his body exists to be "used up." Historicism and New Historicism reach equally grim conclusions: to borrow a line from Prime Minister Margaret Thatcher, there appears to be no alternative to the violence that we inherit.

Torching History: From King to Kubrick

To shed further light on the unsavory convergence of the twin impulses behind American History and post-History, we must turn more directly to Kubrick's well-known adaptation of *The Shining*. Kubrick's film dismantles established notions of American History in several significant ways, including its presentation of nostalgia—the suturing of different periods—as a form of heartless, even barbaric exclusion. As we describe in the previous section, although critics routinely separate the novel from the film, in truth both texts track a similar (d)evolution. As Jack moves from custodian of History to a flaunter of the historical order, shifting in tandem with the move from the stagnating 1970s to the rip-roaring '20s, the reader/spectator realizes that there may be no alternative to the macabre machinations of American History. Unlike King's novel, the cinematic version of Hallorann does not offer a truly "alternative" historical consciousness; rather, upon his gruesome murder, he serves as yet another sacrifice to the insatiable appetite of American History. The form of History changes shape, certainly, but *its underlying logic persists in the ruthless degradation of pawns that cannot tell the difference between work and play*. (And do we not tend to resemble Jack Torrance ourselves, typing away on our social media accounts, unaware of the blurred line between leisure and labor?) Ignoring the potential of sideways looks by Hallorann or Danny in King's text, which is to say, his gestures at a historical consciousness better informed by an ethics of the Other, the cinematic Jack remains generally unaware of his impotence within the abattoir.

Under Kubrick's guiding vision, *The Shining* becomes a narrative about more than just the tragic demise of a man and his family, and this key difference has been perhaps King's most unfortunate oversight in his deathless public assault on Kubrick's film. King's self-proposed purity of artistic vision is ironically captured well in Jack's dutiful maintenance of the hotel's History: nostalgia for the Twenties has become an inimitable element of late twentieth- and early twenty-first century Americana. Kubrick constantly harkens back to this point. Some of Jack's behavior might be explained away as a longing for a time when class hierarchies and race and gender categories were more defined and business less regulated; others choose to memorialize the decade as a glamorous belle epoch, one great party, with America apparently still nursing the hangover. Yet in the contemporary era, in which the income gap has become so egregious that it spawned an Occupy Wall Street movement, a portion of President Obama's 2014 State of the Union address, and the election of a billionaire President with a tax reform agenda that has resulted in big tax cuts for corporations and the rich while hacking away at social safety nets, Kubrick's *Shining* resonates for reasons that extend beyond mere nostalgia for the Twenties. Of equal concern to us, though, is Kubrick's endless *deconstruction* of the toxic nostalgia that his film uses as a strawman—a notion captured in Jack's total disregard not only for his family's wellbeing, but also for his responsibility to understand better the (wholly unexplained) chasm between Grady-the-laborer and Grady-the-gentleman elite. In a word, when audiences are invited to react against the oppressive History that weighs Jack down, they risk unconsciously replicating the grotesque revelries of the party-goers that distance themselves from accountability to past or future generations. Upon recognizing this two-sided trap, is there a way for Kubrick's spectator to make sense of the Overlook's bizarre timeline without concurrently submitting herself to the delusional role of puppet or powerbroker?

One of the more intriguing aspects about the controversy over whose *Shining* shines brightest, King's or Kubrick's, is the one-sidedness of the debate, and with Kubrick now dead it will be left to film scholars to continue the discussion. Over the years, King has been so vociferous in his disappointment on the Kubrick adaptation that when he sought to reacquire the rights to *The Shining* in order to make his own cinematic version of it for ABC in 1997, the auteur director insisted that King must cease and desist uttering future public statements. Even as recently as an "Author's Note" at the end of *Doctor Sleep*, King continues to exhibit a surprising tenacity of view, especially if his opinion is based on artistic disagreement, a perceived slight in Kubrick's decision to reject King's initial screenplay in favor of writing (with Diane Johnson) his own, or the inability to recognize that Kubrick produced a masterpiece from reinterpreting King's original material: "[T]here was Stanley Kubrick's movie, which many seem to remember—for reasons I have never quite understood—as one of the scariest films they have ever seen" (529–30). Kubrick's *Shining* may not be a "scary film" in the way that King's novel maintains the potential to shock and frighten, but it nevertheless remains a highly disturbing movie (despite its restraint in refusing to employ the usual claptrap of most horror films, such as an animated fire hose or a diabolical topiary). Moreover, Kubrick's *Shining* is the product of an auteur who understood the legitimacy of his art as an entirely distinctive entity from its primary source. As a result, Kubrick not only chose to place his emphasis on Jack—instead of the novel's focus on Danny and the hotel—he also underscored Jack's disaffection from his family by setting his identity in an era that deliberately excluded Wendy and Danny.

In Kubrick's film, the Overlook Hotel's ghosts and even parts of the hotel itself are all linked to the 1920s and the spirit of Modernism. At first, it appears as though this focus breaks sharply from the post-World War II "index" we have been referencing as the most important context in King's novel. The dress and speech of Kubrick's ghosts connect them with this time period; the romantic big band background music that plays in the scene when Jack collides with Delbert Grady in the Gold Ballroom originates from the early Thirties; Kubrick's heavy reliance throughout the film on selections from Béla Bartók's *Music for Strings, Percussion and Celesta* (composed in 1936) creates fragmented moments of discordant, cubistic sounds that continually reference a modernist aesthetic; with its vaulted ceiling, enormous fireplace, two elaborate chandeliers, and magisterial staircase, the cavernous Colorado Lounge where Jack spends time typing resembles the Gothic architecture of German silent-era cinema; Kubrick has Jack limp like "horror film cripples and hunchbacks of the 1930s" (Nelson 205); the Gold Ballroom and room 237 are decorated in Art Deco motifs; and, in the last scene of the film, Torrance himself appears within a photograph that is dated July 4, 1921.[3] In *The Shining*, as in his earlier film *2001: A Space Odyssey*, Kubrick turns his protagonist into a time traveler, on this occasion, not forward but backward—first, psychologically, but eventually, literally—as Jack's contact with the ghosts at the Overlook essentially extract him from the late 1970s (when the film was made) and suture him back to the Twenties. It is not just his disturbing inclusion in the 1921 photograph that has puzzled critics and viewers alike. Throughout the film, Bartók's nondiegetic musical splicing's as well as Jack's sustained and intimate interactions with the community of ghosts—apparently trapped for eternity in modernist space—suggest a temporal dislocation that strains and eventually severs Torrance from the far less interesting "real time," the time of Ullman and the time that he occupies in the company of Wendy and Danny. Kubrick creates a disjointed sense of history (with a lower-case "h") by speedily relieving his anti-hero of the marching orders issued to Jack-as-Historian in King's version.

What does this disjointed history look and—still more interestingly—sound like? Kubrick's films often employ music as a vehicle for underscoring what Claudia Gorbman has labeled the complex bond between "story world and soundtrack in the Kubrick universe" (12). In *A Clockwork Orange*, to cite merely one example from the Kubrick universe, Beethoven's *Fifth* and *Ninth Symphonies* reflect Alex's inner reservoir of romantic energy as well as feeding his urge for the violent and sexual expression of this energy. It is impossible to separate Alex's character from "lovely Ludwig van's" music, even when the latter is perverted into a source for reinforcing the state's experimental Ludovico aversion treatment that Alex undergoes. In *The Shining*, Bartók's discordant and startling inclusions are also associated with Jack's character, meant to signal his psychic fragmentation (it is as if Jack alone hears these unconnected fragments) as he comes to identify with a time period roughly corresponding to Bartók's. Whereas King might have better appreciated a plot-driven horror story that conformed to the linear narrative of his novel, Kubrick delivers a dreamy, enigmatic allegory that had more in common with the presentation of simultaneous perspectives found in modernist movements such as Cubism and Surrealism. Just as Cubism describes an underlying progression from outer presence to inner shape and the co-existence of multiple and dissonant frames of reference, Kubrick's film evinces a fluid orientation towards time. The white-on-black sequential frames that punctuate *The Shining*, for example, depict a steady "funneling" of chronological time—beginning with the open-ended "The

Interview," "Closing Day," and "One Month Later," then shrinking to specific days of the week, and, by the end of the movie, a compression of time at the Overlook into hours of the day, concluding with "4 pm." Similarly, Kubrick undermines other traditional time and space perceptions in the soundtrack's brief staccato bursts of selected excerpts from Bartók's fragmented score. Far more than what occurs in King's novel, Kubrick twists objective historical time into subjective psychic space, a labyrinth where Jack finds himself sliding seamlessly between the banality of a winter caretaker in the Seventies to an esteemed playboy in the Twenties, a man one moment playing "catch" with Navajo sand people, and the next tracking his wife and child as they somehow occupy "real time" miniaturized space inside the hotel's model of its outdoor maze. To our knowledge, no film scholar has connected events in *The Shining* to the Surrealist movement, but how else do we explain how Torrance manages to free himself from inside the locked food pantry where Wendy has imprisoned him? Through these aesthetic choices, Kubrick develops his vision of history with a lower-case "h" as an artistic method of departure from the History that oppresses Jack throughout King's novel.

The director's deployment of Bartók's nondiegetic music, intruding as it often does on Jack and his family functioning in "real time," is meant to highlight the breakdown of the family as a unit and at the same time place emphasis on Wendy and Danny as separate psychic entities from Jack. The first appearance of Bartók occurs as Wendy and Danny wander inside the hedge maze, making wrong choices leading to dead ends, while Jack broods over their movements from within the hotel's model maze. This juxtaposition takes place via a neat camera trick as all the while the oppressive soundtrack of Bartók's flowing arpeggios in piano, xylophone, and celesta conclude in a crescendo of strings. The fragmented, discordant sounds of Bartók underscore the psychic and historical "fracturing" Jack is beginning to experience in the hotel, the inside of his brain already a maze of hidden chambers and broken corners that keep depositing him back in the Roaring Twenties. While Wendy and Danny appear outside the hotel at play on two separate occasions, Jack is always pictured inside looking out—windows first and then *looking in* on the model maze—refusing to leave the Overlook after Closing Day. Only at the film's conclusion does he venture out of the hotel's labyrinth and into an outdoor simulacrum of it in the snow-covered hedge maze where he ends up freezing to death.

The Modernism of the Roaring Twenties dovetails nicely with Kubrick's postmodern sensibility (a sensibility actually shared by King), a site of overlap that forces audiences to explore these Janus-faced moments in conversation. What does Bartók have to tell us about the Seventies—and, perhaps more importantly, what do the Seventies tell us about Bartók? Just as Bartók's presence always underscores the atomization of the Torrance family, his music likewise serves as an analog to the discordant friction between the film's two separate, open-ended planes of history—the

Seventies and modernist Twenties—being sutured together into an uneasy simultaneity. The careful viewer cannot help but recognize Kubrick's effort to suggest that there are plenty of uncomfortable similarities that link the American Twenties to the Seventies. Moreover, many of Kubrick's other musical selections for the film are popular works from the same historical period as Bartók, such as *Midnight, the Stars and You* (1934) by Ray Noble and his orchestra, and *Masquerade* (1931) by Jack Hylton and his orchestra, which further serve to provide the film with a sense of one chronology co-existing inside—or at least alongside—another. The most unsettling similarity of all, though, may be the failure of artists from both eras (including King and Kubrick) to make a lasting dent in the footslog of an exploitative History that continues to be the representative constant in all discussions of America's past.

On a symbolic level, the maze operates in a way similar to Kubrick's use of time in the film: you can enter it at one place, on one plane, and then exit it someplace else. Historical eras co-exist in an overlapping simultaneity at the Overlook, and underscored as they are by Bartók's dreamy musical fragments, the viewer recognizes that the surreal can displace the real in Jack's mind as well as in the labyrinth of mazes that surround him. History with a capital "H," the structural prison that utterly ruins King's Jack, dissolves before our eyes. In his interview with Michael Ciment, Kubrick suggests his intention to explore "strange things that were happening [supernaturally] would finally be explained as the products of Jack's imagination … the plot is really more important than anything else, perhaps communicating with us on an unconscious level" (Ciment 474). As the movie unfolds, Jack spends increasing prolonged scenes with the ghosts in their epoch and less time with Wendy and Danny in theirs, and it soon becomes evident which of these temporal planes he prefers. When Grady informs Jack in the red bathroom scene that the latter has "always been the caretaker" the only way in which this bizarre occurrence makes any sense is if viewer (and Jack) accept that they are present in a universe with a highly elastic conception of time. As Albert Einstein postulates, time may be bent rather than linear, and understanding its spiral construction keeps us going back and forth—to other times, to other historical moments. *The Shining* follows this logic to the point where today might not necessarily lead to tomorrow, but instead back to yesterday. This represents the same temporal fluidity that is often present in King's work—especially in novels such as *Pet Sematary*, *IT*, *Rose Red*, and *The Dark Tower*. The fact that Kubrick's Jack appears to accept Grady's assertion without argument or need for clarification suggests again his willingness to see himself as unrestricted by recognizable chronological constraints. This lack of restriction makes Kubrick's Jack, from the very beginning, much less inhibited by the corset of History into which King relentlessly presses Jack. When Kubrick's Jack walks into the crowded ballroom, for example, literally crossing over into a party atmosphere directly distilled from the Jazz Age, redolent of smoke, free-flowing booze, flapper fashion, and music, he feels right at home, as unfazed by the simulacrum that absorbs him as he was when he earlier watched miniature versions of Wendy and Danny exploring the hedge maze. The maître d'hôtel greets him by name as he enters the Gold Ballroom, and he happily informs Lloyd the spectral bartender, "I've been away, but now I'm back," indicating that while he may have been away interacting with his family in the Seventies, his preference was to be back interfacing with the ghosts in the Twenties. Only his checkered flannel shirt, casual brown jacket, Lee jeans, and boots are out of place at this ballroom bash, and Jack is self-conscious enough of their sartorial inappropriateness that he intends to change his clothes before the "fish and goose soiree." Later in this scene, after Grady spills Adovcaat, a drink popularized in the Twenties, on Jack's jacket, the two men retreat to the red bathroom that was inspired by a Frank Lloyd Wright men's room Kubrick discovered in an Arizona hotel. Once there, Torrance refers to Grady as "Jeeves, old boy," an indication that Jack has assumed the diction of the Twenties as well as the period's sharply divided class demarcations. Although Torrance is hardly in a position to feel superior to anyone, Grady confirms his greater social status when he acknowledges that Jack is "the important one" whose jacket must be cleaned by the offending valet.

An attentive viewer of the film must ask why Kubrick methodically jams Jack—and Jack alone, as the sole representative from his era—back into the 1920s. As we traced earlier, King's novel barely links that decade with the Overlook, referencing several of the hotel's core epochs, but centering primarily on its immediate post-World War II past, while Kubrick's hotel is solidly foregrounded in a single period, saturated with the sights and sounds of Modernism. The aesthetic similarities between Modernism and post-modernism are, by now, quite clear: abject fragmentation; feelings of deep alienation; a rejection of the "grand narratives" of History. We recognize an enduring sense of futility beneath the surface of both movements, as their relentless breakdown of History and its avatars (like the nuclear family) merely *extend* the painful progression that preceded it. The violent power struggles that define American History persist even in—and, perhaps, *precisely because of*—the inventiveness of artists such as King and Kubrick. Because History cannibalizes Itself, any escape route predicated on the absolute negation of social norms leads us (infuriatingly) back to the beginning of the maze. Whether dressed in modernist or postmodern garb, Jack is always just what the etymology of his name suggests: a human tool; a male animal to be "used up."

Fredric Jameson's essay "Historicism in *The Shining*" offers a fine place to address this issue further, as he argues that the Twenties represents a time in American History where the gap between rich and poor was most acute and uncontested: "The Twenties were the last moment in which a genuine American leisure class led an aggressive and ostentatious public existence, in which an American ruling class projected a class-conscious and unapologetic image of itself and enjoyed privileges without guilt, openly and armed with its emblems of top-hat and champagne glass, on the social stage in full view of the other classes." Jameson is interested in exploring the ideological parallels that exist between the Overlook and an emerging corporate capitalism, the "multinational atmosphere in which Jack Nicholson is hired for a mere job by faceless organization men." His analysis of the film thus engages issues of community and the individual, opining, "whatever possibility this particular family might have had, in the social space of the city, of developing some collective solidarity with other people of similar marginalized circumstances, is henceforth itself foreclosed by the absolute isolation of the great hotel in winter." However, Jameson rarely touches on the impact of Kubrick's critique of History on Jack himself, acknowledging only that he is possessed by History writ large, "by the American past as it has left its sedimented traces in the corridors and dismembered suites of this monumental rabbit warren" (94–5, 90).

There is perhaps a more personal and specific rendering of the Twenties and their impact on Jack that needs to be explored: where does Jack fit into the ideology of capitalism, particularly in the form it occupied during the Twenties? And how do work and the importance of social status aligned with work shape Torrance's identity and historical configuration? It is rather odd that Jameson's Marxist reading of *The Shining* contains so little about the film's constructions of work. Jameson does argue that Torrance "is not a writer, not someone who has something to say or likes doing things with words, but rather someone who would like to *be* a writer, who lives a fantasy about what the American writer is, along the lines of James Joyce or Jack Kerouac" (93). While this is an intriguing point to which we will return, we would remind viewers that Wendy is the only person in the film who is pictured performing *actual* work (e.g., preparing meals in the kitchen, serving Jack breakfast in bed, checking on the status of the electrical systems in the hotel basement, maintaining contact with the forest rangers during a snowstorm, and supplying the protective childcare that an abused and catatonic Danny requires). We may witness scenes of Jack at his typewriter typing (one recalls Truman Capote's condemnation of Kerouac's *On the Road*: "That's not writing, that's typing"), but as Wendy discovers late in the film, all his work is distilled into a maze of words, an "All work and no play makes Jack a dull boy" manuscript. Hardly a magnum opus.

Unless, of course, you happen to be a member of the leisure class in residence at the Overlook Hotel during the Twenties. Kubrick's spectator discovers what will prove to be the seeds of an information economy, in which the leisurely (though endless) typing of words reveals itself to be grueling labor, cleverly disguised as the opening of creative floodgates. What is Twitter but a vast restaging of the film's infamous typewriter scene? Jack has literally typed the same characters in various permutations, signaling to both Wendy and the audience that his mind now belongs, or at least is in intellectual harmony with, the collective persona of the hotel. For it is the hotel itself that has instructed Jack to type and retype this third-person proverb, as if he must inculcate it into his psyche a thousand times, like some errant schoolboy at the blackboard, until he has absorbed its meaning fully. More insistent than a mere chastisement, the declaration is the hotel's demand that Jack must abandon all *work*—from writing, to hotel maintenance, to parenting, to his job as a husband—if he wishes to *play* alongside the juvenile revelers who frolic at the Overlook. For an alcoholic, this compact is the supreme temptation: a "forever and ever and ever" party with a deathless supply of free Jack Daniels and sexually available bathtub women. And what better era in America to locate and enjoy these vices than the Twenties—with its reputation for excess and decadent self-indulgence? It nearly goes without saying that Jack's fundamental confusion of artistic self-expression and empty-headed compliance to the shifting demands of the Overlook goes on to characterize an entire generation.

Pictured in Wendy's (brief) review of Jack's manuscript are the standard forms of language arrangements on the page that a writer employs in defining himself as a poet, dramatist, novelist, or essayist. In misusing and subverting all of these genre forms to reproduce the same mindless cant over and over, the Overlook is playing with the very "work" of a writer's livelihood and potential future. Correspondingly, the mocking diction of the typed proverb—stated from the same upper-crust persona that Jack assumes when he first encounters Grady entering the red bathroom, condescending and judgmental—belongs to the jet-set guests who reside permanently at the hotel. The upper-class ghosts at the Overlook are products of the severe class demarcations that Jameson references in his discussion of the income gap separating the absurdly rich denizens of the hotel from those who are their servants. Like the ghosts themselves, Jack's career as an important writer is an illusion, a fanciful image that he would like to assume in order to elevate himself beyond his present status as a *dull boy* caretaker and towards the rarified air of the wealthy trust fund party brats and corporate millionaires who paid no taxes in the Twenties, who never had to work, and who spent all their time perfecting play. The connecting points between Kubrick's postmodern *The Shining* and Fitzgerald's modernist *The Great Gatsby* make for a multifaceted discussion, but in the end both film and novel come back to a shared design: they are highly nostalgic texts that speak to the inimitable American need—and this need, unfortunately, is not restricted to the Twenties—to establish rigid class distinctions in lieu of an entrenched aristocracy. Fitzgerald's novel and Kubrick's film are throwbacks to a distinct American epoch. At the same time, however, they are also indictments of that era so devoid of a moral base that the elusive Jay Gatsby himself emerges as the one character "'worth the whole damn bunch put together'" (Fitzgerald 103).

Kubrick's film therefore advances a crucial thesis that King's novel generally "overlooks": by escaping from the dutiful labor of the Historian, and by embracing the hotel's free-wheeling post-History (unencumbered by attention to cause-and-effect), Jack immerses himself within the playful system of value extraction that continues to haunt this place. Said another way, whether reified (Kubrick) or burned for fuel (King) —whether the object of modernist or postmodern experimentation—Jack always ends up being consumed. History and post-History reach the same dead-end and so, at the twilight of the twentieth century, work becomes play and play becomes work. In an economy largely based upon information sharing, the two concepts grow indistinguishable. In Jack's refusal or inability to perform the hard work of sustaining History, whether it be the work of a writer or a hotel caretaker, Kubrick signals both Torrance's separation from the sphere of the living as well as his affiliation with the playboys from America's past. Reflecting their own class prejudices, the ghosts at the hotel have filled Jack with the terror of becoming a "clockwork" man, fearful of being reduced in stature to the proletarian tasks of "shoveling out driveways [and working] in a car wash."

This helps to explain why the film ends with the photograph of Jack situated in 1921. It is a confirmation that Jack has completed his journey back in time. The hotel's tacit promise of a position elevated above and outside of History—an erasure of cause-and-effect that allows the ghosts to jump from period to period—leads, ironically enough, to Jack's paralysis. Whereas he has perhaps secretly identified with the values of the Twenties as they are embodied at the Overlook, no doubt concurring with Ullman's obsequious perspective on the hotel's "illustrious past" as a "stopping place for the jet set, even before anybody knew what a jet set was ... all the best people," Torrance's death sets him free to complete his own transition back to the Overlook's past. The bleary-eyed hours that he spends alone with the hotel's scrapbook are, from the moment he starts to research the selected details from the Overlook's past, indistinguishable from the hours that he later spends with the hotel's jet-set revenants. As film critic Jason Sperb speculates in *The Kubrick Façade*, "It could just be the only place, cognitive or otherwise, where Jack possesses a sense of place and time" (Sperb 102). Through chronology or collage, drudgery or deftness, Jack the Historian obediently completes the tasks to which he is assigned. In contrast to his frozen, grizzled visage out in the hedge maze, in the 1921 photograph we witness a younger, vital, clean-shaven, tuxedoed, and manically grinning Jack Torrance, comfortably situated; he is centered among a group of Roaring Twenties party revelers, all of them young, meticulously groomed, and exclusively white, embracing Jack into their fold. Everyone pictured is smiling, convivial, and safely ensconced within the nostalgic dreamscape of America's past—a time that exists only in photographic memory, when head chefs at the Overlook were called "nigger cooks" without fear of retribution. The fact that the Great Depression was just around the corner, lurking in the shadows at the decade's end, was easily dismissed as the prognostication of some "dull boy." By suturing the Twenties to the Seventies (both decades that embody a spirit of menace hovering like smoke over their party atmospheres), Kubrick's film exposes American History, even in times of absent-minded revelry, to be a narrative of violent exclusion.

Kubrick's *Shining* is less a ghost story than a tale of repossession. The spectator feels that beginning with the very first occasion that Jack pulls up a barstool in the Colorado Lounge and begins to decant himself to Lloyd the spectral bartender, he's already a ghost in his own tale. One of the ways in which *The Shining* distinguishes itself from the conventions of the classic haunted house/ghost story is that Torrance adheres to a supernatural version of Stockholm Syndrome, identifying and bonding with the revenants that plague him and his family; he desires nothing more than to become one with them. Their sudden supernatural manifestations do not terrify him, as they do Wendy and Danny and most other protagonists who are trapped in narratives of gothic haunting.[4] Instead, by the end of the film, Jack's antipathy centers on whatever is human, an inversion of the survival struggle practiced by most characters in the horror genre. When he finds himself lost in the frozen hedge maze, Reason has left him (he could simply follow his son's example and retrace his steps out of the maze). However, Jack simply surrenders to the cold confusion; he collapses in on himself in an act of *suicidal resignation*. He is attracted to the dead white males that inhabit the Overlook for exactly the reasons that Wendy, Hallorann, and Danny are not: his core definition of masculinity is exclusively aligned with status, career, race, gender, and access to the trappings of privileged success. He obsesses over prestige, money, illicit women, alcohol, and a feckless, particularly American 1920s sense of masculine independence, which is to say, he is already, prior to his arrival at the Overlook, an effective agent of American History. It is not so much a society as it is a fraternity that Jack joins in the Overlook's *demimonde*. He enters a white, affluent patriarchy where women exist primarily as cosmetic decoration and men are free to drink and carouse with each other. In contrast to the unstable Seventies (exacerbated by the advent of American feminism) of Jack's own "real time," Kubrick depicts the Twenties as an era where blacks, children, and especially wives "knew their place" (unlike Wendy's role as the "old sperm bank upstairs" who, as Grady reminds him, stands in severe need of Jack's masculine "correction"). It may not be a coincidence, then, that Kubrick configures Jack's Overlook photograph during a July Fourth fete, seeking to capitalize on the ironic significance of that date in American History. Although neither King nor Kubrick provide us with much information about Jack's politics, we would speculate that he is far more likely to be a closet Republican, replete with an earlier era's faith in an uninhibited venture capitalism, than any stereotyped version of a progressive writer-private school academy English teacher. Jack merely lacks the financial wherewithal, class birthright, and marital independence to come out of the closet and join the deceased heiresses, junk bond traders, and monopoly capitalists of an earlier American era, who lived to play and party every night while mocking all the "dull boys" outside their elitist circle who had to get up every morning and work for a living. While the Overlook's ghosts are meant to be memories from past eras of the hotel in King's novel, in Kubrick's film adaptation these ghosts are better understood as projections of Jack's wishes, fantasies, and a struggling writer's vain longings for fame and fortune. In Surrealist fashion, there is no meaningful distinction between within and without the subject. For example, throughout the film, Jack asks Lloyd to serve him bourbon as his drink of choice, a working man's whiskey; the advocaat, transported by Grady, in contrast, is an effete cordial preferred by the cultural elite. When these two liquors come together in Jack's collision with Grady, the resulting blend symbolizes Jack's desire to be part of the Overlook's exclusive guest list, even as his roots remain in the material world of menial servitude. This veritable cocktail of different histories reveals a base ingredient of American History: like Jack, the twentieth-century American worker has had to resign himself to participating in both manufacturing as well as information economies controlled by faceless multi-international corporations operating in distant cities, shaping the violent forces of History as they consume the American middle-class for fuel. These phantom elites would, of course, have no problem with Jack's gradual retreat into his own head; after all, a subjectivity unfettered from external reference points can be more easily plugged into a volatile, hyper-speculative economy. Whereas King's Jack is coopted into maintaining delusions of mastery and coherence that stem from Henry Ford, John Maynard Keynes, and world wars (and this cooptation sparks his downfall), Kubrick's Jack is already—from the opening shot—a sign of what comes next: a postmodern playboy immersed in the party atmosphere of a world functioning without History.

The period (1980) in which Kubrick's film was released coincided with the rise of Reaganism and the Right's unleashing of a deregulated capitalism reminiscent of the monopoly system that gave birth to the Rockefellers, Carnegies, and Fricks in the Twenties. During both of these eras, the gap separating rich from poor in America widened dramatically. As Jameson reminds us about the Twenties, in the age of Reagan it was not only permissible to be wealthy, it was also encouraged to flaunt this wealth whenever and wherever possible. When Jameson published "Historicism in *The Shining*" in 1990 he could not have foreseen that the American Twenties would soon be rivaled in greed and decadence by a generation of Wall Street bankers and junk bond speculators spawned during the Reagan era of deregulation, their nefarious and illegal schemes fueled with borrowed money, just as they were in the Twenties, to the point where these money manipulators were responsible for producing the global recession in 2007. And as they were held unaccountable in the Twenties and Thirties, none of them went to jail after the financial meltdown in 2007. By providing Jack with images of a Twenties' celebrity lifestyle that contrasts so fatally with his "real time" existence as a struggling writer, unemployed English teacher, and abysmal father and husband, the hotel ghosts pull him into their collective milieu, like a perfume advertisement relying on glossy photography and exceptionally attractive people to produce a fantasy of beautiful romance (it is, by way of extending this analogy, worth noting that the modern advertising industry was conceived in the 1920s). This hegemonic design has traditionally been employed to manipulate, while also enticing, the lower classes, to the point of psychic exhaustion and physical extermination—promising the democratic American Dream of instant happiness via tremendous material wealth for everyone while, in reality, depositing this money into the coffers of the ruling class, the one percent of the American populace that controls over ninety percent of the nation's wealth. Unable to see beyond History's mutable façade (another faux motility, like the bricolage that makes up the nest of White Anglo-Saxon Protestants), Jack is seduced by images of the past just as he is by the illusion of the beautiful bathtub woman in room 237. At the closing of the day, we might ask if there is a historical consciousness that could avoid conforming to the dominant ideology of the era. Even as King and Kubrick attempt to outpace the tempo of an Anglo-militant History, they only succeed in reflecting its brutal constancy. Not unlike the followers of Reagan, King reflects a desire to decamp from the plotting of a military-industrial complex; not unlike the generation of hedge fund managers to come, Kubrick employs a deconstructive impulse that actually *supplements* the financial shifts taking place at the time of the film's release. In brief, these visions of history (with a lower-case "h") do not map a path forward so much as they reveal a terrifying consistency: a violent History that, like the Overlook itself, fools us into thinking it has amended its ways.

With varying degrees of self-consciousness, both *Shining*s allow us to inspect the shimmering allure of toxic nostalgia as well as (illusory) escape routes offered by capitalists run amuck. Jack either submits to decadent dreams of "American greatness" by entering into frozen animation, or he dissolves into a form of liquefied human capital, the warp and woof of rampant post-war financialization. In either case, *The Shining* presents twentieth-century American "progress" as an accumulative, bloody force that leaves only debris in its wake. Moreover, the many false hinges that would shift us from History to post-History—Watson's dramatic departure (King); the photograph that memorializes "independence" (Kubrick)—bring us right back to the point from which we launched. Perhaps the one thing that Torrance shares most in common with the ghosts in residence at the Overlook is their restive discontent with the mundane. Like Jay Gatsby before him, Jack willingly sacrifices his present-tense identity in order to recast himself into an image of success and importance. At the same time, however, Gatsby recreated himself out of love; Jack's goal is not nearly so noble. His quest (and the quest of King and Kubrick, to some degree) more accurately resembles the restless discontent that fuels the self-centered energies of a Horace Derwent. Suffering from a terrible case of writer's block, hyperconscious that he is inappropriately dressed in denim while the *demimonde* wears formal attire, dissatisfied with his place as a sexist male trapped in the era of second-wave feminism, Jack looks to relocate in a more predictable past. While the American has always looked to the future for self-definition, Jack so prefers the past that he willingly sacrifices both himself and his family in the present. Jack's is the worst case of nostalgia since Gatsby's misguided dream to recapture Daisy. But as Jack and Jay discover, albeit too late, the reason the American has always looked to the future is because History itself is a powerful illusion. The hyperbolized time frames that consume Jack in these two respective narratives—the Twenties as well as the post-war Forties—simply cannot sustain themselves. The Twenties crashes headlong into the Great Depression, while the post-war American "Colossus" sinks eventually into the mud of Vietnam. Kubrick and King possess the benefit of this grim historical consciousness and they recognize in Jack a tragic figure: a man out of place and out of time.

An even more paralyzing realization takes hold of us as we recognize that both *Shining*s yearn to access a point of impossible critical distance and join Hallorann and Danny in their shared postmodern revelry. Yet even as King attempts to outwit History (with a capital "H"), and Kubrick attempts to outwit King's naïve confidence in a history to come (with a lower-case "h"), both figures overlook how late capitalism converts wit into weaponry, thus transforming aesthetics into a war that is violent in its own right (hence the acerbic feud over which *Shining* shines brightest). Therefore, although they aspire to articulate a different sort of history, modernist or postmodern (or somehow both at the same time), each version instigates another "fish and goose soirée": a mere variation of the windmill against which they have been tilting. With varying degrees of self-consciousness, both works imply that, whether we like it or not, we are all Jack in the end, and American History proves to be a ruthless shape-shifter that can make tools of us all. In response, King spends the next four decades attempting to abscond from History's maze.

Notes

1 New Historicism, by blurring the line between history and literature, encourages readers to understand history as a project without predetermined contours, and not as a rigid, imposing metanarrative that custodians like Jack are forced to maintain.
2 See also Christopher Norris's *Uncritical Theory: Postmodernism, Intellectuals and the Gulf War*.
3 In his 1980 interview with Michael Ciment, Kubrick speculates that "the scope and flexibility of movie stories would be greatly enhanced by borrowing something from the structure of silent movies where points that didn't require dialog could be presented by a shot and title card" (Ciment 480).
4 Patrick Webster's chapter on *The Shining* from his book *Love and Death in Kubrick* claims that "In *The Shining*, to some extent, [Kubrick] reinvented the

horror genre, just as he had previously reinvented the science fiction genre with *2001* ... although we were offered a cross-section of horror film archetypes: the ghosts, the haunted house, the 'vampiric' attack to Danny's neck, the idea of selling one's soul to the devil: all these instances were, in some sense, subverted" (Webster 89–90).

This chapter's discussion of Kubrick and Modernism was first articulated in Tony Magistrale's essay "Sutured Time: History and Kubrick's The Shining" in *Stanley Kubrick's* The Shining*: Studies in the Horror Film*, edited by Daniel Olson, Lakewood, CO: Centipede Press, 2015, 151–66.

4 The Vietnamization of Stephen King

It would be difficult to overstate the impact of the Vietnam War upon Stephen King. As a college student at the University of Maine at Orono (UMO) from 1966 to 1970, he was utterly transformed by the conflict, torn apart—like many members of his generation—by a growing chasm between the comfortable fantasies of middle-class America and the grotesque realities of combat. The crisis in Vietnam would prove to be King's crucible, the event that most dramatically transformed him into the contemporary chronicler of America's nightmares. And yet, surprisingly, there exist no sustained critical analyses of how the Vietnam War shaped King's fiction, or what his works reveal about this grim interval in American History. There are occasional brief references to the event, such as Simon Brown's reminder that the televised miniseries of *The Dead Zone* (2002–2007) updates the World War II context for the film (1983) to Vietnam, replacing the movie's Dr. Weizak with the younger, Vietnamese Dr. Tran. Or Caleb Crain's intriguing book review of *Hearts in Atlantis* that muses insightfully, "maybe Vietnam is the archetype not only of the otherworldly … but of all King's supernatural horror." This is, however, the extent of current King scholarship on the subject. In this chapter, we examine how two of King's novels—*Hearts in Atlantis* (1999) and *Dreamcatcher* (2001)—explore America's deep psychic wounds that have not yet healed. Few King scholars and readers appreciate sufficiently the degree to which both his fiction and his life have been influenced by the political consciousness that emerged during his formative years at UMO. While many Americans politicized in the Sixties had by the Seventies and Eighties rejoined the mainstream establishment in order to make money and advance careers, King has held true to the political awareness he incurred as an undergraduate, and novels such as *Dreamcatcher* and *Hearts in Atlantis* reflect this awareness.

America's involvement in Vietnam began in the years following the Second World War. As France sought (brutally) to retain control of its colony, America—now a superpower with considerable global influence—was drawn in to support both sides. Officially, it did not want Southeast Asia to succumb to communist rule, and it preferred French colonialism to Chinese or Soviet expansion. Concurrently, however, the Vietnamese struggle for independence under the charismatic leader Ho Chi Minh was closer—ideologically, at least—to the American mantras of freedom and self-determination. In fact, Minh so admired the American model that he sought American aid as an ally in his country's fight for liberation. As the years passed, and the bloodshed continued, America's role in the region grew ever murkier. By the war's ignoble end in 1975, hundreds of thousands of soldiers and civilians had died, and the scope of American imperialism was being called into question at home as well as abroad.

According to King, the horrors experienced in Vietnam disrupt the "normal" flow of American History. The war rips a gaping hole into the presumed rationality of American "progress"—ripped so irreversibly, in fact, that King remains disoriented to this day. The chaos of the conflict consistently ruins his own efforts to look back upon his youth. With his recent retrospective on the war, "Five to One, One in Five: UMO in the '60s" (2016), he offers an intentionally disjointed text, one that jumps around in time, with an unreliable narrator that admits his memories of the era will never be entirely clear. The war in Vietnam thus reveals how any effort to interpret American History as a coherent whole remains *a fundamentally impossible task* (a realization that directly influences King's writing style as well as his recollections of these formative years). As a senior in high school, he expressed interest in going to Nam—because, in his mind, the "great Vietnam novel was still waiting to be written"—but he narrowly escaped being drafted for health reasons (King "Five" 30). When he arrived at the campus in Orono, a product of backwater America in a state with one of the smallest minority populations in the country, the politics from his blue-collar upbringing were appropriately conservative and benign, and he remained relatively supportive of America's military presence in Southeast Asia. Very soon after his arrival, though, King was confronted by protestors and activists, both in and outside of his classes. King let his hair grow long, experimented with drugs, and identified—especially during his last two years as an undergraduate—with the Students for a Democratic Society (SDS) movement against the war in Vietnam and other American social ills: "While I began college with political leanings too far to the right to actually become radicalized, by 1968 my mind had been changed forever about a number of fundamental questions ... I did not and do not believe that the hands of the Rockefellers were utterly clean during this period, nor those of ATT; I did and do believe that companies like Sikorsky and Douglas Aircraft and Dow Chemical and even the Bank of America subscribed more or less to the idea that war is good business" (King, *Danse* 296–7). Readers familiar with King's body of work discover in his retrospective the seeds of a long-lasting cynicism regarding "the establishment." To put it bluntly, his fiction from this point forward fuels a "perception of the federal government [that] borders on paranoia" (Magistrale, *Landscape* 35). That is to say, as a result of the paranoia bred during the war in Vietnam, King's narratives routinely return to the oppressive weight of a bloated military-industrial complex, gesturing at vast cover-ups and heartless bureaucracies while fanning the flames of conspiratorial sentiment.[1]

King's first short story collection, *Night Shift* (1979), reveals the extent to which the war influenced his earliest publications. "Children of the Corn"—ostensibly a story of religious fanaticism dedicated to a malevolent deity—can be read as an allegory of the Vietnam experience transported to Middle America. Nebraska and its corn are located in the "heartland" of America, its moral epicenter, and out of an effort to reestablish the purity and innocence of an earlier era, both the corn and the land itself can be interpreted as demanding penance for a sin that originated in 1964, the start of American involvement in Vietnam (see Magistrale, *Landscape* 78–83). "The Boogeyman," also in this collection, tells the story of a shell-shocked man in a therapy session as he laments a situation familiar to many anxious parents of the era: his children are being killed off under mysterious circumstances. Although the tale only mentions the conflict in Vietnam in passing ("the war in Vietnam was still going on," the narrator notes as an aside), the connections to Southeast Asia are everywhere. A boogeyman stalks the man's home in a fashion that clearly calls to mind guerrilla warfare of the Viet Cong: "You could hear something moving in a stealthy way. But not too stealthy, because it wanted you to hear it" (*Night* 156, 160). In the end, the real enemy is disclosed as the therapist: a bureaucratic, establishment-type covertly responsible for the death of the man's children. And, finally, in "Battleground," an "infallible predator," John Renshaw, receives a package labeled "The Vietnam Footlocker," the contents of which turn out to be toy soldiers that launch a surprise attack on their unwitting recipient. Renshaw represents the American juggernaut—armed with "superior firepower" and a bellicose attitude with "no intention of being turned away"—who finds himself suddenly ambushed by an antagonist whose aggressiveness he failed to anticipate. Much like an American solider entering the rice paddies and jungles of Vietnam, Renshaw's mind cannot quite adjust to "the real or unreal aspect of what he was seeing," and he is shocked to find himself at a disadvantage against a foe that he (fatally) underestimates: "I'm losing!" (183–6). At the very dawn of King's career, his readers discover the tentacles of the Vietnam War as they work their way subtextually into the author's different story lines.[2]

Few of King's scholars appreciate sufficiently the extent to which both his fiction and his life were impacted by the political consciousness that was raised during King's formative years as an undergraduate at UMO that happened to coincide with one of the major events in the twentieth century that challenged America's conception of itself. According to King, the Vietnam War will remain, long after 1976, "the steady drumbeat of our lives ... always there" ("Five" 47–8). Indeed, it was this relentless beat, he insists, that first brought him to "political awareness." As a result, his fiction possesses two faces: on one side, it is passionately anti-establishment, expressing sincere convictions about the many failures of the federal government; on the other side, it is weary of activism and advocates a reclusive suburban existence in which we forfeit our (futile) attempts to change the world. The duality of these positions prodded him into activism as a rabble rouser with the campus paper; at the same time, it revealed to him that protestors such as the Students for a Democratic Society were "humorless," inauthentic (because of their endless posturing), and unwilling to conform—to "clean up"—and get a job. For every incisive attack upon the barbarity of the American war machine, King's texts condemn those for whom "the traditional values of family, fidelity, and personal honor have not all drowned and dissolved in the trendy California hot tub of the 'me' generation" (Underwood 53). This acute ambivalence, which plays such a constitutive role in King's corpus, has its origins in the larger context of Vietnam. The fissures that run through the pages of his works can be traced back to the divisions of American society created by this conflict.

Hearts in Atlantis and *Dreamcatcher* present a divided America in proximity to the war that shattered the nation's optimistic vision of itself. In these novels, the superficial cries of patriotism and the underlying assumption of unity run up against rogue characters, veterans, and counter-cultural figures that have been cast aside and left to deal with this trauma, alone. How, then, are King's readers to interpret the war in Vietnam? Viet Thanh Nguyen posits that "all wars are fought twice, the first time on the battlefield, the second time in memory" (Nguyen 4). The issue gets even cloudier in the context of King's contemporary readership, insofar as many are too young (or were not yet born) to possess any kind of memory to play off King's fictionalizing. Or, perhaps more to the point, how is it that we have managed collectively to forget the war so well—to erase the atrocities and persist in the long walk of American empire? Although the ghosts of Vietnam linger throughout King's fiction, his multiverse appears to be hopelessly mired—much like the nation's History that it often references—within a perpetual loop of imperial violence. King captures this sense of paralysis, of being stuck in a perpetual loop, in his recently released story "Squad D," which ends with a young man killing himself because he can never escape the trauma of Vietnam and a clock in his parent's home simultaneously coming to an eerie standstill. King therefore views the conflict in Vietnam as emblematic of an America History doomed to replay its mistakes forevermore. By investigating the role of the war in these novels, we begin to understand why its phantoms are both nowhere and everywhere in American life—consistently repressed and habitually returned.

Hearts in Atlantis as Vietnam Allegory

There are several recurring characters who make their way through the five chronologically sequenced, yet distinct, sections of King's *Hearts in Atlantis*. One way of reading this fragmented narrative, of attempting to pull together its disparate parts and the fluid movement of its characters, is to recognize that Carol Gerber, the novel's central female, is the locus around whom all the other characters gravitate. She is the metaphorical prism through which to view the males with whom she interacts. First, she is the sole romantic interest for three of these males in three separate sections of the novel: Bobby Garfield, Pete Riley, and John Sully Sullivan. Additionally, because of his active participation in a beating she incurs as a child, "Blind Willie" Shearman spends his post-Vietnam life engaged in a bizarre ritual of penance: "God marked him in 1960, when he first helped Harry Doolin tease Carol and then helped Harry beat her. That occasion of sin has never left his mind. What happened in the grove of trees near Field B stands for everything else" (576).

Because all of the protagonists in this book are in some way tainted by their exposure to the Vietnam War, none of them gets out with their sanity intact. This is a novel filled with wounded and fragmented identities, characters unable to fix what the war has done to them (directly and indirectly). It is no coincidence that Sully references having read Hemingway's *The Sun Also Rises* three times (617). Like the role the Vietnam War plays in *Hearts* and *Dreamcatcher*, World War I is the subject of Hemingway's novel; both wars function as much characters in these respective texts despite the fact that it is the aftereffect of combat that emerges as their truest subject. In the first great war of the machine age, mechanics were more important than the men killing and being killed by them. Vietnam was also a war of technologically-based machines as well as interpersonal weaponry—such as mines and booby traps—where war was fought against an invisible enemy, and where soldiers were likely to be killed—or not killed—quite by accident. Like the "lost generation" in Hemingway's earlier book, the protagonists in *Hearts* bear psychic wounds (Sully even resembles Jake Barnes insofar as he has also suffered a crippling injury to his groin) that makes it impossible for any of them to function in conventional society. Just as Hemingway's world-weary war veterans no longer feel connected to their respective societies because of the dirty business those societies foisted upon them through war experiences, King's dysfunctional characters have all lost their faith and been rendered impotent by the war. Sully dies in the embrace of the ghost *mamasan* who was executed in front of him in Vietnam. Willie has become a bifurcated personality—one part of him goes home to his loving wife Sharon every night, after his other self spends the day "working" as a phony panhandler by performing acts of contrition for his adolescent violence against Carol and as a soldier in Vietnam. Bobby Garfield disappears from the text after part one, but returns in the novel's coda to reunite with what may or may not be—Bobby's consciousness is so distorted by this point in the book that King leaves his sense of reality in doubt—a scarred and burned vision of Carol in a surreal scene where the two adults look back at their childhoods and lament their tragic outcomes. Dieffenbaker, who fought with Sully in Vietnam, acknowledges at the end of the book a sentiment that Hemingway's lost men and women would have understood intimately, "'our generation died [in Vietnam]'" (640). *Hearts* is King's testament to this mass casualty.

Like Bev in *IT* (and likewise Lady Brett Ashley in *The Sun Also Rises*), Carol Gerber's role in this novel is as a pivot or fulcrum for the action that revolves around her, and to which she plays a highly interactive part. In addition to being a good girlfriend, she is also the figure who is most radicalized by the Vietnam experience. "Carol was the one who didn't sell out" (523). These are some of Pete Riley's final words in *Hearts*. After dropping out of school to join the anti-war movement full time, Carol emerges as the most unequivocal presence in the novel. She is also the most authentic and patriotic character in the book. Her patriotism, however, is not the knee-jerk response of a right-wing supporter of the war, such as Sully-John who initially enlisted for the same reason other naïve boys went to Vietnam—because they believed in the rhetoric of the cause. Instead, her protest against America's involvement in Southeast Asia is based on a personal awareness of victimization and bullying that she recollects from childhood. In the sincerity of her moral commitment we witness the potential Stephen King once recognized in his generation from the Sixties. The severity of Carol's beating at the hands of Harry Dolan and his two friends raises her sensitivity to other injustices and cruelties that go unpunished in the world. More specifically, the older boys who abused Carol were armed with superior strength and firepower; they attacked her without cause and then left her alone and suffering. Their lack of mercy and misuse of force later forges a parallel in Carol's own moral schematics with the overwhelming resources of the American *Wehrmach* in Vietnam. Her childhood violation forms a nexus to the indigenous Vietnamese people and their struggle against a foreign invader who will "'pay a price for hurting people'" (418). Her anti-war sentiments are as close as King gets in this book to articulating the "other side" of the war's combatants, the Vietnamese people, who were similarly victimized in a war that was foisted on them. Moreover, Carol shares some of the same resolute determination that energized the struggle of the Vietnamese in her efforts to shut down the war. Although this connection is not explicitly developed in *Hearts*, Carol is the one character (in addition to Pete Riley in Chicago) who takes her commitment into the streets—shedding her own blood in a confrontation with police—in terms that suggest an identification with oppressed "'people who are smaller than you and don't mean you any harm'" (418).

Carol's loss of innocence affects her both as an American citizen and an anti-war protestor, who makes the mistake of taking her ethical outrage to a level of militancy wherein she accidentally kills an innocent student with a bomb meant to blow up an empty building. As such, her tragic trajectory serves as the operative paradigm that all the other characters in the book either respond to directly or follow unwittingly. Moreover, her personal experience reflects and parallels the loss of innocence that came home with American veterans, such as Sully and Bill Shearman, and shaped as well the anti-war movement for those Americans who never went to Vietnam, including King himself. When Bobby Garfield loses his father-figure Ted Brautigan in the first section, his life collapses abruptly, leading the formerly sweet boy down a path of delinquency and violence. Garfield's spirit is corrupted by the work of the "low men in yellow coats," a mysterious cadre dressed in yellow suits and driving large garish automobiles who bear something in common with both supernatural revenants and secret governmental agents. In their relentless pursuit of Brautigan's "Breaker" abilities, the "low men" utilize the same manipulative and duplicitous methods the Sixties revealed about American governmental agencies. Although Bobby's descent into nihilism occurs in the final pages of section one, it speaks to the transformation that occurred to so many of the American boys who came home as broken men after witnessing the horrors of engagement "in the green." Bobby exits part one a victim of PTSD, a condition that will eventually affect all the characters in *Hearts*. At the heart of Bobby's despair is the learned evidence that life is not fair; that adults cannot be trusted (he witnesses his mother's sexual violation at the hands of her boss, aptly named Biderman, and her subsequent betrayal of Brautigan to the "low men"); that his childhood friends Carol and Sully cannot follow him into adulthood; and that growing up in Sixties' America necessitates forced exposure to a dark and violent reality that lurks just beneath the placid (and false) surfaces of small-town American life.

The characters in *Hearts* are initiated into an adult world that is often emblematic of the corrupting force of History in King's multiverse. Good men, like Ted Brautigan, are sacrificed to the tyranny of "low men." And the novel's implication is that the "low men" also represent the politicians and patriots who misled American youth about the nobility of purpose, the strategic importance behind nearly a decade of carnage in Vietnam, and the specious reasoning that commands everyone and everything to be sacrificed in the support of some vague concept of cosmic "Beams" or against the advance of an abstract world communism. In this way, *Hearts* is arguably King's most pessimistic book, for none of its characters find reason to temper the "information" that arrives from their loss of faith in American institutions: school, the military, the legal system, family, even friendship and love. The child not only gives way to the adult in this text, but the adult then gives way to despair. Perhaps the operative metaphor for such American nihilism is the final image of Sully Sullivan just before his death on a Connecticut interstate, ducking a "noisy hail of falling televisions and backyard pools and cartons of cigarettes and high-heeled shoes and a great big pole hairdryer, ... all things American falling out of the sky" (647). These are the symbolic objects America sent its youth to protect and promulgate in a war that King insists destroyed the dream of Atlantis. Like *Dreamcatcher*, *Hearts* is without much commentary about how this war impacted the indigenous people of Vietnam itself. But it has plenty to say about its impact on the children of Atlantis, who afterwards came away from this shameful moment no longer capable of viewing American History (via icons like the nation's flag) without an admixture of contradictory sentiments: "Sully couldn't think of a single man he'd served with, including himself, who would want to be buried in an Army uniform" (601).

The weakest section of *Hearts* follows Pete Riley, as we have alluded to already, an autobiographical portrait of King himself at the University of Maine, Orono, in 1966. Riley's obsession with the card game Hearts occupies way too much of the narrative action. But if we read the sophomoric obsession with this silly game as a distraction from what could, and perhaps should, be occupying Riley's focus, it makes more sense in the context of the rest of the novel. Significantly, his girlfriend Carol keeps urging him to give up playing cards in order to concentrate on school and the war that in 1966 began to taint the edges of Atlantis. As the section unfolds, Pete does move the discourse away from playing cards and towards Vietnam, but he is able to do so only because of Carol's inspiring influence: she becomes his conduit to an anti-war consciousness. Each of the two news photographs in which Carol is featured protesting—the first in a peaceful confrontation, the second, with blood on the side of her head as a barometer to the conflict's escalation level—forces Pete to recognize her commitment to the protest and, in turn, because he respects her so deeply, to challenge his own conservative apathy, a similar political transformation which, as we have alluded to already, occurred to King himself. Carol helps to motivate Pete's embryonic upsurge in political consciousness, a process that is symbolically signaled when he scrapes the Barry Goldwater bumper sticker off his car while she looks on approvingly (423). Thus, even after Carol terminates their romantic relationship at the same time as she leaves school, Pete continues to evolve politically: protecting Stoke Jones' First Amendment right to political expression and, by the end of the section, becoming an integral part of the protest movement itself, locked in a Chicago jail for demonstrating at the Democratic National Convention.

The strangest and most philosophically convoluted section of *Hearts* is titled "Blind Willie," and it takes place years after the war has ended. While the Vietnam War was over by 1983, its aftermath rages on inside Willie Shearman's haunted psyche. To capture that, King creates an unbelievable, almost cartoon-like scenario that is meant to exaggerate reality to the point at which it is only believable as metaphor. Unable to express his remorse for past behavior in a more conventional and constructive manner, Willie choses a bizarre daily ritual of putting on brown (appropriating the role of blackface, or of a grunt out in the bush?) makeup, an Army jacket and fatigues, dark sunglasses that blacken the world, and spends his workweek begging for money in front of St. Patrick's cathedral. Before then going back to his suburban world each night, he also writes in a bound ledger the phrase, "*I am heartily sorry*"; he has, "to the best of his reckoning, written this over two million times" (543). As a boy raised in parochial school, it is possible to view Willie's secretive actions as a form of self-punishment for past sins, an act of contrition in order to regain some sort of ethical equilibrium through a daily program of expurgation: "These days he does penance instead of confession, and his certainty of heaven is gone" (556). Just as he failed to confront the bat-wielding Doolin when young Carol Gerber was placed under siege, Willie again neglected to give voice to his conscience during the massacre of the Vietnam village where he witnesses a helpless old *mamasan* murdered by Ronnie Malenfant.

Hence, Blind Willie's "blindness" extends not only to the momentary vision loss he experienced during a blast-flash that took place "in the bush" after the massacre, but also to his moral blindness on each of the aforementioned occasions. Moreover, his blindness extends beyond these past events and into the present, to a level of self-deception that may find value in acts of perpetual restitution, but then is undercut as it turns into "pure, selfish self-indulgence" (643). Instead of following the Roman Catholic prescription of confession for his sins and the determined volition not to repeat them, Willie compounds his past offenses. The money he makes panhandling as Blind Willie—"there's four or five hundred dollars in all, which puts him on the way to a three-thousand-dollar day" —is garnered at the expense of decency and humility: preying on the open grief of other Vietnam vets, a sympathetic and guilt-riddled street public, and his duped wife who believes he has an actual job in Manhattan (558). And rather than giving the money he makes to a veteran's organization, the Vietnamese people themselves, or even a local charity, his racket funds his middle-class lifestyle in Connecticut, "there are compensations for even the blindest life" (589). Willie's corruption overwhelms any purification effort to exculpate his misdeeds; while he may sincerely lament his past criminal actions, his street theater panhandling, which he apparently has come to enjoy, implies that he has gained no authentic self-insight, no shot at redemption despite his self-designed masochistic catechism. His monologue is trapped in theatricality, something orotund and empty: a performance for only himself and some imaginary sympathetic reader. Indeed, his bound penitent ledgers filled with "pages of densely packed writing" remain housed inside stacks of office cabinets, unseen and unread by anyone else (542). Even Willie's wife is excluded from the grand design of his morally inert effort. It is clear that Willie has chosen to put himself through this elaborate daily drama of humiliation, but to what end? Is it to honor Carol, or to make money? Both? How do readers measure its level of sincerity since he literally sheds his skin each afternoon to become again the bourgeois gentleman of Connecticut? What else can a reader do but annotate the contradictory ironies of Willie's daily rituals with multiple question marks in the margins?

Behind the blindness of Blind Willie is King's larger, metaphoric condemnation of the Atlantis failure. The condition of blindness is meant to extend beyond Willie himself to include those Americans who willed themselves to believe that this war was just, and forward to those who failed to learn anything from the sacrifice in blood, credibility, and dollars that were wasted in Vietnam. Rudyard Kipling's "Epitaphs of the War" may well serve as the ultimate and most trenchant comment on America's involvement in Vietnam: "If any question why we died, / Tell them, because our fathers lied" (Kipling). As Victor Howard posits, "I don't think that any of us knows exactly what happened to America across that terrible time. Nor do we yet comprehend the cost of the war both then, now, and for the future" (Howard 57). Just as Carol's childhood assault enlarges for her to become an allegory for American violence in Vietnam, Willie's split selves convert into a commentary that addresses his generation's core hypocrisy. King's novel asks explicitly: does his entire generation view the past with any more integrity than Blind Willie? After all, placed in a position to learn from its tragic mistakes in Vietnam, America continues to pursue a feckless foreign policy; while the generation of peace and love "'had the opportunity to change everything ... Instead we settled for designer jeans, two tickets to Mariah Carey and retirement portfolios'" (643). In other words, the Vietnam War left its scars (literally on Carol Gerber's face) on those whom this nation sent to fight and die, but also on the psyche of the generation that lived its horror vicariously. The children of Atlantis are really not so distinct from the self-duplicitous Willie. While many in his generation look back on Vietnam with sincere regret, they also own stock in the corporations that made this war (and others to come) profitable. We honor our warriors and war casualties each Memorial Day and Veterans Day, but we rarely debate what their lives were sacrificed for (much less how to avoid creating future war dead). Present-day historians may judge the Vietnam experience to have been a horrible mistake predicated on lies and misguided patriotism, yet the descendants of Atlantis continue to elect politicians who conduct unchecked covert actions at home and abroad in flagrant violation of the War Powers Act, while American tax dollars fund a military that is bigger and better equipped than the world's next seven militaries combined. Nguyen argues that the most important legacy of the Vietnam misadventure was that it "was one conflict in a long line of horrific wars that came before it and after it" (2). Sometimes it seems as if the most important lesson the Pentagon took away from Vietnam is the critical value of censoring graphic images and unsanitized scenes of carnage from the eyes of the American public. America remains blind to—when it should be haunted by—the amount of money it has squandered on wars from Vietnam to Afghanistan. What kind of place might Atlantis have become in the past half century had its national treasury gone instead towards improving its schools, cities, infrastructure? These are issues that still ghost the socially-conscious Stephen King. As Jessica Mathews notes, "At home, defense spending crowds out funds for everything else a prosperous economy and healthy society needs. Abroad, it has led us to become a country reflexively reliant on the military and one quite different from what we think ourselves to be" (23). Perhaps this gets to the relevance King invests symbolically in Willie's misuse of monies he garners panhandling. At any rate, these are the contradictions most of America has learned to live with quite nicely, just as King's Blind Willie goes home each night and has no problem sleeping peacefully in his suburban bed.

Only two short years after the publication of *Hearts*, King releases *Dreamcatcher*—a novel that addresses many of the same themes: the breakdown of the American social order during as well as after the war; the hypocrisy of post-war America; and feelings of guilt mixed with practices of conspicuous consumption. Each text concerns itself with the influence of the conflict upon the collective psyche of the nation more than twenty years after the collapse of Saigon (although certain sections of *Hearts* were written earlier in King's career). At the close of the millennium, King seems particularly interested in relitigating the core debates that surrounded the war in Vietnam, and he does so by reconsidering American life in the years prior to the conflict—in the "Low Men in Yellow Coats" section, for instance—as well as in the years that follow its ignoble end. As we will see in the following section, *Dreamcatcher* is ultimately less retrospective than *Hearts*; it adopts a broader and still more allegorical viewpoint by exploring how American imperialism consumes everything in its path. The novel's style also remains more symptomatic of the concerns of its unique historical moment. Crafted as a postmodern epic, *Dreamcatcher* reflects a major preoccupation of the 1990s in its blurring of fantasy and reality. Despite these minor differences, *Hearts* and *Dreamcatcher* both force readers to consider how America's mnemonics of the conflict have come to look a lot like forgetting. On multiple levels, these interlocking texts ruminate upon how keepers of American History coopt tropes from the war and, in the process, blind us all.

Dreamcatcher and Memories of War in Vietnam

King's *Dreamcatcher* builds upon a connection between American History and the impulse to create war that we discuss in earlier chapters concerning *Pet Sematary* (1983) and *The Shining* (1977). King once more returns to a thinly-veiled drive to military combat, exploring in detail how American society remains stuck in cycles of violent confrontation. Consider, for example, the myriad wars that America has fought since Vietnam, and how many of them closely resembled Vietnam in terms of invading a sovereign nation state without establishing beforehand either a clear justification for the incursion or an exit strategy. To convey this paralysis, *Dreamcatcher* touches upon a number of American military exercises, including the Civil War (the invading aliens are called "grayboys"—a term used to describe Confederate soldiers), World War II (the relentless references to concentration camps), as well as the more recent excursions into Bosnia in the 1990s. Upon sojourning to a cabin in the woods on its annual retreat, a small group of hunters discovers that an alien species has begun to take over the bodies of rural Maine residents. The federal government subsequently sends in hawkish commandoes to transform the little hamlet of Jefferson Tract into a blood-soaked war zone. Despite its otherwise generic restatement of the body snatcher narrative, *Dreamcatcher* probes into why American History has been punctuated by ceaseless war, and—more pointedly—the text forces readers to grapple with the residual psychic effects of the Vietnam conflict. As we've seen in our discussion of *Hearts*, King's allusions to Vietnam in his fiction often occur in the form of mnemonic allegories actually set in America. He transposes horrific events through time and space, thereby suggesting parallels for readers to pull together.

Dreamcatcher revisits America's involvement in the conflict in Vietnam, a connection that it makes quite explicit: "Vietnam comes to northern Maine." The novel cautions against a "panic-stricken" government that too eagerly sanctions a "My Lai massacre," and it constantly draws upon the imagery of "Vietnam War movies" to give more vibrant color to its sketch of Jefferson Tract (*Dreamcatcher* 289, 524, 341). As we will see, *Dreamcatcher* gestures at the crisis of Vietnam in broader ways as well, such as its general anxiety concerning communism and a well-camouflaged enemy. Like many contemporary body snatcher narratives, King's text fears the unseen enemy. By inhabiting its host in ways that cannot be spotted by the naked eye, the aliens foster a dread felt widely during the Cold War, which is why horror film scholars often interpret movies such as *Invasion of the Body Snatchers, Cat People*, and *Alien* as political allegories of their respective eras. Transmitted through air-born spores—spores that are, unsurprisingly, reddish in color—this alien life form sneaks into unsuspecting victims before fundamentally altering their character (*Dreamcatcher* reflects upon the absurdity of this premise by referencing Stanley Kubrick's 1964 film *Dr. Strangelove or: How I Learned to Stop Worrying and Love the Bomb*, in particular the film's hand-wringing over the imagined attack by communists upon the "precious bodily fluids" of Americans). The conflict in Vietnam was (ostensibly) about containing communism before its reach could extend too far. Of course, the trope of the invisible enemy becomes even murkier in the thick foliage of Vietnam—an environment famously exploited for ambush by Northern Vietnamese soldiers as well as the Viet Cong. The tactics of guerilla warfare further heighten the terror of an enemy lurking just out of sight. In short, *Dreamcatcher* restages the tensions of so many of America's recent wars by dropping its protagonists into the middle of Maine's overgrown terrain and then demanding the impossible: that they somehow figure out a method with which to discern friend from enemy.

The ensuing struggle takes on a very definitive shape. Specifically, as a surfeit of detached officers rely upon industrial mechanisms to achieve ever greater efficiency, King's novel presents the nature of modern war as thoroughly bureaucratized, hitched to a phenomenon described by James Gibson as "a technobureaucratic force" (101). "The most fundamental incompetence in Vietnam," psychologist Jonathan Shay writes, "Was the misapplication of the social and mental model of an industrial process to human warfare" (17). Secretary of Defense Robert McNamara, a former executive in the Ford Motor Corporation, famously utilized systems analysis logarithms to chart the course of the conflict, setting the stage for an engagement driven at the highest levels less by ethical concern and more by the gathering of data. Consequently, to be promoted, officers were expected to inflate kill counts in the name of greater efficiency: "United States military officers conceived of themselves as business managers rather than combat leaders. Enlisted men were seen as a kind of migrant labor force ... traditional military social bonds between troops and their commanders deteriorated. Soldiers instead became 'costs of production' for Technowar" (Gibson 121). In *Dreamcatcher*, the American commander Kurtz exemplifies this tendency: "Kurtz had the build of a bureaucrat. Yet something about him was terrible" (285).[3] In Kurtz, the military-industrial complex dons perhaps its most grotesque mask, fueled by what Hannah Arendt deems the "banality of evil." King's image of war oscillates between abject violence and the business-like tedium of recording death counts on a clipboard. Kurtz (rather gleefully) does not think for himself, but simply does what he is told, a mere functionary of a much larger apparatus. In the name of greater cost-effectiveness, the system imposed upon Jefferson Tract leads to clinical precision, embodied in concentration camps for potentially infected Americans as well as the widespread dehumanization of residents. A character responds to the industrialized warfare undertaken within this police state by radically devaluing his own life. He strips away romantic delusions of his place in the universe before admitting that he is "nothing but a heap of tasty white meat" (285, 160). By underscoring a bureaucratic ethos on display in Vietnam, *Dreamcatcher* amplifies a growing disconnect between "reality"—in this case, a reality replete with horrific carnage—and official accounts of the conflict (consider, for instance, attempts by the U.S. government to censor the pictures of war in Vietnam produced by American journalists).[4]

King's novel highlights the wedge driven between perception and reality in Vietnam, as well as the subsequent disarray experienced within American culture, by making the case that this conflict ushers in the postmodern condition. Due to the heavy concealment of the enemy, the nature of combat in Vietnam forced soldiers to question if they could trust their own perceptions: "In such warfare nothing is what it seems; all certainties liquefy; stable truths turn into their opposites" (Shay 35). On the home front, citizens are bombarded with conflicting reports, as the government tries to spin losses into victories and journalists consistently seek to expose the truth (whatever that means). At the height of the fighting, what commonly held truths, if any, remain? Ever diligent concerning public relations, Kurtz understands the problem of "too many watching eyes," and so carefully manages the narrative of Jefferson Tract—a lesson that he learns from the failed media campaigns of Vietnam. His media savviness results in a world that would closely resemble the interior workings of a Trump presidency: without an agreed upon method for establishing veracity, a world that starts "getting the truth and the spin mixed." When the name Kurtz turns out to be "a prop," and his professed Christianity proves to be mere "plumage," *Dreamcatcher* encourages readers to interrogate their faulty perceptions and, subsequently, to wonder what is *really* happening in the battle with alien invaders (290, 446, 424–6). The novel's state of disorientation steadily works its way into the consciousness of the protagonists, in particular, Jonesy, whose consciousness resembles a Hollywood film that has been edited in an unorthodox fashion. Decoupled from his own mental processes, Jonesy cannot tell where his thoughts end and the thoughts of his alien invader begin. *Dreamcatcher* contemplates a post-Vietnam universe in which neither soldiers nor civilians can regain a foothold on common ground (collectively or within their private lives).

As a result, this novel, like *Hearts*, focuses extensively upon Post-Traumatic Stress Disorder (PTSD). Jonesy, for one, has a near-death experience that neatly splits his life into two segments: in the first, Jonesy is bold and decisive, whereas in the second, Jonesy is timid and fearful. *Dreamcatcher* attends to a shell-shocked Jonesy that struggles to put the pieces of his life back together and suffers from extreme bouts of withdrawal. Unlike soldiers in previous wars, soldiers in Vietnam were often alone. Influenced by a climate that fosters extraordinary levels of anxiety, they were inserted (in a transactional fashion) into units, and then re-assigned or pulled back individually. Absent a "living community" upon their return, many veterans withdrew into themselves, opting not to participate in the daily routines of their former lives (Shay 198, 180). Jonesy similarly evacuates from the "real world" to take cover in a literal Cartesian attic, where he is able to observe the foreign entity as it infiltrates his body. Hidden inside of himself, "too deep, too small and powerless," he feels as though he has been left "on his own" to fight his inner demons—a condition that closely mirrors the experience of a high percentage of Vietnam veterans (*Dream* 328, 665). In related ways, Jonesy's comrade Henry becomes mistrustful, estranged, and hopeless (the "Group Skeptic"). He obsessively contemplates suicide to escape from what he perceives to be an increasingly untenable situation. Living "deep inside his own head," Henry shares with Jonesy "a sense of utter disconnection," and even though he is a practicing and successful psychologist, he cannot shake his oppressive loneliness (178, 271, 842). Through the PTSD of these men, King's novel stresses the long-term impact of the war in Vietnam by tracking individuals that strive to reconnect with one another, but experience very little success.

Following in the paths of his earlier namesakes from Joseph Conrad and the film *Apocalypse Now*, by the close of the text, Kurtz "goes bush," which is to say, he becomes a rogue that acts without the express approval of hyper-bureaucratic superiors. Filled with vitriol and rage, he nearly poisons the Boston water supply in order to purge the U.S. of its internal enemy. With a common trope adopted from the conflict in Vietnam, King's text depicts Kurtz retreating from industrialized warfare in an attempt to reclaim primal potency. The most visible example of this tendency, of course, remains the film series based upon the character of John Rambo. The novel directly references this series when a protagonist tells one of Kurtz's men: "'Go on, Rambo, do your thing.'" As the military-industrial complex loses its grip upon the situation in Jefferson Tract, Kurtz steadily takes matters into his own hands, before at last going AWOL and declaring himself to be a Jayhawk on a personal quest for righteousness. In a moment of surprising lucidity, he proclaims: "I am that post-industrial post-modern crypto-fascist politically incorrect male cocka-rocka war pig" (438, 311). In fact, his condition of extreme individualism is never far afield of the symptoms shown in Jonesy or Henry. All of these men are altered by the toxic environment of Jefferson Tract, molded by horrific conditions that germinated in Vietnam into a grotesque form that erodes their social order.

Through its interrogation of the war as well as its aftermath, *Dreamcatcher* sheds light upon America's hotly-contested role in Vietnam and, by so doing, rekindles fiercely fought debates from the era. For example, as the American military methodically disposes of citizens potentially contaminated with alien spores, readers are pushed to ask: "Was this murder, pure and simple?" Was the cost in human life really worth the possible benefits of containing communism? Or, because of the enemy's effective concealment, how could the military even begin to distinguish "civilian causalities" from the enemy body count? In turn, *Dreamcatcher* brings to the surface inquiries regarding the supposed righteousness of America's intervention in Vietnam: namely, even if we assume that the American government had only the best of intentions, should we still conclude that it acted improperly? One of Kurtz's former foot soldiers begs, "Tell what that makes us—I need to hear it," and a beleaguered companion warily obliges: "It makes us heroes" (304, 606). The novel thus combines a perverse thirst for heroism with a sense of utter exhaustion at the prospect.[5] As a result, King's book asks us, when does "defending liberty" start to look an awful lot like "expanding control"? By refracting these pressing questions of contemporary American History through the prism of the war in Vietnam, King's text assesses the nature of American imperialism, especially trenchant since the novel was published just prior to September 11, 2001 and the resulting military missions in Afghanistan and Iraq. The novel's political implications prove prescient as they foreshadow the other wars that unfold in the decades that follow.

Attendant to issues raised in the first chapter's discussion of King's relationship to the American transcendentalists, *Dreamcatcher* also ruminates upon the fraught dynamic between individual and community—in this case, to investigate the deep fragmentation experienced during the post-war period. "Brought to their units one at a time," Fred Turner comments, "many grunts of the Vietnam era, unlike their fathers in World War II, [see] little connection between their personal tours of duty and the aims and scope of America's national commitment to the war." King's novel follows a small band of individuals that cannot seem to stick together; the unit dissolves, time and time again, in the face of unspeakable atrocities. King appears to be aware of the U.S. system of troop rotation in Vietnam that offered "men in combat a strong incentive to retain an emotional distance from one another" (Turner 5, 28). Moreover, the countless clashing narratives of the era prompted some citizens to distance themselves from "official accounts" (a version of things that regularly turns out to be yet another example of deceptive propaganda). Jonesy's break from the alien broadcast that infiltrates his mind, for instance, offers "resistance on a whole other level," with an important reminder that "opposing voices" are essential to a functioning democracy (476, 765). At the same time, *Dreamcatcher* magnetically pulls its protagonists together by endowing them with a telepathic link that proves to be one of their greatest assets. As such, the text performs a vital role—a role that many other Vietnam War narratives perform—when it suggests to readers that "in the real world too, Americans have always found—and will continue to find—ways to maintain their national unity" (Turner 135). For King's crew of hunters, "What held the spokes together was the center—the core where they merged" (*Dream* 812). Following the war in Vietnam, Americans both lack and yearn for communal ties that have been badly damaged as a result of the fighting abroad as well as at home. As *Dreamcatcher* aggravates old wounds *and* supplies a metaphysical balm, the novel reveals a fundamentally divided nation desperately trying to make some sense of its legacy in Vietnam.

In sum, *Dreamcatcher* focuses upon America's *benevolent tyranny*. By aggressively spreading "freedom and democracy" into all corners of the globe, does the United States unconsciously deny the very values that the nation ostensibly promotes? King's novel raises this concern through the metaphor of the dreamcatcher. On the one hand, the dreamcatcher allows readers to witness collective dreams—national myths—as a troop of men share an "American dream" and create a "force" to bewilder the enemy. On the other hand, the dreamcatcher reveals itself to be toxic, coercing individuals into actions that they later regret: "They all caught the same terrible dream." In their youth, King's hunters dream of liberating a stranger with Downs Syndrome from a bully (a dream that—when fully realized—becomes a genuine nightmare). Together, through their joint dream, they (unwittingly) murder the bully, and so their "best" intentions cannot be isolated from their "worst" deeds: "Every dreamcatcher was also a trap." Although it undoubtedly remains their most potent weapon, the telepathic bond that joins this group also unnerves them by showing how "freedom" slips readily into its opposite—an oppressive grip that rejects all signs of autonomy. In King's story world, a patient possessed by the alien species proves to be healing well only when they start to lose their telepathic capabilities. Patriotism remains a "sword with two edges" (533, 702, 875).

According to the logic of *Dreamcatcher*, the war in Vietnam signifies the endurance of a unified America (compelled by its self-described role as global savior during the Cold War) that stands at odds with the dissolution of the American *mythos* (which manifests as an imperialist web of dreams that compulsively snares unsuspecting victims).

In King's novel, then, the inner workings of American imperialism prove to be analogous to the inner workings of cancer (in fact, *Cancer* was King's original title).[6] Like an alien spore, American ideology—aided by its persuasive military muscle—expands into new territory, absorbing fresh victims in its attempt to dominate the entire globe. Cast as unwelcome invaders, Americans resemble cancer "with teeth"; they are less like Dracula, a character in *Dreamcatcher* comments, and more like leukemia. America starts to resemble the colonial French that were ignobly dispelled from Vietnam. *Dreamcatcher* contemplates the unquenchable appetite of the United States when, like an aggressive disease, the nation expands its influence by projecting, always and everywhere, a binary of "infected versus immune." *Dreamcatcher* suggests that there may not be a tangible distinction between infected and immune; instead, the cancer metastasizes until it has nowhere else to go and, finally, begins to consume even itself, like a sort of "autocannibalism" (249, 261, 59, 183). Composed during the post-History era, King's novel recognizes in American-style globalization a parasitic quality at long last come home to roost. *It depicts a country unwittingly at war with itself.* Because the aliens may be figments of America's collective imagination, the ruthless destruction of the aliens is actually (at a primary level) the destruction of its own life. With nowhere left to go, the cancerous body politic unwittingly reverses its assault to attack its own defenses before ultimately recognizing (in horror) that the enemy has always-already been within. Indeed, the American imperial machine in Vietnam resembles a cancerous invader as it helps to pit the Vietnamese against one another, and then napalms the friend as well as foe until everything burns. Meanwhile, on the home front, in the name of ideological "purity," the nation attacks itself—generations devour one another; both the establishment and the counter-culture will accept nothing less than the total abolition of the other—until it gasps its last breath. With precious little self-reflection or apparent sense of irony, Kurtz boasts, "We'll napalm their amber waves of grain." He recruits alien invaders to his cause because they are single-minded, they do not ask questions, and they take no prisoners. To defeat the enemy, he mutates into the enemy that he has always-already been. There is no meaningful distinction between the infected and the immune in the final tally. All that remains is what the commander represents: "The cancer" (431, 319). *Dreamcatcher* excavates from the memory of the war in Vietnam the self-destructive DNA imagined to be lurking behind American History as a whole.

To complicate things a bit, we might consider how imperialism's cancerous associations spread even further, into King's representation of the war. In its most intriguing moments, *Dreamcatcher* serves not only as a passive, detached chronicle of a pernicious, violent tendency in American History, but as a viral agent that (perhaps unconsciously) extends the story's autocannibalism outward. Again, according to Nguyen, wars happen twice: in actuality, and then in memory. With its impressive global power, Nguyen argues, the United States may have lost the physical combat in Vietnam, but it subsequently "wins" the battle over the memory of the conflict—a victory that demonstrates "the industrialization of memory... where the actual firepower exercised in a war is matched by the firepower of memory that define and refines that war's identity." The Vietnamese, who have been completely erased from King's retelling, remain a looming absence. Without Vietnamese memories of the atrocities, it can be argued that *Dreamcatcher* offers what countless modern fables of the war offer: a self-involved, self-gratifying exercise that has been stripped of its international, or more basically relational, dimensions. The novel prefers to imagine the war as "a conflict not between Americans and Vietnamese, but between Americans fighting a war for their nation's soul," a recollection intended to provide insight into "the white man's heart of darkness, where he is both human and inhuman" through a "spectacle to be enjoyed and regretted simultaneously" (Nguyen 13, 110, 121). That is, in classic Gothic fashion, King's story exposes the darkness within by treating the memory of the Vietnam War as yet another opportunity for self-scrutiny (if not outright catharsis). While this mode of inquiry need not be denounced in full, King's readers must interrogate an increasingly thin line between moralism and the pleasure of spectacle. Does the "industrialization of memory" in *Dreamcatcher* limit our ethical vision by turning us perpetually back upon ourselves? Not unlike the imperialist apparatus that it references metaphorically, *Dreamcatcher* exploits a particular recollection of the conflict in Vietnam, and it does so in a manner that renders the Vietnamese people faceless. Ever parodic, the text is a memory machine on overdrive that repurposes familiar stock footage and cannibalizes itself until reality becomes so distorted that it is no longer recognizable.

Yet perhaps the autocannibalism of American History has, at least to a certain degree, been programmed into the genetic makeup of King's novel. According to Nguyen, the way in which most Americans continue to remember the war in Vietnam implies that "we win even when we lose"—proof, he claims, that memories of the conflict are churned up regularly into an omnipotent, all-encompassing imperial vision (124). King's alien visitor, Mr. Gray, expresses a similar sentiment: "We always lose and we always win." By revealing how foreign invaders claim victory even in defeat—by showing how the "industrialization of memory" obliterates borders that work to preserve an ethical means of engagement between nations—*Dreamcatcher* is finally a novel about the inherent slipperiness of remembering Vietnam. The terror of the invasion does not end in 1975 with America's withdrawal; no, if King's text teaches us anything, the invasion persists today, like that belligerent cancer, Kurtz (a simulated caricature based upon a simulated caricature; the symbol of an America that feeds gluttonously upon its own excesses). Our last remnant of hope, King's novel implies, is *to remember through the eyes of the Other*. The protagonists of *Dreamcatcher* must recall how the young man that they saved felt love for them by telegraphing themselves into his mind and then looking back at themselves (*Dream* 414, 845). The potential of a genuinely expansive ethical vision (albeit one that teeters always on the brink of self-indulgence) lies at the heart of the text, as Mr. Gray and his host, Jonesy, each struggle to come to terms with the viewpoint of the Other. What might it mean to remember the conflict in Vietnam without colonizing the memories of others? What could it mean to dream together without simultaneously catching individual dreams up into a singular, oppressive totality? Perhaps more than any other, this residual crisis characterizes American culture in the wake of the war. It defines the deficiencies of American History as a discipline (one that we have been tracking throughout King's fiction as an imperial enterprise in its own right). By blurring the artificial boundary that demarcates historical events from the mode(s) with which they are remembered, *Dreamcatcher* has much to tell us about the unsettling persistence of the Vietnam War—or, as Vietnamese call it, the American War—and its continued presence in our collective imagination.

With *Hearts in Atlantis* and *Dreamcatcher*, King paints a compelling portrait of how the war in Vietnam continues to infiltrate our national psyche. Characters in both novels lose a clear sense of connection to their respective communities as they scatter across a post-war wilderness, barely clinging to their sanity. This sense of alienation underscores one of the primary casualties of the conflict. For Sully, who cannot bear the thought of being buried in his uniform—or Henry, who cannot bring himself to feel real hope in the future of Jefferson Tract—the promising trajectory of American History arrives at its terminus in the blood-soaked bush of Southeast Asia. King's nihilistic survivors sit in their suburban homes, at once apoplectic and numb, unable to process the atrocities that they have witnessed. Meanwhile, characters such as Jonesy and Blind Willie exist in two worlds: engulfed in self-hatred and clinically detached, they view the aftermath of the fighting alternately from a comfortable perch and through bizarre acts of contrition—at once far removed from the grotesque reality of the situation at the same time that they are immersed in it. The fundamental divisions seen throughout King's fiction begin right here, in the schisms caused by this war (the so-called American Dream as promise and peril; the desire to remember and the drive to forget). In these texts, King choreographs once more the nation's masochistic ritual of penance, in which Blind Willie's private ceremony becomes part of America's imperial grieving, part of the repulsive process in which the caricature of Kurtz is consumed, regurgitated, and then consumed once more. *Hearts in Atlantis* and *Dreamcatcher* expose the cannibalism of American History, with its expansive appetite and its unwillingness to accept responsibility for tragedy. The whole of King's work argues that we habitually forfeit the opportunity to learn from our historical past. Only at the outermost limits of this struggle can King's readers start to conceptualize something like redemption—in Carol's struggles to defend the voiceless, or in efforts made by Mr. Gray and Jonesy to see the world through one another's eyes. These vestiges of an ethical fulcrum are undoubtedly faint, but in King's post-Vietnam multiverse, they may be all that remain of a long-forfeited City on the Hill, buried now beneath snow and crashing surf.

From his Vietnam experience, King's post-Vietnam fiction was shaped by a genuine distrust of all American social institutions—politics, school, church, the prison system—but especially a skepticism towards the corporate-military-industrial nexus. King's perception of the federal government has always bordered on paranoia. His fictional characters can expect to find no sanctuary from its agencies and officials, and have every reason to fear its tenacity and penchant for violence. America emerges as a nation marked by the rhetoric of free markets, equality, and democratic ideals, but defined by the violence it perpetrates at home and abroad. While he remains one of the most popular writers in America, for the past half a century Stephen King has also served as a critical spokesperson for its (repressed) conscience. These national considerations represent core, recurring concepts that pervade the King oeuvre. And they are all products of the writer's post-Vietnam malaise, as is the fundamental distrust that King incorporates so frequently to demarcate the difference between childhood and adulthood. In reaction to parental values condemned as materialistic and hypocritical, the youth generation of Atlantis celebrated its agelessness. "We ain't never, never gonna grow up," promised Yippee Jerry Rubin in his pre-corporate finance days. "We're gonna be adolescents forever!" (qtd. in Richard 320). Late in *Danse Macabre*, King posits a fundamental difference he discerns distinguishing the child from the adult, and this imaginative gap is not merely observational so much as it becomes a core narrative impetus driving the first two decades of King's writing: the power of imagination is "an eye, a marvelous third eye that floats free. As children, that eye sees with 20/20 clarity. As we grow older, its vision begins to dim ... [t]he boundaries of thought and vision begin to close down to a tunnel as we gear up to get along" (378). In the Sixties, those who governed the nation—the adults—became the enemy; they had perpetrated the war in Vietnam, had lied to the American people about its progress and purpose, and had sent America's children to perform the killing and dying. They revealed the boundaries of their collective imagination, their lack of thought and vision, and a separation from a Wordsworthian benevolence. Above all else, Vietnam was the sacrifice of the children, just as the trench warfare of World War I was; a needless sacrifice, certainly—and even worse, an aimless one. There exists, therefore, a clear historical line that can be traced through from Vietnam to the many instances of child abuse which appear throughout King's canon and the duplicitous behavior associated with American adulthood and its institutions. The conspiratorial destruction of its own progeny becomes one of the greatest indictments of King's portrayal of America's postmodern legacy.

If the war left this post-war novelist with anything positive, it may be a reaffirmation of King's fundamental Yankee faith in the vitality of the individual, their ability to retain a moral center at variance with examples of communal and institutional group think stifling dissent. This faith constitutes the best part of what remains of the anti-war movement.[7] And in spite of King's disillusionment with how that movement turned out, its residue energies helped produce what we call the "anti-Historians" who appear elsewhere in this book: those characters in the King canon who seek alternatives to the negative arc of American History.

Notes

1 For examples of this phenomenon, see *The Stand* (1978), *The Long Walk* (1979) published under the pseudonym Richard Bachman, *Firestarter* (1980), and *Under the Dome* (2009).
2 King's *Firestarter* (1980) similarly dwells upon a disaffected veteran of the war in Vietnam, John Rainbird, as he silently broods over—at the same time that he serves under—the omnipresent gaze of the military-industrial complex.
3 Just as King references *The Sun Also Rises* in *Hearts*, his choice of the name Kurtz in *Dreamcatcher* is no less deliberately literary. The officer in Joseph Conrad's *Heart of Darkness*, a novel of colonial depredation, is also named Kurtz. He has gone rogue into the forests of Africa. The name establishes an even more direct parallel with the Vietnam War in the film *Apocalypse Now*, where Kurtz, an American commanding officer, goes renegade insane in response to America's universal loss of authority and sanity in Vietnam.
4 James Gibson highlights the gap between "scientific-looking production indices" and the "reality of lived experience" (Gibson 128–9).
5 Fred Turner writes, "Like the heroes of the ancient plays, many [Americans] did what they thought was right, only to discover that they had committed horrible wrongs" (Turner 189).
6 The metaphor of cancer pervades King's multiverse. For instance, novels written under the pseudonym of Richard Bachman, such as *Roadwork* (1981) and *Thinner* (1984), prominently feature characters—indeed, entire societies—ravaged by the illness. The widespread malady is so much a part of the makeup of Bachman's novels that King declares Bachman to have died by "cancer of the pseudonym." Later, in *The Green Mile* (1996), cancer signifies the fallenness of humanity in a racially divided society. As Susan Sontag has argued in *Illness as Metaphor*, cancer is the most modern of diseases. It not only continues to deplete the world's population in defiance of society's attempts to conquer it, but it also serves as a convenient metaphor for our times. It is the shadow attendant to the affluent lifestyle Americans cherish and pursue. King's fiction employs the disease to call attention to the broader social ills of a society cannibalizing itself through gentrification, the relaxation of regulations governing pollution and toxic waste, Wall Street excess, and American imperialism.
7 The counter-culture gave shape to King's political consciousness. The Tabitha and Stephen King Foundation continues to be one avenue that reflects this influence through charitable acts that are funded by ten percent of the King family's pre-taxable income every year. While the Kings tend to support Leftist organizations and political candidates, their foundation fills community needs that are not restricted ideologically. The counter-culture's blend of social activism, liberal social causes, and ethical outrage—the brew that helped radicalize King back in the Sixties—remains a distinct feature of his subsequent writings and personal life.

5 Outing Stephen King and the Queering of American History

The American Gothic routinely unsettles established boundaries of human sexuality. "Gothic resolutions repeatedly insist on order restored and (often) on reassertion of heteronormative prerogative," George Haggerty observes. At the same time, "Gothic fiction is about reaching some undefinable world beyond fictional reality, and that 'beyond' can never be pulled back into narrative control. That is why Gothic fiction remains as queer as it is" (Haggerty 10). In other words, readers discover in Gothic works—including, prominently, works penned by Stephen King or adapted from his words to celluloid—a conservative assertion of heteronormative prerogative as well as the transgressive potential to violate this suffocating order. Due in no small part to its Gothic character, King's multiverse oscillates between homophobia and its rejection, between *the monster as homosexual and homophobia as monster*. This oscillation enables us to explore the sexuality of his corpus from two different positions. When we read his monsters as homosexual, a correspondence takes shape: "queer" History is monstrous because it refuses to reproduce itself in a "healthy" way. When we interpret King's considerable output as homophobic, a perverted sense of History appears in parallel, one that can be (at least partially) blamed upon impediments to the "normal" propagation of the species. At the same time, when we analyze these tales with homophobia as the monster, we walk away with a distinctive impression that History is stuck in an entropic loop precisely because of its so-called normal propagation. History with a capital "H"—a dominant, heteronormative construct—rubs up against histories with a lower-case "h"—accounts made "queer" due to their rejection of any singular Historical (or sexual) consciousness. As Andrew Smith and William Hughes write, "The very presence of the queer makes the assigning of absolutes ... a futile act" (Smith and Hughes 5). That is to say, by reclaiming the "queerness" at work in King's vision of American history, we might be able—at last—to imagine a future beyond our limited horizons. With this duality in mind for the chapter as a whole, let us consider first the nexus King often offers between homosexuality and monstrosity.

"Queerness" as Confinement

To begin, let us not equivocate: King's treatment of homosexuality throughout his literary career has been less than enlightened. There exist no gay male or lesbian relationships that are portrayed as mature, morally responsible, or loving. There exist, on the other hand, plenty of examples of King employing homosexuality as a metaphor for oppression and otherness, a point that is acutely apparent in his treatment of adult male homoeroticism that crosses into the worst stereotype of male homosexuality: predatory pedophilia. Many of King's most perverted adult male figures (and their supernatural avatars) underscore their mental instability and social pathology through an out-of-control compulsion to rape boys and sexually naïve heterosexual men. Their dictatorial violence expresses itself most essentially through homoerotic coercion. More specifically still, the monster throughout King's canon is frequently coded "queer" even when its sexuality remains indeterminate: Pennywise (*IT*), Barlow (*'Salem's Lot*), Bogs and the sisters (*Shawshank*), Sunlight Gardener (*The Talisman*), Gasher and Tick Tock Man (*Dark Tower III: Waste Lands*), Horace Derwent and many of the other ghosts at the Overlook (*Shining*), Percy Wetmore and Billy the Kid (*Green Mile*), The Kid and Trashcan Man (*The Stand*), and Todd Bowden and Kurt Dussander (*Apt Pupil*). As earlier chapters have already demonstrated, King perceives American History to be stuck in a self-defeating loop, and this loop appears to be propelled along by a corrosive "queer" undercurrent.

To examine the "queer" side of American History in King's texts that feature the monster as homosexual, let us begin with *Apt Pupil* (1982), the story of a young man named Todd Bowden who forces a former Nazi soldier, Kurt Dussander, to tell him all about the atrocities that he committed in World War II. *Apt Pupil* is, first and foremost, the story of an aspiring Historian (reminiscent of our discussion of Jack Torrance in his role as a writer).[1] While Torrance is pulled into the role of sympathetic reader as he uncovers the Overlook's documented History, Todd's involvement is far less passive, eventually birthing an Americanized version of a "Hitler Youth." Todd's drive to master all of the secrets of Dussander's History quickly proves to be transgressive, if not downright perverse. "Things would come into focus," he assures himself. "Things always did." The boy's effort to uncover, document, and organize unsavory events into a neat-and-tidy History proves similar to Dussander's "German efficiency," which is to say, in both cases the compulsion to arrange things systematically proves to be utterly dehumanizing (116, 112). *Apt Pupil* intersects Todd's misguided codification of World War II with King's codification of a certain view of human sexuality—a connection that remains highly problematic.

Put simply, King's text sexualizes Todd's drive to expose the innerworkings of History. "'I really groove on all that concentration camp stuff,'" Todd remarks. "'I get off on it.'" He's not alone, of course—as King's story notes, "a *lot* of people" today seem to "get off" on images of the Holocaust, feeling an odd combination of repulsion and sadomasochistic titillation. Todd's obsession with exposing all of the secrets of WWII appears as a pathology, faulty wiring, or—more likely still—the result of bad parenting. Practicing relaxed parenting methods associated with the 1960s, Todd's father shrugs off the possibility of his son reading *Penthouse* magazines, claiming that the boy should be encouraged to "poke around." Because of the state's reputation for liberal politics and a sunny American disposition, it appears to be no accident that both novella and film choose California as their locale. In related ways, *Apt Pupil* lays a good deal of the blame on secular American culture, with its embrace of "easy sex" (119, 122, 263, 136). According to the logic of *Apt Pupil*, to understand our obsession with World War II requires that we interrogate America's half-baked high school History as well as sex education curricula. In the end, Todd's problem seems to stem from dual over-exposures: to sex *and* to History. He suffers from a desire to uncover forbidden knowledge, as he consumes images of the Holocaust as though they were pornography, as though his over-heated appetites should never be repressed but always indulged. Perhaps when it comes to knowledge of History and sex, the novel suggests, we should avoid consuming too much of a good thing (in our Introduction to this book, we discuss this proposed moderation as an effect of King's tacit alignment with New Historicism).

Historians, in King's estimation, possess an unhealthy libido. Dussander's instant recall of the war strikes readers as "*perversely* clear," and so the drive to leave no stone unturned, to pry into every taboo, reveals itself to be transgressive on multiple levels. As Todd transforms into his childhood fantasy (a detective), he plunges into puberty, a shift that pushes him to blur the line between "all-American boy" and grown man with carnal impulses. Due to his free-thinking parents and his liberal culture, he is never chastened; in fact, he is rewarded for his curiosity with good grades and academic accolades, such as becoming the Valedictorian of his graduating class. There is nothing foreign to his imagination, super-charged as it is by raging hormones and a prurient fascination with the darkest propensities of the Nazi regime. That these elements overlap into a perverse sexuality remains one of the more compulsive aspects of the novel and film. *Apt Pupil* declares the violence of American History to be, at its root, kinky. Todd cannot neatly separate his jingoism from his poisoned Historical consciousness or his abject sex drive. The film highlights this admixture in its frequent associations between Todd and baseball and basketball, Todd and the "Dare to be a leader" slogan linked to the presidential figures on Mt. Rushmore in his high school hallway, Todd and the American flag in his driveway at the end of the movie. In the novel, after he dreams of having sex—while Dussander drones out statistics in the background—he mistakes his ejaculate for blood, misreading his personal climax as the climax of History, "the end of the world thundering" (193). *Apt Pupil* therefore presents the border between sexual lust and blood lust as a confused hinterland, diagnosing (in the process) a psychosis that characterizes King's over-zealous Historian (we might gesture here at the "inappropriate" arousals experienced by Jack in *The Shining* or Louis in *Pet Sematary* as the two men pursue mastery of History).[2] In the novella's final scene, Todd seizes a (phallic) gun and begins a killing spree—an "ecstatic" moment that resembles the young men that gleefully run into deadly conflict throughout American History, proclaiming themselves to be "king(s) of the world." King's pubescent protagonist mounts an orgasmic charge into certain death and, after he murders for the first time, promptly masturbates (193, 240, 216).

In addition to the homoerotic bond that is cemented between Dussander and Bowden in the evolution of their "History course," King and director Bryan Singer likewise associate the isolated and isolating act of masturbation with the arousal of pathological impulses. There is a scene [52:00] in the film version that could be easily overlooked: Dussander has donned again for a second time his Nazi uniform and cap and stands erect in front of a bedroom mirror. On this occasion, he is alone in his house and has chosen to wear the uniform voluntarily. The camera opens the scene with a slow pan right beginning with a view inside Dussander's open closet; it stops on the old man securing his cap and taking in his mirrored reflection. In a film where various "doors" serve throughout as metaphors for a forbidden knowledge of History as well as violent indulgence, Dussander's open closet door proves no less significant.[3] The symbolism is clear: Dussander has released his closeted (Nazi) self, discarding his old man (American) pants in exchange for the German uniform, and, like Jekyll's transformations into Hyde in *The Strange Case of Dr. Jekyll and Mr. Hyde*, he desires a mirror to bear witness to the emergence of his doppelgänger. Underneath the open window, Archie roots in Dussander's garbage cans for empty liquor redemption bottles. As he confronts his reflected image in the mirror, Dussander's left hand begins a slow descent down the front of the uniform until it hovers over his crotch.

Just as he appears about to touch himself, he is interrupted suddenly by the sound of Archie's clanging bottles. There are several conflicting aspects associated with this scene, the most glaring being the sexual arousal Dussander experiences while wearing the Nazi uniform, especially because he is further stimulated by the pseudo uniform that has conferred a higher military rank—"I see I've been promoted," he tells Todd—than the one he had during the war. At the same time as the image he views arouses him, he is also shamed by it. When he realizes someone is lurking below his window, Dussander's immediate reaction is to hide himself in the room beyond the scope of the window. Just as Stevenson's Jekyll rushes away rudely from the window in the chapter "Incident at the Window" when he feels himself unwittingly transforming into Mr. Hyde in front of his friends, Utterson and Enfield, Dussander fears his own exposure as Nazi *and* masturbator.

Figure 5.1 Former Nazi Kommandant Dussander is alone with his thoughts admiring his uniform in *Apt Pupil*.

Both novel and film go to great lengths to trace the steady process of character inversion taking place between the teenager and old man: Todd finds himself encumbered with adult burdens—lying, murdering, sexual impotence, restive sleep—as his affiliation with Dussander and a shared Nazi past deepens; conversely, the "stories" from this past (stories that he is at first coerced into telling, but then gradually revels in exposing) reactivate the repressed Nazi underneath the "tax paying" American citizen. Dussander's return to his dark past fills him with a degree of shame, as when Archie catches him wearing the uniform, but more so it reinvigorates him: regaining his pride as a Nazi officer, he surges with the life and death power he once wielded as the *Kommandant* at various concentration camps; in King's novel he goes on a killing spree of "undesirable" homeless men (while murdering only Archie in the film adaptation). It is therefore in keeping with these inverted transformations that Singer visualizes the reawaking of Dussander's sexuality at the same time that Todd's is adversely affected when Becky attempts to fellate him in the front seat of her car. Both Dussander and Bowden manifest warped sexual responses because of their "secret bond," which includes a pronounced homoerotic component.[4]

Singer's film adaptation explores how Todd desperately attempts to achieve mastery through what we might call *an eroticism of vision* (a connection that stresses the dual meaning of "pupil" as a student in pursuit of mastery as well as a core component of the eye).[5] As the movie's opening credits appear on screen, we watch Todd combing through photographs from World War II, eagerly absorbing grotesque images, moving smoothly from English to German language texts. Through the magic of film, on several occasions during this montage the viewer watches Todd literally page through History—his boyish American face aligned with head shots of the most infamous German officers from the *Wehrmacht* and figures from a book entitled *Hitler's Henchmen*. Todd's eyes are frequently juxtaposed with Nazi eyes that appear through the transparent pages of the History that he peruses. On at least two separate moments, the viewer finds it difficult to distinguish Todd's eyes from those that are staring out of the past from young faces of Nazis not much older than Todd. As early as this opening montage in *Apt Pupil*, the past merges with the present and overwhelms it visually. In Freudian terms that the film appears eager to recycle, the eye possesses phallic attributes because it serves as an individual's most potent sensory organ: "What has been called the expansion of our 'exosomatic organs' has meant above all extending the range of our vision, compensating for its imperfections, or finding substitutes for its limited powers." Subsequently, a number of feminist critics, including Luce Irigaray and Laura Mulvey, address a pervasive correlation between ocularcentrism and phallocentrism (Jay 3, 526). From this standpoint, Todd's (impossible) quest to know all of the secrets from Dussander's historical mnemonic takes on a uniquely cinematic quality. The film longs to see what remains barely visible, what is tantalizingly revealed only in glimpses—Dussander, partly obscured by a filthy screen door; Dussander, partly obscured by a lace curtain that divides rooms; Dussander, partly obscured in the shadows of Todd's dreams. Singer's *Apt Pupil* remains singularly obsessed with a boy's frustrated desire *to see everything*, a perverse scopophilia that the audience shares: when a shade is drawn, the film cuts in a similar fashion, forcing spectators to endure Todd's experience of (highly sexualized) frustration. At the climax of the film, the teenager encounters a pigeon with a broken wing, a stunning shot framed by the otherworldly light coming through an open gym door. As he smashes the pigeon with his basketball, everything glows. An ecstasy of total vision accompanies Todd's decisive entrance into the field of violence—an intimate exposure, blinding the spectator with its dramatically heightened radiance.

In the novel, Todd's climatic End of History raises important questions about the intersection of sex and Historical consciousness. If Todd's perverse desires lead him to a (grim) totality, that is, to a sense of absolute mastery over the past that marks the final "thundering" days of the species, what are readers to make of the treatise on sexuality that *Apt Pupil* grafts onto a treatise on the (sadomasochistic) discipline of History? King's novel—unlike the film adaptation—reaches a dead-end, as the all-American boy dies before he can become a man and the corrosive elements of American society march forward, more or less unchanged. The text thus perpetuates a thesis that our book has been tracking: American History remains stuck in a violent cycle, hyper-sexualized and—as a result—unable to "move forward." As Dussander forecasts in his dire warning to Todd about possessing secret knowledge of the past: "It never goes away. Not for you." Figuratively speaking, we can read Todd's nocturnal emissions as blank bullets, fired aimlessly in the isolation of his bed, lacking any future-oriented purpose. Because the future is always already mired in the past, Todd's future is a crypt that should have been "left shut" (*Apt* 201). When *Apt Pupil* likens a failing model of understanding History to intercourse without germination, we glimpse the homophobic and anti-gay underpinnings of King's story (and we also begin to understand how these underpinnings influence King's understanding of American History as a noxious construct).

After all, King's narrative renders Todd's notions of History visibly "queer." His relationship to Dussander is infused with homoeroticism (e. g., he loves when Dussander begs). The two males come to possess one another's secrets, intimate details that they use to playfully tease one another as if engaged in a kind of foreplay. In the scene where Todd "gifts" Dussander with the Nazi costume uniform, Todd forces him to put it on for the boy's visual pleasure. While Dussander prepares himself upstairs out of sight, Todd is shown eagerly anticipating his return in the kitchen. It is a sequence suggestive of a lover awaiting the emergence of his beloved, adorned in s/m fetish clothing out of *The Night Porter*, purchased for the purpose of sexual arousal. Indeed, the fact that the old man is initially repulsed when he sees it and reluctant to wear it allows Todd the opportunity to exercise control over Dussander, further enflaming the boy's homoeroticism. Singer's camera actively invites such a reading as it tracks Dussander's black-booted ankles descending the staircase in a slow rhythm. The Nazi assumes the position of the feminine object of the male gaze, appropriating the role of the female whose legs would be typically adorned in sheer stockings and high heels, as is the case in countless heteronormative iterations of similar scenes. As feminized object of the gaze, Dussander is side-lit in blue lighting, while Todd is back-lit with the natural light source entering behind him through Dussander's window and the kitchen's yellow paint (see Picart and Frank 112–3). Todd's response to this fetishist indulgence is clearly meant to contrast his interaction with Becky in her car: when Dussander arrives in front of him, Todd abruptly rises phallic-like from the chair he is sitting in and engages the Nazi directly, first telling him to "shut up" when he complains that the uniform makes him itch, and then dominating him further under orders to "perform" a variety of military signatures. When Becky seeks to arouse him sexually in her car, on the other hand, Todd remains passively disengaged, asking her to blow marijuana smoke away from him, slumped into the corner of the girl's passenger's seat, and more interested in seeking clarity to his moral confusion—"Do you ever wonder why people do the things they do?"—than focusing on the orgasm Becky wants to provide him.

Todd is at least subconsciously aroused by the uniformed Dussander because the boy is in control—he has constructed the entire scenario; with Becky, his libidinous urge is diminished accordingly because she is female ("Maybe you just don't like girls," she mockingly snorts) and because she seeks to establish herself in control of their sexual agenda. If Todd's encounter with Becky suggests history with a lower-case "h"—a reminder of the individual's impotence before forces that he cannot hope to grasp—Todd's connection to Dussander presents History with a capital "H"—an invitation to impose one's personal preferences as if they are universal; a call to sustain (the delusion of) control over invisible forces that surge through the frame. In the novella, Todd almost immediately recognizes his relationship with Dussander in these sexualized terms: "'He was holding my balls ... I was holding his.'" To which Dussander adds: "'He and the boy were ... feeding off of each other ... eating each other.'" Importantly, readers cannot interpret this relationship as romantic in any traditional sense; even beyond the pedophilic elements, their depraved bond lacks any redeeming qualities. It is a tale of domination, pure and simple—a tale of self-flagellation as well as abject humiliation. In novel and film alike, Dussander eventually cries out: "'We are fucking each other—didn't you know that?'" (178, 150, 197). Consequently, there is neither a future for this relationship nor for either one of them. The experience ruins Todd completely, violating all of the salutary boundaries that would have kept his libido alive. He has seen and felt it all now, and so he must perish, as he does in King's novel. But in the film, Todd's survival bodes badly for the future, pointing the way to what Dennis Mahoney envisions as Todd's graduation into an American "bogeyboy" (39). In its literary and cinematic iterations, *Apt Pupil* culminates with a dismal foreclosure common to both horror literature and film: monstrous homoeroticism, "properly articulated and fully identified, can only mean the end of (H)istory" (Haggerty 128).

It is nearly impossible to interpret *Apt Pupil* as in any way friendly to the cause of the LGBTQ community because the story incessantly portrays its homosexual undercurrent as deviant, evil, and violent—like AIDs, a manipulation of a contagion that threatens to contaminate "our children." We cannot ignore how the overt homosexual subtext that courses throughout Singer's film led to a real-life lawsuit (eventually dismissed) where attorneys for the plaintiffs argued that the teenage actors who played Todd's classmates were victims of pedophilic exploitation and that Singer (and the film's production company) deliberately reworked King's tale into a homosexual story line. As we have seen, King's novella can be read as complicit in inspiring similar charges. As Todd and Dussander purportedly take pleasure in "unhealthy" expressions of sexuality (expressions directly linked to the boy's reprobate understanding of History), King's reader could reasonably walk away from the story associating homosexual desire with Nazi criminality. Simply put, King's novel demonizes homoeroticism by virtue of its association with Nazism. Joan

Picart and David Frank argue convincingly that "the historical malevolence of Nazi atrocity as a social and ethical problem is conveyed and constructed as a sexual problem" (102). Todd's final words in the film—"You have no idea what I can do"—complete the demonic trajectory of the text as a dark *Buldungsroman*: Todd inherits the Nazi mantle from the dying Dussander, signifying his "graduation" to a higher level of evil. At the same time, his intimidation of the guidance counselor Mr. French, reminding a historical-conscious viewership of how easily the Nazis first dominated France militarily and then subjected the country to the humiliation of the Vichy puppet regime, succeeds because Todd pushes the film's homophobic subtext to a more overt level, employing the threat of false homosexual accusations as a means for securing French's silence.[6] Though the novel details explicit homoerotic dream sequences to underscore the corruption of the Bowden-Dussander union, the film offers a broader array of implications—and almost all of them are negative. The brutal murder of Archie, the homeless man with clear homosexual (or at least bisexual) inclinations, is reduced to a rite of passage for Todd: Dussander queries him "How did it feel?"—a final test of Todd's Nazi education and the completion of the extermination pie chart that includes a category for homosexuals in the opening of the film. Archie's murder takes place in Dussander's basement, a dark cellar illuminated with a glowing red furnace meant to suggest concentration camp ovens. Archie's last words—"Why are you doing this?"—indicts not only Todd himself, but likewise the boy's unholy relationship with Dussander and the entire Nazi regime. After the murder, Todd's face is streaked with Archie's blood, raising the unconscious specter of AIDs as the homosexual again bleeds into both victim and murderer, the monster that creates and perpetuates the disease.

Beyond the sheer profligacy of male-male desire, *Apt Pupil* enlarges to address the "queerness" of an American History that fails to reproduce itself. In other words, American History lacks the "proper" orientation required for advancement, for either successful development or expansion. In the versions told by King and Singer, this "queerness" stops the supposedly natural trajectory of History in its tracks. When Todd engages in "real sex" in King's text—defined as heterosexual congress—he finds it distasteful and devoid of any meaning: "Her breasts were bags of meat. No more" (255). In this exact moment, *Apt Pupil* solidifies what theorist Lee Edelman calls "reproductive futurism": through its absence, the text gestures at the interdependence of a "natural" Historical imagination and a "natural" sexuality. King's reader witnesses how heteronormative assumptions inform dominant constructs of human (in particular, Nazi as well as American) History. Pointing at Todd's "wasted" seed, in tandem with his apparently warped proclivities, the reader is asked to draw a concrete conclusion: "If [...] there is *no baby* and, in consequence, *no future*, then the blame must fall on the fatal lure of sterile, narcissistic enjoyments understood as inherently destructive of meaning and therefore as responsible for the undoing of social organization" (Edelman 13; author's emphasis). If Todd could only have engaged in a "normal" mating ritual with a female, his masculine urge for mastery might have been tempered, and his ejaculate would have been put to better use: namely, to fertilize an egg and form a child. In turn, the self-enclosed (and self-indulgent) loop of American History could have been broken and the species would have flourished once more—moving its focus from the crypt to the crib. Due to its unsavory "queerness," then, *Apt Pupil* can be read as a representative example of the homophobia in King's multiverse, and, subsequently, as an affirmation of the implicit "reproductive futurism" that informs so much of America's heteronormative culture.

When placed in conversation with *Apt Pupil*, the novel *IT* further confirms the homophobia attendant to many of King's works. Once again, the writer invokes queerness to deepen a character's connection to monstrosity. Like *Apt Pupil*, *IT* tracks History stuck in a loop—a town doomed to replay its prior traumas, over and over again; adults who must return to their old stomping grounds and confront an evil that, like clockwork, re-emerges. Echoing the obsessive chain forged between Todd and World War II, Derry cannot engage in a forward trajectory as the city remains mired in the past. This paralysis again has clear sexual undertones: the arrested development of the town parallels the infertility of the Losers' Club, none of whom can bear children, leaving them to serve as sacrifices to be made to Pennywise. Disguised in his most terrifying avatar as a clown, Pennywise's link to a lethal orality that is coded gay is emphasized in an expanding mouth filled with razor-sharp teeth and its particular desire to consume male children, such as Georgie. Importantly, Pennywise's emergence in the novel, signaling the commencement of another cycle of terror against Derry's children, coincides with the torture and eventual murder of a gay man, Adrian Mellon (a scene erased entirely from the 1990 miniseries based upon the novel). While none of the perpetrators of this crime remember the event with absolute clarity, and Mellon's lover, Don Hagarty, was preoccupied with his own terror and searching for rescue, several of them see Pennywise lurking in the brush under the bridge from which Mellon was thrown. In the various descriptions of the clown offered to the police, Pennywise is pictured as an active participant in completing the job of killing Mellon. In the process of claiming Adrian's body for itself, the observers all emphasize the clown's mouth filled with "bared teeth—great big teeth." But several of the boys also recall the attentive body language that Pennywise applied towards his wounded gay prey, "shoving one of Adrian Mellon's arms back so it lay over his head." Pennywise offers his victim an intimate embrace, signaling a mixture of vicious cruelty and homoerotic arousal: "The clown, [Hagarty] said, was standing near the far bank with Adrian's dripping body clutched in its arms. Ade's right arm was stuck stiffly out behind the clown's head, and the clown's face was indeed in Ade's right armpit, but it was not biting: it was smiling." The clown places Mellon in a position that resembles a feminizing swoon as much as a death throe. And of course, Pennywise's involvement remains the only secret left undisclosed: "At the major trial—that of Garton and Dubay—no one mentioned a clown" (35–7).

Pennywise's lair is located in the brush of the Barrens, and underground, specifically the sewers of Derry. It's affiliation with the literal "bowels" of the city links the clown with a secreted homosexuality—the anus of the city—a place where the heterosexual adults of Derry are never pictured, but perhaps the only public place in the town where gay men dare to express themselves sexually. Pennywise's fierce orality again finds another parallel in the disturbing homosexual interlude that takes place down in the Barrens between Henry Bowers and Patrick Hockstetter later in King's novel. Both of these young adults are aligned with It and exist, like the clown itself, in opposition to the Losers' Club. Although fully aroused by Patrick's hand, "Henry's [penis] had grown amazingly. It stood up stiff and hard, almost poking his bellybutton," Bowers' reaction, as it is for everything in his life, is to view his sexual response with a combination of denial and fury: "'I don't go for that queer stuff ... And if you tell anyone I did, I'll kill you, you fucking little pansy!'" (821–2). The ferocity of Bowers' homosexual panic explains his relentless antagonism towards Mellon earlier in the novel. But even more relevant, it highlights his and Patrick's link to Pennywise: their mutual duplicity, fear, random anger, and mental instability. Once more King aligns homosexuality with pathology; in fact, one appears to feed into the other: "[Hockstetter] was a sociopath, and perhaps, by that hot July in 1958, he had become a full-fledged psychopath" (825).

Throughout the King canon we find a repetitive triad of mental illness, homosexual desire, and a loss of moral compass in the writer's constructions of monstrosity. A significant number of King's monsters—be they human or supernatural—bear disturbing similarities that conform to this description. Perhaps King relies on such stereotypes to establish clear-cut portraits of malfeasance for a popular audience in order to forge a sympathetic bond between reader and the monster's victims. Just as It is a compendium of monsters from popular culture and the personal nightmares of the Losers' Club, the writer's appropriation of homophobic stereotyping may be an effort to incorporate monstrous figures such as John Wayne Gacy, a homosexual serial killer readily identifiable to King's readership who, like Pennywise, also employed a Pogo the Clown avatar. As a horror writer seeking to provide an essentially heteronormative readership with associations designed to inspire fear and loathing, King's reliance upon a nexus between homosexual terror and monstrosity is especially effective. His readership can repress and deny identification with the "queered" outsider. Consequently, when such figures appear in King's plotlines, gay desire, as it does in the "torture porn" genre, conflates with a love of torture, violence, and murder. The love that cannot be spoken destroys binary oppositions, linking itself to Julia Kristeva's definition of the abject, and thereby threatening the constructed idea of normative heterosexuality. King's "queer" monsters exploit the audience's own homophobic prejudices in order to associate them with beings made ever creepier. Whatever King's reasoning, he is creating monsters, such as Bowers and Hockstetter, that are neither nuanced nor multidimensional; having fallen off a moral continuum, they exist solely to foment cruel violence and crude destruction. They are unburdened by any self-doubt that might complicate their warped visions of reality. The fact that evil in the King universe frequently forms a bridge with undiagnosed mental illness may be mysterious (and thus appropriately terrifying), but its link to a sadistic homosexuality remains exploitative. The joining of mental illness with perverse sexuality—a violent brand of homosexuality, specifically—equates the two in a reader's mind, ultimately defining monstrosity in King's fiction as both "queer" and insane.

IT's resolution is once more inseparable from "reproductive futurism." The future stems from heterosexual copulation, the novel suggests—a relationship that the text solidifies with the infamous encounter between the male youths and their lone female friend, Bev. Each boy must have sex with Bev (but *not with each other*) to pass from their stunted development—away from the fixed eddy of American History, with its constant return to violence and perversion—to a survivalist tomorrow. It is as if by confirming their heterosexuality via intercourse with Bev that the boys become insulated from Pennywise's homoerotic drive at the same time that any hint of homosexuality (among the boys themselves) is displaced through the presence of Bev as female. Similarly, in King's *The Shawshank Redemption*, the same-sex bond between Red and Andy is diffused and normalized by the "poster girls" that Red shares with Andy to put on the wall of his cell. Like Rita Hayworth's erotic presence, Bev serves as a "sexual conduit" for legitimizing expressions of male homosocial bonding and love. Her active presence eliminates the homosexual threat that, as we have traced, signals corruption in King's world. Eve Kosofsky Sedgwick describes this process in *Between Men*, that "we are in the presence ... of a desire to consolidate partnership with authoritative males in and through the bodies of females" (38).

Given the heightened degree to which King treats sexual expression in his fiction, some of the strongest and most life-affirming bonds that occur in his books take place (ironically) between men in strictly homosocial relationships. The numerous male-bonding permutations found in work as diverse as *The Stand, IT, Shawshank, The Green Mile, Stand by Me*, and *Dark Tower IV: Wizard and Glass* are intensely intimate, but never sexual.[7] King habitually appreciates the value of same-sex bonds; they represent some of his most compelling fictionalized portraits. Yet he steers clear of investing any of them with a homoerotic charge—at least overtly. When characters in his texts do cross the line from homosocial to homosexual, they risk an opprobrium apparently summoned from King's own inherited past. The severity of King's judgment might be tied to his career-long affiliation with the Gothic, wherein transgressions against the status quo—particularly sexual transgressions—result in horrific consequences (at least, within the framework that we have been tracking of homosexuality as monstrous); or perhaps it is the lingering influence of the writer's strong Methodist upbringing, his long heterosexual monogamous marriage, or the regional ambiance of New England Puritanism with which King has lived his entire life. In a *Playboy* interview published in 1983, early in his career, King was remarkably candid on the subject of sex, acknowledging his own personal conservatism which, in turn, has likely filtered into his treatment of the subject in his fiction as well: "I think I have pretty normal sexual appetites, whatever the word normal means in these swinging times ... There's a range of sexual variations that turn me on, but I'm afraid they're all boringly unkinky" (Underwood 45). This comment, particularly the last half of it, goes a long way towards explaining why any expression of "kinky" sexuality that breaks against "normal"—masturbation, bondage, cross-dressing, fetish wear, adultery, pornography, oral sex (recall the disastrous consequences of car sex in *Thinner*), and particularly homosexuality—is viewed as deviant in the King universe. More often than not, when human sexuality makes an appearance in a King text it signals at the least unresolvable complications for the characters involved, and more often than not, their fall into corruption.

At the close of *IT*, the reader realizes that its protagonist, Bill, has chartered a successful escape route because, as he peddles his catatonic wife down the hill (and away from his past), he achieves an unexpected erection. King's narratives in this way conceptualize American History as "queer" in a homophobic sense and appear to prescribe heterosexual coupling as a sort of panacea. His works reveal the extent to which America's dominant Historical consciousness remains caught up in a certain paradigm of sexuality, anchored (unconsciously) to a set of assumptions about the value of procreation, including the ideal of child-bearing, that offers a "libidinally subtended fantasy ... to screen out the emptiness" (Edelman 7). *Doctor Sleep* likewise correlates the claustrophobia of History with what it posits as perverted expressions of sexuality. A sequel to *The Shining*, this novel begins by remembering how the Overlook once demanded that Jack forfeit his offspring in exchange for intimations of glory, a transaction that also occurs in Derry and fuels the hotel and town's inability to "move on." *The Shining*, we will remember, also advocates reproductive futurism when the owner of the Overlook, Horace Derwent, reveals his terrifying homosexual proclivities through his dalliances with a violent dog-suited man named Roger, who (not unlike Dussander) threatens to "eat" Jack's son Danny, starting with his "plump little cock" (*Shining* 494). Now an adult, Danny goes to battle in *Doctor Sleep* against a group of marauding vampires that calls itself the True Knot. Rather than make its own future, the True Knot takes the future away from its victims by consuming them within an incestuous loop. Perhaps unsurprisingly, the text identifies this inward-looking consortium with a homosexual meeting between two stereotypical "men-haters" (lesbians, it is worth noting, that appear to have *chosen* their sexuality due to the bad behavior of men). The True Knot perpetually indulges itself, recalling the decadence of *Apt Pupil*, in "meaningless" foreplay that leads to nothing but pleasure: "Life was ... their only reason for living" (*Doctor* 154). Put a bit differently, these vampires simply vamp, without advancing anything, including biological life itself. Their personal enjoyment cannot be linked to the perpetuation of the species, and so they "queer" what the novel implicitly understands to be a "normal" Historical consciousness. From *Apt Pupil* to *Doctor Sleep*, then, King's story worlds demonize homosexuality by evincing that the growing impotence of American History will only be "corrected" through *even more* heterosexual coitus.

One of the only scholars to address the issue of homosexuality in King's fiction, Douglas Keesey, attempting to rescue *IT* from charges of homophobia, argues that "[I]f society is disturbed by homophobic violence in [King's] fiction, it should recognize and criticize its own homophobia rather than blame the writer for it" (189). This position completely lets King off the hook. As John DeLamar counters, "Keesey spends more time arguing a defense of King, the author, than he does examining the novel's embedded homophobia [by] claiming the text is a satire of homophobia" (DeLamar 4). As we have shown, King's literary and cinematic narratives regularly equate homosexuality with monstrosity (a harmful caricature with real-world consequences that must not be overlooked, especially when perpetrated by a writer with King's cultural clout). They codify American History as sexually perverted, deviant, and corrosive, suggesting—at times, quite directly—that the failings of History and its chroniclers can only be "corrected" through a return to heteronormative prerogatives.

At his most restrictive, King associates a deviant sexuality, as he does especially in *The Stand, IT, Gerald's Game*, and *Apt Pupil*, with the moral degradation of the individual. In *The Talisman*, for example, King and Straub create a dual universe that is imperiled by men such as Sunlight Gardener, an evangelical preacher who is also a homosexual pedophile. Like Pennywise, Gardener emerges as a homophobic portrayal of viciousness whose lust for male children is made even more odious in the delight he obtains in traumatizing them further through acts of fear and sadistic torture. King and Darabont's highly popular and powerful prison narratives, *The Shawshank Redemption* and *The Green Mile*, eventually locate criminality and evil not in Andy Dufresne and John Coffey, who, respectively, are falsely convicted and incarcerated for murder, but in each text's representative homosexual men: the sisters, Percy Wetmore, and Wild Bill. While Percy Wetmore may not technically be gay, he is certainly coded as "queer"; highly effeminate, he is the only guard on the cellblock excessively attentive to his physical appearance (e.g., meticulously combing his hair or adjusting his tight uniform). His name, Wetmore, underscores his propensity for hysterical panic during crisis situations resulting in wetting his pants. Percy's outsider status and lack of competence at his job is glaringly obvious when contrasted with the albeit unrealistic hyperbolized kindness and commitment to justice (e.g., Brutal's fierce assertion that Bitterbuck's execution leaves him "square with the House") associated with the other guards on the cellblock. In contrast to Wetmore's outwardly effeminate traits is his baseline sadistic personality—while he freezes in terror during active moments of Wild Bill's random acts of violence and sexual harassment, Percy luxuriates in the power he imposes over the other prisoners, especially savoring Delacroix's protracted misery. Thus, Wetmore is an exemplar of King's gay monsters: coded homosexual—even effeminate—but expressive of a vicious cruelty rather than tenderness towards other males.

King's portraits of homosexual men always contain a profound element of sadism. The sisters in *Shawshank* ("Go ahead and struggle; it's better that way") and Wild Bill in *Green Mile* are "bull queers" who force their sexuality onto others. While their intrusive violence leads Red to acknowledge that they "have to be human first" to qualify as homosexuals, the fact that both the novel and film define Bogs and the sisters solely in terms of their sexuality works as an implicit indictment of their homosexuality. In *Green Mile*, Wild Bill is an omnivorous rapist: he may prefer little girls, but is also highly attracted to Percy's prissy presence on the cellblock. Notably, Bill is unattracted to the heterosexual guards he finds working there; he recognizes the "queerness" of Wetmore, whom Bill demeans as if he were female, stroking his crotch and whispering in his ear that he is soft like a girl, that he wants to fuck his asshole, and later invites Percy to "suck my dick." Wild Bill's felonious crimes are murder and pedophilic rape, but he is actually a compendium of psychosexual perversions, and King and Darabont make it clear that homosexuality is among them. In the *Playboy* interview, King goes on to opine that "I'm not into the sadomasochistic trip either, on which your competitor *Penthouse* has built an entire empire ... despite all the artistic gloss, it's still sleaze; it still reeks corruptingly of concentration-camp porn" (Underwood 45). King proves to be a chaste taskmaster when it comes to expressions of sexuality. This translates into a somewhat contradictory stance from such a politically progressive thinker, as one might expect such stringent sexual conservatism from a religious zealot or an ultraconservative ideologue. The writer's attitude towards sexuality may in part explain the deep-seated antipathy he has consistently shown Donald Trump in Twitter posts, as the president is a good example of King's propensity to view a person's (especially a male's) sexual proclivities as a barometer for his morality.

"Queerness" as Liberation

It is through a reinterpretation of *The Stand* that we might start to complicate the analysis of King's depiction of the homosexual as monster. Upon an initial reading, *The Stand* upholds many of the problematic aspects addressed above: in particular, its villainous forces are branded as "queer" by practicing sadomasochistic sex (as when The Kid anally rapes Trashcan Man with his gun as the latter orally pleasures the former) as well as by admiring the novel's central antagonist, Randall Flagg, with "something like love," something that blurs the line between the ecstasy of worship and the ecstasy of orgasm (587, 358). However, a careful reading of *The Stand* cannot bypass the text's core conundrum: how is it that "normal" American society keeps recreating its own destruction? Of even greater interest to us, is it possible that a "queering" of History with a capital "H," which results in more expansive as well as inclusive histories with a lower-case "h," may not lead to society's ruin, but to something else entirely—a kind of renewal? After all, Flagg's vulnerability is initially exposed by a bisexual woman, Dayna Jurgens, whose suicide thwarts the Dark Man's apparent omnipotence and his desperate efforts to extract information from her. "She had gone, perhaps in triumph" (965). Although a minor figure among the novel's cast of hundreds, Dayna does stand out as the first to disrupt Flagg's plan for dominion over the Boulder Free State. Instead of focusing exclusively upon the novel's virulent association of corruption with homosexuality, then, it may prove fruitful (or—indispensably—fruitless) to dwell upon the invaluable role of "queerness" in disrupting the delusional march of History. Sam Miller proposes just such a reading while examining the horror film genre as a celebratory alternative to hegemonic sexual and social order: "The queer monster not only provides [the LGBTQ community] an opportunity to identify with someone on-screen, it also allows us to vicariously live out our rage against a social order that oppresses us" (Miller 221).

As we invert the core argument of this chapter so far, we must not dismiss out of hand the various ways in which King's works present heterosexual "norms" as poisonous. Interestingly, instances of homosexual rape and heterosexual marital sex are often disturbingly similar in King's world. King's gay men are typically aligned with a fascist agenda, preying on the young and vulnerable. The husbands that populate this writer's "domestic fiction," beginning with *Cujo* in 1981 and culminating with the 1990s novels of patriarchal abuse: *Dolores Claiborne, Gerald's Game, Rose Madder,* and *A Good Marriage,* underscore similar horrors in marriage and heterosexuality. Susie Bright recognizes that King's "men, exemplified by Daddy and Husband, are pretentious brutes who are impossible to identify with" (Bright 54). And King's women are often only "liberated" once they extricate themselves from sexual relationships with these husbands and fathers, instead embracing lonely, sexless lives. The few successful marriages and sexual unions that occur in King's world are so traditional that they harken back to the 1950s (King's own childhood reference point). His fictionalized sex is either cloyingly romanticized—locked in the domain of rarified white, bourgeois marriages, such as those found in *Bag of Bones* and *Lisey's Story* (where, coincidentally, a spouse has died, leaving the remaining partner to indulge a Poe-like romantic cliché of a lost perfect union deathlessly immolated at the altar of memory)—or it sinks to the level of vulgar appetite, in the form of brutal rape assaults, both heterosexual and especially homosexual. While partially attuned to negative abuses that can stem from sexual compulsion of all stripes, King seems closed off to the idea of liberated constructions of either homosexual or heterosexual unions. It therefore falls upon inventive readers to reclaim the "queerness" in King's works for productive, even redemptive, ends.[8]

Although *The Stand* does end with the much-ballyhooed birth of a Child, this particular child hardly resolves things for the novel's central community; in fact, the child's life teeters on the edge, and the reader cannot be certain that it survives at all. Michael Collings comments that, in King's fiction, "only rarely does the [C]hild become instrumental in restoring order" (Collings 17). On this front, *The Stand* subverts a common expectation of post-apocalyptic art, such as in the film *Children of Men* (2006): the tendency to hinge hope habitually upon a miraculous birth. At his worst, Flagg treats the continuation of the species in a shockingly clinical fashion, declaring Nadine Cross, his female slave, to be nothing more than an "incubator" (*Stand* 976). *The Stand* fears—perhaps above all else—the reproduction of the status quo, a fear that it links directly to the (mistaken) belief that the arrival of a Child will fulfill the society's fallacy of instant renewal. A very different picture of Randall Flagg emerges in this reading: his inherent "queerness"—as a rabble rouser, he lives to overthrow the accepted way of doing things—may prove to be *an essential component of King's multiverse*.[9] He does return incessantly to undo stale social orders. Could it be that the King reader errs in the urge to reject all of what Flagg represents? While *The Stand*'s "crew of light" seem intent on recreating the *ancien régime* (through committee assignments, the return of law, and democratic processes, etc.), and retaining faith in the coming Child, it may be Flagg alone that recognizes a need for radical social change (even as he seeks to recreate a fascist regime that employs all the deadly hardware of the past under his personal dominion). As the Gay Liberation Front states in its 1971 manifesto, the "complete sexual liberation for all people cannot come about unless existing social institutions are abolished. It's not a question of getting our piece of the pie. The pie is rotten" (Serinus). When read in this fashion, Flagg's recognition to rebel against the pre-plague status quo alerts King's reader to the cycle of doom aligned with American History. At the end of the novel, Flagg is emblematic of a self-destructive urge—the Freudian death drive—inimitable to American society. He embodies a compulsion to undo dominant cultural narratives that survive in many of King's works produced in the wake of *The Stand*.

Before returning to texts discussed earlier with this alternative framework for analysis in mind, let us briefly pause to unpack how "queerness" might function as a requisite part of historical consciousness rather than an abject aberration. The fantasy that the arrival of a Child will fulfill all of the desires of an ailing society—underwritten by a deep-seated belief in the supposedly divine mandate of heterosexuality itself—is a dangerous one, Edelman warns. Such a belief equates the child with "Imaginary Wholeness" and promulgates "[H]istory as the continuous staging of our dream of eventual self-realization" (Edelman 10). This perspective provides a secular theology of sorts by supporting two delusions: first, that society could be perfected, and second, that humans could consciously plan this perfection. As a Gothic author, King's works are antithetical to a utopian vision—from the anti-heroes of his pseudonym Richard Bachman, to the misguided transcendentalism of *IT* and *Dreamcatcher*, to the innate corruption of the American suburbs, punctuated by Todd's gunfire (*Apt Pupil*) and Blind Willie's doubling (*Hearts of Atlantis*), King argues time and again that an ideal society can never exist. The flaws of human nature stand in the way of such social amelioration. The purpose of King's spokesperson Glen Bateman in *The Stand* is to remind us that the individual can maintain his or her moral freedom and dignity only as long as he or she remains an individual. Once a social relationship advances beyond a small group, the dangers attendant to conformity and institutionalization grow progressively stronger, transforming a social microcosm into a macrocosm. King deflates delusions of perfection in a variety of manners, including (one could argue) with his "queering" of History as a heteronormative absolute. "The queer must insist on disturbing, on queering, social organization as such." Said another way, the image of the "queer" reminds us of our "inescapable failure" in breeding an all-American boy like Todd in the first place (Edelman 17, 26). The "queer" ruptures the dream of bureaucratic Nazis everywhere, offering in its stead a death drive to undermine fantasies of total fulfillment, or imaginary wholeness. In King's story worlds, the best way to dismantle a "reproductive futurism" is to privilege "queerness" as a negativity that marks the short-sightedness of any imagined path to the End of History.

In *Doctor Sleep*, Danny's faith in the determinism of genetics, which is to say, his mistaken investment in the internal logic of human breeding as a form of self-realization, proves to be deeply corrosive: "In human affairs, the only real king is genetics," he laments. "There's nothing but family history … blood calling to blood." But, in the end, Danny proclaims: "I am not my father," a sentiment that undermines his previous statement (189, 523, 499). What ultimately drives historical imagination, Danny begins to realize, is not the venerated birth of a child, but death. At the close, his contribution to society is not through heterosexual partnership, not through "getting regular with somebody," but in his willingness to work in a hospice lending assistance to individuals in their last moments of life (178). The final reversal of *Doctor Sleep*—from birth to death—exemplifies the "queerness" of King's alternative American history (with a lower-case "h"), a model that rejects patriarchal inheritance in favor of ceaseless transgression.

IT can be read through a similar "queer" lens because we might interpret Bill's "sexual awakening" at the novel's terminus as just another one of the text's many delusions. Indeed, the cosmic cycle in Derry can never truly end. The city crumbles to pieces in order to be rebuilt (*ad nauseum*)—such is the death drive of the place as well as its people. The story necessitates a lack of heterosexual libido to gather the adults together and guide them to save the day; if the adult members of the Losers' Club are not impotent (or unhappy in their partnerships), they would have had no reason to return to Derry. To interpret *IT* in this fashion, we shift from Freud's pleasure principle—in which heteronormativity is the presumed means and ends of a healthy society—to his death drive—in which the figure of "the queer" plays a pivotal part in prolonging desire by maintaining dissatisfaction, thwarting the allure of *The Stand*'s first Child, and insisting that a perpetuation of the status quo never delivers what it promises. Although *IT* can be interpreted as a shining example of reproductive futurism, the novel can also be read as debunking the notion that procreation and the forward movement of History, together, form a meaningful *mythos*. When Adrian—the gay man murdered in the opening of the text—demonstrates his civic pride by wearing a Derry hat, *IT* suggests a different historical understanding, one in which the city might achieve a pluralistic sense of continuity *without* the repugnant aspects of American History that are at the center of much criticism throughout King's fiction (i.e., violent, imperialistic, and exclusively heterosexual). Adrian's legacy endures in the novel's penultimate scene: when Bill grabs his friend Richie's hand and feels that he is wearing his wife's wedding ring, it amplifies their fraternal bond and empowers them to enter into battle with Pennywise (*IT* 769, 1020). Decoupling the urge to be an actor on the stage of History from the institution of marriage as existing exclusively between a man and a woman, *IT* charts a different course in which homoeroticism is not the End of History but *its moment of rejuvenation*. The film adaptation directed by Andy Muschietti, *IT Chapter Two* (2019) picks up on this theme and suggests that Richie (Bill Hader) is a closeted homosexual. In one scene, Pennywise torments Richie by threatening to expose his secret to the rest of the town. Ultimately, Richie finds some kind of peace in his sexuality, as he is empowered to finish carving the name of his love interest at a visible town site. (Nevertheless, we must ask why Muschietti's film seems to have little compunction in portraying grotesque homophobic violence, but it remains unwilling to declare Richie's homosexuality in any kind of overt way.)[10]

With this pivot, we may inquire into what the "queering" of American History in *Apt Pupil* can tell us about the complex imbrication of sexuality and historicity in King's multiverse. In a sense, the crypt actually turns out to be better than the crib (as a compelling rejoinder to heteronormativity, the pathological mastery embodied by straight white males). The death drive of American History does reveal itself to be "queer," but not in a fashion that needs to be dismissed as homophobic; rather, the death drive of *Apt Pupil* might be read as instrumental in preserving King's fictional universe against the threat of annihilation. *Apt Pupil* choreographs the death drive in several specific instances. When Todd invites Dussander for supper with his parents, it disappoints him that everything goes off without a hitch. After he extends the invitation, he (unconsciously) longs to "let the cat out of bag," for his visitor to blow a hole in the naïve iconography of his all-American image of his family and himself. Meanwhile, Todd's father (unconsciously) wants his son to cease being "perfect" and violate the clean-cut, obedient ideal. He gleefully imagines Todd's secret urges in a way that undermines his son's stagnant "normalcy," thrusting him into a manhood defined by its dysfunctionality. Neither Todd nor his father, then, truly want to maintain their efficient, well-manicured façade. Instead, they are driven to "queerness" in order to escape from the oppressive hold of their sanitized and sanctimonious lives. Unaware, Todd is also driven to failure at school, a failure that threatens to expose his charade with Dussander and, mercifully, eviscerate his storybook paralysis: "A part of you wants it to end. *Needs* for it to end" (*Apt* 183, 145; author's emphasis). Faced with the nightmare of complete exposure—a totality that would end his desire because no secrets would remain, and there would be no unfulfilled fantasies left to pursue—Todd the Historian *needs* to fail. The "queerness" of his experience with Dussander may have been his sole opportunity to decamp from the self-perpetuating, oppressive narrative called American History.

Because King's long-standing account of American History is built upon the promise of greater acquisition and absolute mastery, Todd can escape from this loop only with the (re)introduction of blind spots, forgetting, as well as the inability to expand, germinate, and bear oneself forth, over and over again. A "queer" American history (with a lower-case "h"), shorn of the "evil" connotations foisted upon it, would remain *always-already transgressive*. A "queer" American history would not reproduce itself; it would forever negate its own delusions, undermining its own "libidinally subtended fantasies" and "disturbing … social organization as such" (Edelman 7, 17). Rather than look to the future Child (a static ideal, unable to grow or change), we might consider what life might look like beyond the enclosures of reproductive futurism. From this alternative vantage point, Todd's downfall stems less from an excess of "queerness" than from the shortness of its supply.

To accentuate this alternative, Singer's adaptation contemplates a "queer" mode of seeing. The film repeatedly lingers upon obscured windows through which the audience must strain to comprehend what lies beyond. These opaque apertures challenge the film's spectators to reflect upon their own narrow, heteronormative viewpoints as well as to consider the pleasures to be found in a different erotic visuality. At one point, Dussander watches Mr. Magoo, the famous cartoon character who is visually challenged. One "queer" mode of seeing proposed by the film is *blindness*: the inability for the eye to penetrate the world, to master it, to bring forth knowledge. The eye finds new delights in distinctive forms of engagement. When the authorities apprehend Dussander and they are pictured standing at his hospital bedside, the camera looks up through a blurry lens at the assembled faces as Dussander rushes to put on his glasses; at last, he is genuinely seen by others, and the power dynamic has been fundamentally reversed. If American self-confidence is bloated, as Dussander claims to Bowden, the unexpected inability to thrust his penetrating eye outward evokes an alternative ethical vision (alongside an unexpected kind of eroticism).

The second "queer" mode of seeing in Singer's film—arguably the more enduring mode of the two—is achieved through the extensive use of superimposition, in which one scene overlays another (a palimpsest that refuses to freeze events and arrange them into a chronological sequence). Martin Jay writes, "Ocular-*eccentricity*... is the antidote to privileging any one visual order or scopic regime" (591; author's emphasis). Unlike the sense of mastery that accompanies classical Hollywood editing, Singer's *Apt Pupil* recalls the ocular-eccentric juxtapositions of Soviet montage: a mode of seeing designed to make meaning in the poetic spaces between images (not through their seamless accumulation). The film's "queering" of vision challenges an assumption that cinema must operate in a linear fashion by steadily exposing everything until the engorged spectator is at last sated. In the clashing cacophony of Singer's text, pleasure comes from the disintegration of coherence, from a *rejection* of absolute vision accompanied by the elevation of the blind spot. This "queer" mode of seeing opens the future to radical discovery by departing from cinematic norms.

Apt Pupil closes with a close-up of the crystal blue eyes of Dussander's corpse as they stare blankly out at the audience. Uncannily, these dead eyes still seem to see outward, uncomfortably penetrating the spectator—but they do so in a "queer" sort of way; that is, their familiarity (as eyes that can see) rubs up against their unfamiliarity (they should not be seeing anything at all, at least not in any neurobiological sense). The final shot of the film captures a genuinely "queer" mode of seeing as sight becomes blindness and blindness becomes sight, all at once. In our book's final chapter, we further unpack this sort of divergence as a critique of American History, given by King its fullest articulation in the wake of the events of September 11, 2001. King's reader might opt to reclaim the "queerness" of his texts as a force for social uplift—a death drive to alert us when our naïve hope for utopia has become genocidal, and to signal the strong presence of Nazism inherent in our own reproductive futurism. A

Figure 5.2 Dussander's death stare at the conclusion of *Apt Pupil*.

"queer" American history (with a lower-case "h") subverts our blind march into tomorrow by exposing the emptiness of our declared destination as well as the barbarity of History's established cadence. "Queerness" thus fractures the imaginary wholeness associated with procreation and, in turn, alters our attenuated Historical consciousness, which can no longer function like a gilded roadway. King's readers might also reconsider the innate "queerness" of his texts in order to challenge noxious heteronormativity. By so doing, readers of Stephen King might work to open a future with greater possibilities for a plurality of the American populace.

Notes

1 Dennis Mahoney connects the opening History book photographs of the film version of *Apt Pupil* with the "infamous scrapbook" from *The Shining*, a connection that underscores the commentary we associate with both films (29).

2 For instance, see Jack's kinky encounter with the beautiful, rotting corpse in Room 217 (King's novel) and 237 (Kubrick's film) or Louis's complicated arousal/impotence in relation to the burial ground: the pull and push of the eerie woods into which he sojourns to "neck" with a young woman, only to be rebuffed by the acidic undertones of the place; his ability to become "hard and erect" after visiting the forbidden area set against an icy rejoinder—"the winterwhine" of Death that serves as a constant murmur under the sounds of his love-making (King *Pet* 158, 278).

3 In an attempt to provide Todd with an explanation for Nazi excursions into perversity, Dussander remarks in the film adaptation that "a door was opened that could not be shut." The boy and the old man first meet with an amber-colored screen door separating them. And when the Nazi proves physically unable to complete the murder of Archie, he tricks Todd into going down into the basement to finish the job, "Now we'll see what you are made of," and locks the door behind him. In this scene the boy and the Nazi are separated only by the door between them, which functions again symbolically as a mirror as much as a door.

4 In keeping with a fascist aesthetic, which overemphasizes physical beauty and militarism associated with the male body, fascist art worships masculine form. It would appear that fascists are confronted with a core paradox: the fetishization of masculinity at the same time that overt homosexuality must be repressed to avoid undermining the masculine ideal and to permit heterosexuality. Ironically, then, the Nazis were obsessed with rooting out homosexuality within their ranks and punishing it in the camps, forcing gay Jewish male prisoners to wear pink Stars of David. The Gestapo was infamous for blackmailing Army officers who had become disposable with the charge of homosexuality. And yet Hitler had known all along, from the earliest days of the National Socialist Party, that many of his closest and most important followers were gay. As William Shirer documents in *The Rise and Fall of the Third Reich*, "It was common talk, for instance, that Heines [one of the leaders of the Brown Shirts] used to send S.A. men scouring all over Germany to find him suitable male lovers. These things Hitler had not only tolerated but defended; more than once he had warned his party comrades against being too squeamish about a man's personal morals if he were a fanatical fighter for the movement" (Shirer 225). *Apt Pupil* maintains the tension in this conundrum throughout as Todd swings back and forth between Dussander and Becky Trask, secret fetish idol and high school girlfriend.

5. The film's singular focus on vision works both overtly and covertly. It returns, obsessively, to images that resemble the eye (including a clouded window in the wooden door of a concentration camp that Todd configures in one of his dreams). At one point, we see Todd sporting a Vuarnet t-shirt—a French brand of eyewear developed by opticians. The interrogation of sight is everywhere in *Apt Pupil*.
6. Picart and Frank delve into the bond shared between French and Bowden and conclude that there is a strong homoerotic tension between the two that exists *even before* Todd's concluding efforts to manipulate French's silence. Citing a missing scene in Boyce's script that was excised from the movie, Picart and Frank argue that "French's fondness for Todd may extend beyond mere professionalism" (123). J.M. Clark likewise detects that "Singer plants doubts in us as to whether French is gay and whether his concern carries with it a hidden agenda" (18).
7. The majority evidence for positive homosocial bonds in King's canon are male-to-male centered. But there are some interesting exceptions found in *Gerald's Game* and especially *Dolores Claiborne*, where female-to-female bonding forms an important alternative to abusive heterosexual marriages. Nonetheless, King's opprobrium against homosexuality holds firm here as well, as Dolores' relationship with Vera is similar to the homosocial bonds we find among the male heroes populating King's canon. The two women live in the same house and take care of each other for decades, yet despite being alone and friendless all this time, there is no hint of a sexual component to their relationship. Selena is right in the film adaptation when she claims they "love each other," but as friends and co-conspirators only, never as sexual partners. Although Jessie's connection back to Ruth, the latter a radical feminist lesbian in *Gerald's Game*, helps the former to confront and overcome her situation handcuffed to the past, their bond is strictly maintained as a consciousness-raising friendship, even as Jessie departs the novel, like Dolores and Vera, an asexual woman no longer interested in men.
8. When King does consciously attempt to uplift the LGBTQ community, his efforts lead to problematic results. For instance, in *Elevation* (2019), a straight white male literally sacrifices himself to save his lesbian neighbors, affirming a white (heterosexual) savior complex. One of the grateful lesbians fawns over her hero: "'What you did ... made it possible for us to stay in Castle Rock ... without you, part of my beloved would have always remained closed off to the world'" (*Elevation* 134). Even use of the word "beloved" seems out of place and time, diction that sounds artificial and stilted.
9. For instance, Flagg's propensity for disruption is on display in King's *The Eyes of the Dragon* (1984), a fantasy novel in which Flagg foments insurrection against the "good king" and seeks the destruction of the latter's kingdom.
10. In his interview with Hader about the film, Marc Malkin writes, "While Richie doesn't discuss his sexuality in the film, Hader said of Richie, 'Hopefully, he has an understanding of, an acceptance of who he is'" (Malkin). We might wonder why his self-knowledge must remain a "hopeful" undercurrent, rather than made manifest.

6 The Events of 9/11 and Stephen King's Evolving Sense of History

As this book has argued, Stephen King repeatedly narrates American History as a kind of endless cycle: the circular—rather than linear—depiction of a nation that cannot get out of its own way in order to "progress." Due in part to his status as America's most popular horror writer, King obsesses over figures as well as communities trapped in repetitive loops in which the future is only ever the reiteration of a self-destructive past. Here we find the prevailing metaphor of a gothic haunting, embodied in a fictional landscape plagued by phantoms. In King's multiverse, this entropic vision of American History stems from a variety of sources: toxic masculinity (*Pet Sematary*), class and capitalism (*The Shining*), a fatal obsession with bio-technological destruction (*The Stand* and *The Mist*), and imperial lust (*Hearts of Atlantis* and *Dreamcatcher*). Earlier chapters have sought to illustrate how King's novels present American History as horrifyingly and deathlessly repetitive.

However, as we suggest in the previous chapter concerning the possible reclamation of a "queer" history, King's works also harbor optimistic alternatives to this doom-and-gloom model. Specifically, this chapter considers the ways in which King's more recent texts diverge from his initial star-crossed loops by examining unique moments in which his corpus seems to suggest alternative kinds of histories. Interestingly, King gestures at these alternatives by summoning a major figure from the annals of the American Gothic, Edgar Allan Poe—in particular, his famous detective, C. Auguste Dupin. As we demonstrate in the first chapter, King is both shaped by, and dramatically distinguishes himself from, the authority of his forbearers in American literature by expressing a keen anxiety of influence when it comes to the transcendentalists. So, too, did Poe maintain ambivalent feelings towards his contemporaries. Through his prototypical detective Dupin, Poe explores (as well as transcends) mere faith in Western Reason, undercutting the presumed capacity of the dutiful Historian to piece together a puzzle and arrive at a rational conclusion. Unlike Jack with his scrapbook in *The Shining*, or Todd with the jigsaw puzzle in Dussander's kitchen in the film version of *Apt Pupil*, Dupin rejects the notion that Reason will incrementally lead humanity to total mastery. Quite contrastingly, the diligent labor of Poe's police/Historians reveals a form of blindness, as the bumbling policemen that surround Dupin in stories such as "The Murders in the Rue Morgue" (1841) and "The Purloined Letter" (1844) can never spot the solution so plainly in front of them. While he operates within a rational comprehension of observable facts, Dupin is also a poet and a fantasist who relies on imagination/intuition to transcend the limits of Reason that restrict the Prefect and his police force. Equally at odds with the metaphysician and the empiricist, Poe imagines a different kind of detective, and so King too imagines a different kind of historian, one that remains open to unexpected possibilities against the grain of a gross instrumental Reason. In his more Poe-like moments, King offers readers an *anti-Historian*. In this, he provides a divergent template for thinking about American history (with a lower-case "h"): a blueprint for emancipation from the doom experienced by less fortunate characters like Jack or Louis.

According to King the anti-Historian neither attempts to plan nor to plot the future in accordance with the past; instead, she prepares herself to react to unanticipated events that change everything "on a dime" (a phrase repeated often in King's fiction over the last two decades). The anti-Historian closely resembles what Michel Foucault calls the genealogist—a figure interested in radical disruptions that redirect a lineage and move it in quite unexpected directions. She rejects metahistorical narratives by arguing that nothing remains "timeless and essential." There is no History with a capital "H" but only lower-case "h" histories, which is to say, competing stories told between competing historians. King's anti-Historian can dismantle the "suprahistorical perspective" of entities like the Overlook (a self-enclosed totality) in favor of identifying "the accidents, the minute deviations—or, conversely, the complete reveals—the errors, the false appraisals, and the faulty calculations that birth those things that continue to exist and have value for us" (Foucault 79–81, 86). In other words, rather than track a smooth, chronological unfolding of History, the anti-Historian draws attention to singular events—true accidents—that force individuals away from social norms, and establishes a new, more individualistic set of norms. As a result, *things can never be the same again*. Although King's corpus arguably attends to these apocalyptic ruptures from the beginning (think, for instance, of the meltdown that initiates *The Stand*, or the rift that opens up in "The Langoliers"), his contemporary work dwells to a much greater degree upon incalculable events that his earliest fiction gestures at only obliquely.

King shares his anti-Historicist perspective with a number of twentieth-century thinkers. Because the past and the future remain irrevocably tied up in the prerogatives of a postmodern present, we "have nothing to go upon but present perception." According to this logic, temporal markers serve as "performative utterances" that—Michael Oakeshott posits—render the past "neither true nor false," but practical and useful to individuals living in the present: "The practical, so-called living 'past' is not significantly past at all. It is that part of a present-past ... recalled for use ... and valued for what (it has) to offer in current practical engagements" (8, 33, 35, 41). Another critic in this vein, Karl Popper, contends in *The Open Society and Its Enemies* (1966) that it remains impossible for us "to understand the meaning of the play which is performed on the Historical Stage" (8). Like Oakeshott and Popper, King's new millennial work paints "an order of space and time that is enchanted by spirits other than those of metahistory" (W. Brown 15). From King's vantage point, then, history becomes a present-day struggle between storytellers—a vulnerable, if playful, narrative to be rewritten whenever something sudden happens that tips the balance in power. Decoupled from the weight of a History that has been heavily scripted, this sort of play must be intentionally and continually improvised.

Before exploring the ramifications of this shift in King's work, we must pause to define the notion of *the event* (a philosophical premise with considerable currency in our contemporary climate). The trouble today, Alain Badiou maintains, is that we cannot easily extricate ourselves from a consensus view of History. As King's early work contends, we remain stuck in a terrible wreathe, repeating the atrocities of yesterday. Only an unexpected event can shake us loose from this prison: "An event is something that brings to light a possibility that was invisible or unthinkable ... a possibility that wasn't calculable in advance" (Badiou 9). Badiou offers a number of examples, including the story of Jesus Christ and Darwinism. Before Christ's resurrection, the world was one way; after he rose from the dead, it fundamentally changed (and no one can go back to the previous mode of being). Like a bolt of lightning, the event strikes and—"on a dime"—basic concepts of the law, of life as well as death, utterly transform. Similarly, when Darwin proposes the idea of evolution, historical consciousness cleaves: the prior world that pictured humanity's purpose in a particular way divided from a new world that pictures this purpose in an entirely different light (Foucault classifies these divergent periods as *epistemes*). Random mutations erupt and force us to reframe our understanding of old rules. Unlike the rigid Historians of old, the anti-Historian remains open to these events; after all, if she tries preemptively to absorb its truth into her existing narrative, she will clearly fail, as the entire premise (for example, a world in which death is not the final word) divorces itself from prior constraints (in which Jewish and/or Roman regulations definitively demarcated life from death). Badiou notes, "'To be prepared for an event means being subjectively disposed to recognizing new possibilities" (10–12). If many of King's early Historians destroy themselves by refusing to accept that their universe is (of necessity) punctuated by unanticipated ruptures—opting to cling to an illusion of absolute mastery—King's contemporary anti-Historians prove more willing to accept a vision of history germinated by accidents, by sudden explosions, and unanchored from metaphysical continuity. These figures are "subjectively disposed" to possibilities that characters such as Jack Torrance or Todd Bowden are simply not able to entertain. Of course, it is quite unlikely that King has taken an interest of late in the complex ideas of philosophers like Foucault or Badiou. More likely, the appearance of anti-Historicism in his fiction can be explained within the context of a defining event at the dawn of the twenty-first century: the attack upon the World Trade Center on September 11, 2001. In one of King's first interviews following 9/11, the writer indicated his awareness of the moment as a terror event that would transform the American landscape: "I have noticed the first ripples of awareness in the artistic consciousness—not conscience, it's too early for conscience, that comes much later—that represent the first droplets of a rainstorm that will continue for years" (Magistrale, *Hollywood's* 17). And yet, while the event of 9/11 did appear to change everything "on a dime," to treat it as a random mutation involves at the same time obfuscating important causal factors from the past (such as America's long-standing involvement in the Middle East) and even disincentivizing plans for a more peaceful future.

Nonetheless, following the shocking events of 9/11, King's fiction more deliberately re-examines the nature of historical consciousness and proposes a substitute formula in which the chastened witnesses of a highly variable, unstable American history learn, at long last, *to expect the unexpected*. *Under the Dome* (2009) contemplates this shift in both its content and its form. The novel's subtexts speak to the offenses of the Bush regime through a reflection upon the ways in which Americans lost sight of their founding principles in the aftermath of the attacks. The text opens on Route 119—a number readily reversed to read 9/11. And the event that occurs on this stretch of road provides a not-so-subtle allusion to the atrocities of the day in question: without warning, a plane crashes, and the town of Chester's Mill becomes an authoritarian state run by an oil-hungry tyrant. Although as a bald allegory *Under the Dome* remains too reliant upon black-and-white caricatures and readymade catharsis for a grieving audience, the first few chapters of the novel do provide an interesting commentary upon how unanticipated events drive history. The text opens with two figures—a pilot and a woodchuck—whose lives parallel one another. King describes how the woodchuck perceives its surroundings by "bumbling along" and forming "rudimentary images" of the world. At the moment of the plane crash, right before its debris decapitates the poor creature, the woodchuck thinks to itself: "What happened?" *Under the Dome* thus concerns itself with clean breaks: "what happened" moments in which a community seems to be reborn, "like something freshly made and just set down."[1] Its opening pages circle back incessantly to this cleavage, detailing the plane crash in tandem with a "mushroom cloud" that detonates in a character's head and renders him suddenly "crazy" (a state of being that the local doctor "had never even considered") as well as the exit from the town of a nomad that goes on to serve as the text's hero (*Under* 3–5, 22). This nomadic ethos marks King's character as an ideal anti-Historian. He begins the novel by contemplating a new law—a radical severance of the traditional social order—that would force individuals to move constantly, to travel habitually (rather than to remain rooted in provincial fashion). Beyond just a jab at the provincial character of the town of Chester's Mill, the nomad's law would push readers to depart from the restraints of American History and become "capable of undoing every infatuation," thereby empowering themselves to remain open always to different beginnings (Foucault 79). Before its later chapters mire the text in clumsy allusion, *Under the Dome* manages to capture the slipperiness of historical perspective through its metacommentary. The omnipotent narrator undermines any illusions of wholeness—and thwarts the reader's need for a restoration of order—by gesturing at "the magic of narration." That is to say, by exposing its own internal patterns to the reader, *Under the Dome* breaks from convention in order to reveal a vital gap between the jumbled, messy nature of reality and the false promise of narrative coherence. By the close of the novel, characters resign themselves to a state of constant humility by claiming "just life" (37, 1072). They forfeit the machinations of mastery (harnessed by the barbarous authoritarian that runs Chester's Mill) and choose to embrace instead a life born perpetually anew in the wake of random events. *Under the Dome* makes a statement about the post-eventual subject— the anti-Historian that decomposes History (with a capital "H") in pursuit of an alternative perspective, "freshly made and just set down." King's wandering reader at last recognizes the wisdom in the woodchuck's rudimentary consciousness and bumbling manner.

Like *Under the Dome*, *Cell* (2006) explores how the attacks of September 11 fundamentally rewired the consciousness of a nation. The novel is littered with references to 9/11, including, prominently, when the survivors of another attack must dial 911 to reset individuals that have been brainwashed. An observer notes, "'The dirty bastards are using planes again'"; another character remarks, "'Look what happened to the World Trade Center'" (16, 47). In *Cell*, King attends to the nature of the singular event as well as its influence upon historical understanding by contemplating how 9/11 (or, in other moments, an unexpected weather event like Hurricane Katrina) disrupts the ordinary flow of time, and displaces a generally accepted story of how the world works.[2] *Cell*, too, opens with a radical rupture: in this case, "the event that came to be known as The Pulse" (3). As The Pulse pierces through cellular phones, it transforms recipients into violent zombies. On a dime, "things have changed," just as they did after the attacks of 9/11. A resolution to this problem will not be easily ascertained "as the search for answers must be done without the assistance of God or the most specialized and trained human individuals who are assumed to hold the keys to information and survival" (McAleer 179). In fact, "within ten hours of the event, most of the scientists … were either dead or insane." Without any notice, citizens of the northeastern United States become a dangerous collective connected by a kind of "hive think" (*Cell* 3, 38). The few that escape this brainwashing—namely Clayton Riddell, Tom McCourt, and Alice Maxwell—are uprooted from their lives and forced to search in vain for a central source to explain the madness that surrounds them, all the while performing their own acts of self-protective violence against the murdering collective. In King's telling, the event is always tied to a dramatically heightened individualism (a correlation that hints at the failure of these events to trigger *genuine* social change, discussed at length in the conclusion of the book).

The imposition of a single community mindset, the "hive think," is a core component in earlier King fiction, such as *Carrie*, *'Salem's Lot*, *Storm of the Century*, *The Stand*, *The Tommyknockers*, *IT*, and *Needful Things*, among other examples. In these earlier books, anyone who fails to commit to the "hive think" of the infected communal whole is subject to severe forms of punishment and, more likely, violent death. Such is the violence of History. *Cell* restates this infernal design by transforming citizens into a zombie-like mob stimulated by group conformance to the same technological signal emanating out of cell phones. As in one of King's favorite films, George Romero's *Night of the Living Dead*, a community's citizenry become the walking dead who have sacrificed their sanity, vision, and independence for mindless inclusion into a deadly group identity. King is very much a sociologist of our time, interested in chronicling fictionally again and again the role of the individual or small group subset pitted against the majority whole. This is a dynamic we find at work from *Carrie* to *Cell*. How is it possible for the individual to maintain his or her identity in the context of corrupt social institutions and the mass conformity associated with various forms of "hive think" found throughout the King universe? In his canon, there is a possibility for everything to become a prison. Various destructive incarnations share a similar mode of operation: the insistence that others relinquish moral choices, surrender independent thought, and abandon individual conscience. King utilizes "hive think" to represent one of the great threats to American liberty. And while the writer often associates the concept with single demonic figures, such as Linoge in *Storm of the Century*, Flagg in *The Stand*, and Barlow's vampirism in *'Salem's Lot*, in his post-9/11 fiction the model assumes a more diffused and ambiguous form, such as in the random corruption of cell phones. Our society's unquestioning commitment to and reliance on cell phones, where nearly the entire population owns a device, and the way in which terrorism threatens to exploit our own technology against us, such as creating flying bombs out of commercial aircraft, provide King with the opportunity to explore the paranoia of post-9/11 through the metaphor of degraded technology. On multiple levels, *Cell* is King's allegory on the consequences of 9/11, literalizing a metaphor for the experience: the search for knowledge and understanding in the wake of the apocalyptic, the loss of individual liberties through the enactment of the USA Patriot Act, the uniformity of culture that closes in around us like a prison, the honeycombed network of instantaneous communications, the intrusion of surveillance as an accepted everyday presence in public life, the way in which our reliance on a common technology ironically isolates us from one another, and the free-floating anxiety attendant to insecurity, vulnerability, confusion, and paranoia that has become a hallmark of post-9/11 horror. As a result of an advanced and seemingly connected technology, the global population is now susceptible to the "hive think" of conformity, a condition in which protest is useless. Furthermore, we are all subject to random acts of violence, just as our fellow citizens, classmates, and passengers might turn out to be carrying a gun, a bomb, or a defective cell phone. *Cell* is an example of post-9/11 horror art that does not end in the defeat of the monster and reestablishment of normality; it explores 9/11 through the fantastic, the monstrous, and the horrific. As Kevin Wetmore argues, "The paradigm shift in horror [art] reflects the paradigm shift after 9/11. We cannot return to the status quo" (5). For our purposes, it is worth analyzing how King uses the events of 9/11—and the radical paradigm shift that they initiate—to flesh out his image of an ideal anti-Historian for the century to come.

Against these backdrops of capitulation to "hive thinking," King pits his heroes, individual men and women who are typically working-class people struggling to figure out how to circumvent and survive the unfolding cataclysm that has left him or her so terribly isolated. As it turns out, the central source in *Cell* is not a metaphysical design, but "a mutative trigger" (162). Like the nomad at the heart of *Under the Dome*, the protagonists of *Cell* endure because they too are wanderers that lack self-importance, and because they must also confront this brave new world without the crutch of a suprahistorical framework. "A young man of no particular importance to (H)istory came walking": part woodchuck and part nomad, the anti-Historians of *Cell* repeatedly respond to the attack by eschewing cell phone technology and *not thinking*. Said another way, instead of immediately piecing things together (like Poe's formulaic police operative), King's heroes respond to the explosive event by allowing their "brains to stand off to one side," thus forfeiting what "marginal control" they once thought they possessed (3, 20, 12). This strategy informs a disparate sense of personal and public history. Slavoj Žižek argues, "The ultimate Event is the Fall itself, the loss of some primordial unity and harmony which never existed, which is just a retroactive illusion" (*Event* 50). Indeed, the novel breaks apart the illusion of a rational society by exposing a schism between History (with a capital "H") and the fragile, partial histories of a people living always on a volatile fault line. Riddell, the main character—and a man of no particular importance—realizes that "maybe the big picture was always going to be beyond him. He drew small pictures for a living" (49). When the protagonist realizes a gap between big and small pictures, he underscores a core difference between custodians of American History, like Jack Torrance, and the anti-Historians who populate King's post-9/11 fiction.

Similar to *Under the Dome*, *Cell* closes with an invitation for readers to practice this mode of imagining American history (with a lower-case "h"). By positing that the initial, reactive response to the 9/11 attacks (unwittingly) set the stage for The Pulse, *Cell* reminds its readers that *they too cannot hope to plot the next event*. Each action could spark an unforeseen "mutative trigger" down the road. We must reset our relationship to history. Like Riddell's son, who has been brainwashed and now dials 911 to attempt to emerge from the fog, we must transform ourselves into "a new thing" in perpetuity (347).

11/22/63 (2011) offers yet another treatise in this vein. The novel's protagonist Jake, an English teacher, finds a time portal and decides to go back and thwart the assassination of John F. Kennedy. At first a believer in American History—a custodian in the Todd Bowden mold—Jake must undergo reform because he "thinks too much." Unable to write for himself, he begins the novel in a state of malaise: "The red pen became my primary teaching tool … hopeless trudging work." Because literary analysis—reading and writing with a set of prescribed institutional expectations—imprisons him, his creative flows are stubbornly blocked: "Isn't there a frustrated writer inside every English teacher?" (*11/22/63* 3, 93). Jake attempts to revise History (with red pen in hand) as if it was another student essay and so, to rectify this problem, *11/22/63* advocates a shift away from these structural norms, into a place of "writing more freely" (644). To this point, Jake's life has included one predictable sequence after another; his love interest accuses him of treating his life like a textbook (he does, in fact, employ a text—a blue notebook—to read and write about the past with a stunning degree of certainty). Like the protagonists of both *Under the Dome* and *Cell*, Jake becomes an anti-Historian once he forfeits his delusions of mastery.

In King's multiverse, History and literature share a common characteristic: *neither can be legislated*. "Explanations are such cheap poetry" (*11/22/63* 285). The uniquely portable magic of writing helps Jake to transcend the stale algorithm of cause-and-effect, endowing him with the ability to create/enter into other texts (paralleling his use of the portal to jump from one temporal period to another). He argues from the very start that reading and writing *sans* red pen should be more spontaneous, as when he tells a young man from 1958 that he is overthinking a Shirley Jackson story: "'There's nothing to get … a story's just a story'" (4–5, 40). Later, when Jake revisits the cast of King's popular novel *IT* as a stand-in for King himself, Jake cannot change anything about the narrative, instead choreographing the teen's dance before leaving them without looking back. An unplanned waltz between reader and writer, the story is destroyed if subjected to over-the-shoulder glances (like a secular version of Lot's biblical wife). He must remain open to the event, Jake realizes; the spontaneous dance of personal and public history should neither be planned nor rehearsed.

In short, King's anti-Historians aim to detach themselves from the "power and institution-strewn terrain of [H]istory" (Rodgers 250). They accept a circumscribed position of general unimportance when, deprived of linear as well as cyclical imagination, they no longer aspire to transform the world and embrace instead a "living, unarmored history" (*11/22/63* 56–7). As a text speculating on the assassination of Kennedy, *11/22/63* likewise focuses to a surprising degree upon the *dangers* of trying to shape History. It routinely presents figures that proclaim a (faulty) sense of omnipotence: J.F. K. believing himself to be immortal; Jake comparing himself to the excessively confident presidential candidate Hilary Clinton; a politician claiming that he alone can predict the future (132, 485). Therefore, *11/22/63* defines an alternative sense of history in which a series of ruptures eviscerate over-confidence wherever it appears: "We never know which lives we influence, or when, or why." Only absurdists alter the course of history, and only then by accident (454, 700).

As our conclusion considers in greater length, King's anti-Historicism will seem melancholy to some readers because his protagonists give up holding onto the past, rejecting the German concept of *Sehnsucht*: a longing for unity that no longer exists and cannot be recaptured. Jake goes so far as to write anonymously and bury his text (which becomes the actual manuscript of *11/22/63*). Jake—who purportedly does not consider who will read his book, or when, or to what effect—considers himself to be an "ordinary little guy," now writing without ambition (826). There is something terribly sad about how his final mode of writing abdicates heroism (or, more to the point, how it divorces the ideal of heroism from social responsibility). Perry Anderson summarizes a morose, "post-historical" society: "Daring ideals, high sacrifices, heroic strivings will pass away, amidst the humdrum routines … The cry of the owl is mournful at night" (283). Neither reflective nor forward-thinking, King's "heroes" retreat into self-indulgence, waiting (passively) for the arrival of the next event. The one thing that Jake cannot imagine at novel's close is a better tomorrow: "I was just one more cell in the bloodstream of Transit America … there was no triumph or wonder in the idea" (783). Although hardly unproblematic, King's view of history (with a lower-case "h") does try to shake its reader loose from the self-enclosures of a claustrophobic, violent History examined in our previous chapters. From one perspective, at least King's recent troop of anti-Historicists attempt (however marginally) to escape from the entropic cycles depicted in both *The Shining* and *Pet Sematary*.

Lisey's Story (2006) remains perhaps the most sustained consideration of an anti-Historian among King's post-9/11 works. This claim may surprise readers because, on the surface, the text makes few overt references to the attacks of September 11. In one pregnant exception, a character comments that George W. Bush sports a "God-complex," a stray observation that highlights an ineffective return to History offered by the Bush regime in the aftermath of the event (*Lisey* 518). Yet *Lisey's Story* rehearses a recognizable pattern for readers living in the first decade of the twenty-first century: a tragic, unforeseeable attack (on her husband) leads to Lisey's reconsideration of her own floundering historical consciousness. Unable to move on from her husband's sudden murder, her past and present have joined in an endless loop, and so Lisey must find some alternative model that will allow her to decamp from her corrosive enclosure. Like *Under the Dome*, *Cell*, and *11/22/63*, *Lisey's Story* follows a burgeoning anti-Historian as she revises the detective formula. When Lisey combs through artifacts associated with the attack in search of answers, she learns that the past cannot—indeed, *must not*—be pieced together in the name of catharsis, nor in the hope of mastery. Like the other novels considered in this chapter, *Lisey's Story* charts a different path forward in which the protagonist remains open to singular events, interruptions in the stream of her life that will alter its course "on a dime." Moving one step further, the novel also addresses important questions surrounding memory—specifically, what is it that we are to do with our recollection of horrific events from private and public histories? In short, *Lisey's Story* claims that "vacant, maddening gaps" must not only be welcomed in the road ahead; we must also embrace holes in our memories rather than attempting to plug them up with one more clipping for the scrapbook, or one more anecdote from World War II to "complete" the puzzle (478).

Lisey's Story celebrates a more porous present to pave the way for a truly eventful future. Lisey evades the endless spiral of History by casting off her presumed capacity to create greater order from the chaos of her life. That is, on the stage of her own history, she improvises instead of following a pre-determined choreography. She pursues moments of transcendence in which she is uninhibited by the concerns of what lies behind or ahead of her: "This is now" (284). Early in the novel, Lisey recognizes that because her effort to act as an amateur detective, and to make sense of her troubled past, merges with her need to plot the future, she has been seeking an impossible resolution. "Understanding is vastly overrated," she admits. "Nobody ever gets enough safety" (27). Her attempts at mastery may be comforting, but they are never quite what they seem to be. In truth, she (unconsciously) returns to "vacant, maddening gaps" to keep the desire for her lost love alive.

Echoing the "queer" death drive that we discussed in the previous chapter, Lisey's relationship with history resembles self-cutting (a tendency that runs in her family). She returns to her traumatic past like a tongue that "keeps returning to the surface of a badly chipped tooth" (79). *Lisey's Story* charts a tortured dynamic in which the individual wishes to return to the past yet obscures the memory to provoke further desire, which is to say, *to keep living*. Just as the detective needs a mystery to stay busy—to maintain a sense of purpose—Lisey must restore gaps in her knowledge of the past as well as future in order to sustain herself. King likens memory and foresight to metabolism when life in the present leaves Lisey famished, positively "starving," or when Lisey enters into the world of memory to gorge herself until she is "more than sated for one day" (530, 68). In King's multiverse, to desire to know what happened before, or what will happen next, appears to be an acute hunger. But historical knowledge never genuinely satisfies her because she must forget if she is to remain hungry—if she is to keep her physical and psychical processes churning along and avoid absolute stasis (rendered glaringly visible in Jack's frozen face at the close of Kubrick's film adaptation of *The Shining*). *Lisey's Story* illustrates how the historian-detective does not want to close the case because, without more clues, without "vacant, maddening gaps" in her timeline, she would cease to function as a purpose-driven human being.

Lisey reveals the complex inner life of an anti-Historian living through the aftermath of 9/11. When she unearths her wedding invitation, she feels "the curiosity of an archaeologist and the ache of a lover," a unique combination of scientific detachment and intimate longing (217). Just as archaeologists and lovers feed off of unrequited yearning for buried relics, the anti-Historian thrives upon a lack of understanding. In this way, King reverses common assumptions about what Historian-detectives do. Initially, for Lisey, "remembering was like coming home." As she continues to grapple with the memory of her deceased husband, however, she realizes that it is her *exit* from the proverbial Memory Lane that she actually associates with "going home" (436, 455). Perversely enough, she begins to suspect that she has been forgetting "on purpose"—a recognition that would confound King's obedient custodians of American History, condemned as they are to remember everything (96). In sum, *Lisey's Story* eludes the doomed cycles of King's earlier works by charting a very different path (or, perhaps, pursuing an alternative path that has been there all along).

Like *11/22/63*, *Lisey's Story* contemplates the anti-Historian by reconfiguring the relationship between readers and text. Lisey's husband was a novelist (one of his recent works is appropriately entitled *Relic*), and so she delves into his prose to try and piece together what has been lost. The written word entices Lisey like a scavenger hunt, luring her into a detective game in which she at first believes that she can completely recover her past. Yet her husband's books are only ever tantalizing clues to an unsolvable riddle. Their greatest strength is what they *cannot* tell Lisey, what they gesture at but never manage to reveal to her fully. The text serves as what Lisey's husband calls a "bool": an exercise designed to keep the person distracted from the grim reality of her life. Historian-detectives fall into the trap of imagining a cathartic conclusion to the game (a triumphant mastery of the other person's secrets, their most precious silences), whereas the anti-Historian realizes how crucial it is to resign herself to the unknowable. Louis Creed in *Pet Sematary* violates the border between life and death, past and present, without ever gaining insight into the valuable lesson that Lisey learns. *Lisey's Story* thus responds to the traumatic memories of 9/11 by defying Bush's "God complex" in favor of a chastened way of reading America's painful recent history (one that refuses to solidify an idyllic past or colonize a predictable future). Lisey, in a word, accepts the ambiguous status of the postmodern condition against which King's early protagonists so stridently rail.

A New Kind of Detective

Long ago King proved himself capable of serious and profound art whose terror, like that of Edgar Allan Poe's, "is not of Germany, but of the soul," and whose Gothic preoccupations enabled him to penetrate to the corruption that lurks beneath the American Oversoul. His earliest fiction tended to reflect contemporary American History on an epic scale: the individual caught up in the vast swirl of biological determinism (the Bachman books) or the onus of oppression and destiny (*The Shining* and *The Stand*). King's more recent, post-9/11 fiction inverts this perspective: American history with a lower-case "h" is discerned from the subjective orientation of the individual protagonist experiencing it. History and destiny are still important concepts in his post-9/11 novels, but these topics are defined in terms more relevant to each individual protagonist, and they are more random and less comprehensible. While Jack Torrance and the characters in *The Stand* are, to a large extent, swept up in the machinations of History, by forces that are essentially out of their control, King's insertion of the figure of the anti–Historian/detective (and characters who resemble detectives, such as Lisey and college student Devin Jones in *Joyland* [2013]), pose different solutions to the highly personalized chaos that they confront.

A core concept at work in King's post-9/11 corpus, then, is the omnipresence of the gothic-detective tale. Even novels such as *Cell* and *Under the Dome* owe something to the genre, as seeking an explanation for the zombie apocalypse and the presence of the dome itself propels each respective narrative, despite the absence of a formal detective per se. King has always been an avid reader of hard-boiled detective fiction; Ed McBain and John MacDonald remain writers that he has praised publicly and often claims to reread. In the three novels that represent the Bill Hodges trilogy (*Mr. Mercedes*, *Finders Keepers*, and *End of Watch*), however, readers find not only a retired detective whose "hard-boiled" skills are recalled and put to effective use, but also a man who confirms the moral value system established by the many working-class heroes and heroines who precede him in the King canon. But unlike many of these earlier, more obviously resolute protagonists—e.g., Stu Redman (*Stand*), Paul Sheldon (*Misery*), Dolores Claiborne, Mike Anderson (*Storm of the Century*), even another law officer, Alan Pangborn (*Dark Half* and *Needful Things*) —Hodges's personal malaise borders always on despair. Hodges is a somber version of the post-9/11 King anti-Historian: an admixture of hard-boiled detective and post-9/11 American male under duress. Like Lisey, who learns that her traumatic emptiness will never be filled, or the protagonists in *Cell*, who make progress only after accepting that they must maneuver in an abyss of uncertainty and randomness, King's new millennial detective comprehends that he operates in a broken and volatile world. In his discussion of *Cell*, Patrick McAleer argues that "the characters redirect their efforts from attempting to understand The Pulse and its catastrophic effects on the general population and instead focus on surviving by resisting and even destroying those who have been transformed" (180). Although traumatized and vulnerable, Hodges and his *ka-tet* likewise work within the limited conditions in which they find themselves. One could argue that they proceed from a perspective similar to Poe's Dupin in "The Murders in the Rue Morgue," wherein the detective counters the stale approach to crime solving that has led the Parisian police to a place of frustrated befuddlement. Instead of relying on crime-solving that has been effective in the past, "what has occurred" before, Dupin insists that the better approach is to adapt to the circumstances specific to the particular crime at hand, "what has occurred that has never occurred before" ("Murders" 414). This parallels the point of view available to King's post-9/11 anti-Historians: how to move forward under conditions that have never occurred before. On the other hand, unlike Poe's Dupin or Doyle's Sherlock Holmes, whose omniscience is vastly superior to all the other adults in the room, Hodges is driven by failure and the bare instinct to survive. If not for the immediate threat provided by Brady Hartsfield's taunting and potential for violence, Hodges might have spent his retirement drunk on his sofa, oblivious to life outside his television set, or worse: given in to his darkest suicidal impulses. Brady awakens Hodges's survival instincts to the point that even after the detective loses his lover, Janey Trelawney, in a car bomb explosion meant to kill Hodges, her death fills him with remorse, yet motivates him beyond despair. Like the post-9/11 protagonists we find in *Cell* and elsewhere in King's canon, Hodges doesn't triumph against overwhelming circumstances so much as he endures and plods on against them.

Poised against Hodges and his *ka-tet* of courageous friends, Holly Gobney and Jerome Robinson, is Brady Hartsfield, perpetrator of the Mercedes Massacre and a homegrown American terrorist. Hartsfield is a shrouded figure of the post-9/11 underground: sexually maladjusted, angry and friendless, master of destructive technologies and explosives, his life is dedicated to plotting revenge, not just on Hodges and his friends, but on the populations of entire cities. Brady is the face of postmodern terrorism, although his *jihad* serves no god nor political cause, which makes his nihilistic fury all the more terrifying. In his novels before the 9/11 event, King's ambassadors of evil—Linoge, Leland Gaunt (*Needful Things*), Barlow—may have been preternaturally gifted, but they also possessed a well-wrought design centered around a clear and future agenda: "Just give me what I want and then I'll go away," Linoge reminds us throughout *Storm of the Century*. Hartsfield's evil is more akin to the Crimson King's in *The Dark*

146 *Stephen King's Evolving Sense of History*

Tower: he, too, wishes to take down the Beams of History—a suicide not by cop, but via mass annihilation (once again, we might position King's arch villain Randall Flagg on similar lines, "queering" the rigid worldview of the dutiful Historian). The novels in the Hodges trilogy contain a pessimism characteristic of post-9/11 horror. However, unlike post-9/11 horror films such as *28 Days Later, Cabin in the Woods,* and the many examples of "torture porn," Hodges also resembles at least to some degree Roland the gunslinger from *The Dark Tower*. They both carry hard-boiled attitudes of masculine toughness, an alacrity towards using violence, and, most of all, a reliance on, and willingness to cooperate with, their respective *ka-tet* (indeed, it is Gobney that ultimately subdues Hartsfield after Hodges suffers a heart attack). Roland and Hodges's unsentimental approaches toward the reality of a post-9/11 world contributes to saving the respective worlds they each inhabit. Rather than recapitulate the underpinnings of History, King's anti-Historians evoke something quite different.

Mr. Mercedes gestures incessantly at Poe's prototypical detective, Dupin—a figure most notable, as we have seen, due to his atypical approach to issues of cause-and-effect. Unlike the hapless police officers with whom he competes, Dupin thinks about events and their consequences in undisciplined ways. Reminiscent of Poe's "The Purloined Letter," King raises the idea that Hodges does not actually want to solve the case, which is to say, he views history (with a lower-case "h") as a series of deferrals—a movement driven less by resolution than by *perpetual dissatisfaction*. Cast in the mold of Lisey, Hodges doesn't want Hartsfield to be caught. "It's the wrong emotion to feel," he acknowledges, but he "feels it nevertheless." King recognizes the value of Poe's seminal story about a letter without any real content that nonetheless preserves secrets and keeps lit a burning desire to pursue the (unattainable) truth. In the spirit of Poe, Hodges requires a gaping absence to give his life a sense of meaning: "It's pissed him off in a good way. It's given him a sense of purpose" (173, 94).

The outlook of Hodges directly contrasts with the violent view of History held by his arch nemesis Hartsfield, who holds that "the only thing that matters is making a statement ... Cutting the skin of the world and leaving a scar. That's all (H)istory is, after all: scar tissue" (323). Whereas Hartsfield wishes to leave his mark on American History through violence and a will to power, through the creation of ever more scars, Hodges reframes history as an open-ended process that moves in ways he could never hope to anticipate. Instead of imposing his own will, Hodges deliberately deprives himself of imagined glory: the potential fullness of being an agent that makes History. Just as he gradually learns to stop eating too many sweets and drinking fewer beers, Hodges removes himself from the entropic cycle that claims the lives of King's earlier protagonists. He embraces his traumatic experiences—the loss of his imaginary "completeness," the end of his childlike slumber—by rejecting social commendations that would otherwise cement his status in the proverbial History book. At the close of the novel, he resists the idea of a "medal hung over his neck." King's hard-boiled detective therefore copes with the power of unforeseeable events not by goring one's name into the scar tissue of History, but by tarrying with wounds that can never completely heal (195, 432).

In closing, the shape of King's canon following September 11 habitually addresses possible alternatives to the disturbing loop of American History depicted in his older narratives. Although one could reasonably argue that the seeds of this different approach have been evolving all along—implied in contradistinction to the likes of Jack, Louis, or Todd—these seeds appear only to find soil and germinate post-9/11. Prior to this unexpected event, King seems content to point (obliquely) at the anti-Historian as a ghostly rejoinder to his flesh-and-blood monsters. After the event, King starts to fill out his sketch and give a distinctive shape to his divergent vision. While hardly above controversy—issues to which we will return in the conclusion to follow—King's anti-Historians map a route into the twenty-first century by imagining a consciousness that might empower readers to keep going, despite the innumerable abject forces that work to confine them. The events that took place on 9/11 changed notions of how American History works. And as we have seen throughout this chapter, King's post-millennium protagonists reflect the same vulnerability that have become part of the American psyche after the 9/11 attacks. At the same time, survivors in these books are reminders that to some extent the individual can encounter history on different grounds, as a figure still capable of making moral choices (regardless of how curtailed these choices have become). "Survival," as McAleer posits, "depends upon the choice to be decent and utilize a sense of rationality that often escapes people trapped within irrational predicaments" (McAleer 183).[3] Better equipped to handle the traumatic past (and future), King bolsters his anti-Historians by transforming their blind spots into sources of strength for the difficult days that lie ahead.

Notes

1 "The Langoliers" uses "fresh" and "new" to likewise characterize its post-apocalyptic society: "new people" arrive after the event to populate an "unmarked" world (70, 233–4).
2 Slavoj Žižek describes: "This is an event at its purest and most minimal: something shocking, out of joint, that appears to happen all of a sudden and interrupts the usual flow of things" (*Event* 2).
3 As King argues throughout his fiction, both prior to- and post-9/11, "If the horror story is our rehearsal for death, then its strict moralities make it also a reaffirmation of life and good will and simple imagination—just one more pipeline to the infinite" (*Danse* 380).

Conclusion
The Inconstant Reader

When we situate the works of Stephen King within the sweep of their sixty-year context, we begin to understand his resistance to earlier framings of American History. Specifically, these texts are essential byproducts of the 1970s, a decade that looms large in King's imagination because it saw a number of grand Histories crumble and fall, including the History of America's military-industrial complex (via Vietnam) and the History of America's Great Society (through the impact of stagflation). The nation's metanarratives about where it has been—and where it is going—have had a difficult time sustaining themselves in the wake of these turning tides. A part of its unique moment, King's corpus proposes an alternative consciousness with which readers could (presumably) loosen the stranglehold of History.

King plays an important role in exposing the gaps within American History as it metastasizes, which is to say, as it perpetuates itself in ways that prove damaging to the body politic. We have seen through the preceding chapters how the toxic tendencies of American History—heteronormative machismo, jingoism, corporate greed—drive the national narrative in a Gothic loop that is fueled by bloodshed and social fragmentation. King's stories respond by recognizing the merits of history with a lower-case "h": local perspectives that never claim mastery over the vast machinations of social development. When we Vietnamize King, for instance, we recognize that the writer comprehends that a healthy dose of humility and honesty would have concluded that tragic conflict much sooner and as a consequence might have produced a less disillusioned post-war outcome. Similarly, the ghosts of the Overlook Hotel cling to a rigid hierarchy that still exists long after the edifice of their hauntings has gone up in smoke. In conversation with the decade of the 1970s in which King found his footing, this shift in focus makes a good deal of sense, and it helps us to understand King's wide-scale attacks upon antiquated Histories and Historians.

King's warning that the existence of the tradition of the American pastoral vision has become ever more precarious from the mid-1980s and beyond remains remarkably terrifying, consistent, and prescient. The fictionalized portrait of America found in *The Stand, The Talisman,* the Bachman books, and *The Dark Tower* series, for example, is that of a landscape slowly poisoning itself via potent chemical pollutants, lethal technologies, and a corporate mandate that blatantly defies EPA guidelines. American cities and suburbs in his mid-1980 novels reveal the destruction of the pastoral to the point where characters cannot find wholeness; only in parallel medieval and mythic universes—the Territories in the *Talisman*, Mid-World in *The Dark Tower*, and the American Fifties found in *11/22/63*, for example—is it possible to recapture what a detoxified America used to smell and taste like, and where a measure of psychic unity remains available. However, even these oases prove to be endangered spaces, as the polluted world of postmodern America, like the very progress of civilization itself, is expanding outward to the point where global climate change—viewed as a fantastical threat in the era of the 1980s—has emerged as part of the implacable advance of History. These novels, including several of the Bachman books also published during this period, must be read as journey quests where cancer not only lurks at the periphery of the expedition (e.g., the illness of Jack Sawyer's mother, Lily Cavanaugh, that precipitates *The Talisman*), but expands to become the single operating metaphor for a quest to save the earth. The cancer that metastases all through the King universe of the Seventies and Eighties is the result of both the physical consequence of the polluted landscape his characters must trudge across as well as the symbol of a morally corrupt society. As their contact with greater levels of social and environmental degradation grows, King's characters' connection to the mystery and magic of a diminished technological world becomes more desperate and necessary. Trashcan Man in *The Stand* represents the nihilism of King's postmodern view of America, especially as it is articulated in his novels from the Seventies and early Eighties. He is Randall Flagg's id: containing the same nihilistic impulse that seeks to resurrect the omnipresent lethal military hardware still available; indeed, the exact impulse that turns out to be responsible for the invention of the super flu itself and the near extinction of the human race. And King's vision in books such as *The Talisman* and *The Dark Tower* posits that if the American waste land is to be renewed, that is, if America is to be saved from the entropic cycle of its History, it will take the world-view of a poet or fantasist to do so. This perspective may not be as impractical as it appears; the very survival of the planet may well depend upon just how seriously we are willing to pursue such a radical re-orientation.

From the start, King's novels inherited a world engaged in self-destruction, a reality that since the end of the two world wars has fallen apart at the center (as poet W.B. Yeats claimed looking back at the time of the Victorians). The state of America, beginning with early King's perspective grappling with a post-Vietnam malaise to the status of the things in the new millennium, hasn't appreciably changed. It remains shapeless and rough, even more capable of destroying itself from within than the likelihood of an organized military or terrorist threat from without. As far back as an interview with *Rolling Stone* in 1980, King placed his work in a specific milieu "I maintain that my novels, taken together, form an allegory of a nation that feels it's in a crunch and things are out of control. We're in that situation now ... How do we cope? What do we do?" (rpt. Underwood 94). Not much has transformed the King universe since this interview. The supernatural phenomena manifest throughout his canon are hardly terrifying when compared to his consistently paranoid portrait of "a nation that [is] out of control."

However, because King certainly did not stop writing in the 1970s (and Americans certainly did not stop reading his works), we must question the manner in which he continues to breakdown our dominant Historical narratives. Because of late we have entered into a veritable King renaissance, where many of his older texts are being revisited with fresh eyes, especially in new cinematic adaptations, it behooves us to inquire into the apparent inability of his fictionalized universe to alter (however modestly) the impetus of American History. What, if anything, does his approach have to teach audiences today? Should we, like King, perpetually dismantle History with a capital "H"—or is there a limit to this mentality? If historical frameworks change as material and immaterial conditions alter, what are we to do with King's remarkable consistency of vision? In short, since current readers face a set of different challenges than the Constant Reader that he addressed at the start of his career (his readership might therefore be more appropriately described as Inconstant), King's confrontation with American History stands in need of urgent reevaluation. As a fiction writer responding to his unique era in history, King has always created topical fiction relevant to his moment in time. *Cell* is obviously an example of a book he could not have authored at the beginning of his literary career. And one might make the same argument about the rest of his writing that follows 9/11. Yet there remains throughout these decades a consistency to his multiverse—the residue of a post-Vietnam disruption in the pastoral poised contrarily against King's resolute commitment to hope in a positive future. These binaries are hard to articulate, but worth brooding on. And they may serve as the most trenchant explanation for why King felt the need to invent the apocalyptic pessimist Ricard Bachman as a pseudonym.

It is difficult to separate King's habitual chastening of his reader from the command of the 1980s (and beyond) that readers must resign themselves to an increasingly precarious financial marketplace. Over the past fifty years, Americans have witnessed a dramatic overhaul of their society in which they can no longer depend upon mid-century social safety nets. Conditions force them to prostrate themselves before a mercurial financial system (e.g., the steady convergence of retirement savings into stock portfolios). Guy Standing describes the new American as a member of "the precariat": a group that teeters always on the brink of ruin, ready to lose everything at a moment's notice.[1] Rather than anticipate an economy that assists members in achieving their objectives, the precariat bows down to the capricious whims of Adam Smith's "invisible hand." As a result, unlike his initial audience, King's contemporary readers are less concerned with being drafted, or running up against an excessively bureaucratic state, than they are anxious about having to work for driving services like Uber or Lyft on evenings and weekends to make ends meet or a planet that is on the verge of extinction.

Moreover, King's routine attack upon authoritarians—an attack that was keenly felt in the era of *The Shining* and *Pet Sematary*—has disparate connotations in an age of advanced social media platforms in which users are denied purchase in anything that could justifiably be called the Truth. In an era defined by the spread of "fake news" and elaborate gaslighting strategies, the pressing issue is not so much that mindless citizens buy into the delusions of a well-defined military-industrial complex than that citizen-consumers find it harder to organize a glut of information in a manner that could give assurance to their lives. It's not that authoritarians have disappeared, of course—it's that authoritarianism now arrives in very different packaging. By dismantling our shared capacity to weigh causes and consequences (the very work of history as a discipline), social media fuels an extreme form of anti-Historicism—a denial of the grand narrative of American History that has reached such a fever pitch that we often feel unable to rely on a mutually-determined reality, thereby opening the door for renewed authoritarian abuse. When King condemns the attempt at mastery made by established Historians, his condemnation at least partially lends credence to the hyper-fragmented world of Twitter. Inconstant Readers of King's literary and cinematic texts therefore ask if his static approach to the problems of the 1970s may have worn out its general usefulness.

King's failures are not an aberration; they belong to us all. Given the incessant anti-government message of his oeuvre, we could reasonably ask if the military-industrial apparatus has shrunk over the course of his career. And the answer would have to be a resounding no. King's audience has actually seen the steady *expansion* of the federal government. America's martial fervor has altered shape, perhaps, but it has not cooled. It would be an incredibly onerous task in 2020 to track down a group of Americans that would defend King's degraded secret governmental agencies, like the Shop or the Institute, and yet these sorts of entities do endure (often funded, ironically, by the same demagogues who harangue in favor of "smaller government"). King and politicians like Republican Senator Ted Cruz may engage in knock down fights on social media, but Cruz would certainly find no fault in the "Don't tread on me" individualism promulgated in either King's novels or their film adaptations. Where, then, has this anti-Historical attitude brought us? If we come to view his rhetoric concerning Big Brother as nothing more than a tempest in a tea cup, what does that realization tell us about our culpability in allowing an elite class to sustain—in fact, to augment—their influence over the "regular Joes" that King has ostensibly venerated for nearly half a century?

On a related note, what if there is real value to be found in attempts to piece together the jigsaw puzzle of History, just as there may be merit in efforts to prognosticate upon the future? The push to abandon all efforts at historical logic, or to allow such understanding to be infused with a deconstructive agenda, encourages us to forfeit meaningful control over a shared destiny. While claims of mastery can certainly go too far—we pause to remember Jack Torrance and Louis Creed, transgressors of humanity's most significant limits—a near total absence of mastery relegates King's readers to impotence at the feet of an all-powerful few (similar movers and shakers to those found at the Overlook, the "one percenters" with an even more intimate knowledge of the "invisible hand"). For acutely vulnerable members of the precariat, the dissolution of a collective History since the 1970s has not led to their empowerment; it has led to greater fragility at the hands of forces that are seldom scrutinized, much less comprehended. King's rogue heroes that sever the ties that bind and allow themselves to "float" (figures such as Jake in *11/22/63*, who gives up trying to alter timelines) do not end up any freer as a result. Instead, they drift alone, susceptible to those aggressive actors still privileged enough to go out and make a History that reflects their specific agendas.

Undoubtedly, at the start of King's career, the siege of Fordist and Keynesian bulwarks revealed how a singular American History omitted far too much—the stories of lost soldiers in Vietnam, for instance, or "queer" accounts silenced in order to sustain what Lee Edelman calls "reproductive futurism." But in the years that followed, the declared death of American History by a thousand cuts did not substantively improve conditions for most Americans. While this may have done some important work in advancing issues of *representation*, it did very little to address underlying issues of *redistribution* (the noxious economic machinations that erode American History from within).[2] We now stand alongside King at a significant crossroads. Do we return to History with a capital "H" and risk once more marginalizing the voices of disenfranchised peoples? Or, do we persist in histories with a lower-case "h," forcing humility onto individuals that never had much power to speak of, subjecting them to the will of elites (as the latter builds their preferred metanarrative)? Or is there another way? To address this impasse, let us turn to King's *The Institute* (2019), an anti-Historicist tract that illustrates how his 1970s approach, although partially exhausted, lingers on.

The Institute starts with a motif that King's Constant Readers will immediately recognize: a beleaguered federal bureaucracy, both supremely dangerous *and* utterly impotent. Protagonist Tim attempts to board a plane, only to be thwarted by "functionaries" that muck things up (3). The ineptitude of these functionaries sets the wheels of the narrative in motion by inspiring Tim to take the path less traveled. Indeed, this catalyzing moment establishes the story's central binary between a banal evil (the Institute) and a free, independent wanderer (Tim). King's output habitually revolves around this sort of dichotomy—*Firestarter* (1980) with its oppressive Shop, for instance, or the shadowy government entities of *The Tommyknockers, Hearts in Atlantis, The Regulators,* or *Dreamcatcher* (to name but a few). Described interchangeably as the ineffectual Man in the Gray Coat and a ruthless Nazi, King's bureaucrats are reifying agents of American History, life-long Historians mindlessly maintaining the gears of a pre-determined metanarrative as it unwinds. Although it is meant for readers in 2019, *The Institute* operates in the familiar King lexicon of the 1970s, with its attack in broad strokes upon the military-industrial machinery.

King's portrayal of the titular Institute strikes chords that he has been striking since the dawn of his career. These sentiments are very much a part of the King brand. *The Institute* chastises chief administrator, Mrs. Sigsby, as "the grammar-perfect no-tits" repressed woman, a derogatory smear that manages to be both sexist as well as derisive of Big Brother (66). The Institute supplies bread-and-circus for its prisoners, hooking them on sugar, tobacco, and easy credit in a way that discredits the masses as well as the "Skinner box" in which they are conditioned—recalling for readers King's frequent jabs about heavily-brainwashed populaces in places like Flint City in *The Outsider*, Derry in *IT* and *Insomnia*, or Castle Rock in *Needful Things* (109). King directly states the object of his critique to be an American History that depends upon the absent-minded labor of complicit Historians that have been lured into caretaking a pattern of self-sabotage. "This isn't America; it's the Kingdom of the Institute" (90). Distraught by the "ticky-tacky little houses" of Institute workers (paid for on credit by the Institute), and the grim setting—"It was the very definition of utilitarian, with its concrete floor, curved tile walls, and overhead fluorescents"—King's Constant Readers are meant to reject the bloated Fordist-Keynesian state in favor of "emancipated" individuals that, like Tim or many of King's other heroes, prefers a nomadic life: Barbie in *Under the Dome*; David Drayton in *The Mist* (298). Instead of serving as "another cog in the machine," protagonists of *The Institute* must somehow escape from their brutalist dystopia by cultivating a lifestyle that can be characterized as self-reliant, disembedded, and gloriously precarious (416). As we have already seen, this aspiration makes a good deal of sense in the context of the 1970s. Nevertheless, given its recent publication date, we ought to inquire into the functionality of King's formula for a contemporary audience whose situation has been anything but Constant. After all, hyper-individualism and feelings of instability are less a destination toward which we must turn, and more a distressing condition into which we have perhaps irreparably fallen. The writer's earliest advocacy for independent Americans who eschew the corrupt machinery of society and state appears in 2019 more as a reflection of personal anomie and the collapse of the social institutions that they have tried to avoid.

King's latest answer to the problem of a violent, grinding American History monitored by a phalanx of lackeys is the elevation of a distinctive historical consciousness. As we discussed in the previous chapter concerning the anti-Historians that populate his post-9/11 output, King disassembles the metanarratives of American History that envelop us. *The Institute* upholds this tendency by once again insisting that history with a lower-case "h" shifts gears "on a dime." In King's estimation, history remains a genealogical affair, prone to unexpected mutations—what Alain Badiou calls *events*—that can completely redirect the course of things.[3] For example,

Tim's adventure stems not from the marching orders of a History that has been disseminated by bureaucrats, but from the "single impulse act" that inaugurates his far less predictable state of being (495). *The Institute* repeatedly declares: "Great events turn on small hinges" (9). That is to say, unlike the monolithic mission of total government control—a homogeneous affair in which mastery and absolute power trumps all other concerns—King's novel presents history as a fluid sequence, a counter-hegemony that refuses orderliness and relies upon unanticipated happenings like the resurrection of Christ or the political assassinations of 1968. *Prima facie*, this open-endedness sounds quite lovely. And it resonates well against the backdrop of the Vietnam War, or in service of the disarmament of a reproductive futurism (topics addressed in Chapters 4 and 5, respectively). But, in the present moment, King's obsessive stand against History raises some red flags that we can no longer afford to ignore. For one, his endless negation of America's grand stories may be a sign that the virulent History that once consumed Jack or Louis has not actually been defeated; instead, the malignant undertow may have mutated to continue its macabre work in a different guise.

As an example of this mutation, *The Institute* elevates the power of the internet to forge global connections that defy centralized planning. As the imprisoned children utilize the dark web to gain access to information that they need to escape from their prison, they become information workers within a game that is "not an arm's race but a *mind* race" (117; author's emphasis). The text's protégé, Luke, seizes upon the raw *potenza* of the digital highway to rally his friends and defeat his oppressors: "Mutiny—or revolution … was like a virus, especially in the Information Age. It *could* spread" (487; author's emphasis). Yet Luke's touted globalism—his ability to do many different things rather than specialize; his willingness to reach across borders to network with fellow victims—offers a call to action that, in truth, only affirms the status quo. In a contemporary context, the novel's assumption that we need more digital interaction to facilitate the sharing of individual histories remains deeply anachronistic. After all, King's Inconstant Readers will be well acquainted in 2020 with the dynamic freeways of cyberspace. Furthermore, it can be argued that our ever-growing access to information, and the vast "treasure troves" of an interconnected world, have in truth *extended* the logic of the abhorrent History that once plagued sites such as the Overlook Hotel. Although King's idealized digital highway appears to serve as an emblem of modern progress, of the fast and fluid movements of the anti-Historian (similar to Route 15, the rural road that claims so many lives in *Pet Sematary*), the electronic byway proves to be *just as deadly as the older road*. Both highways remain rooted to the patterns of an intemperate History from which they have presumably detoured. As Luke's romanticized excursions onto the Internet rewire his brain in "productive" ways, King's readers cannot isolate the digital from the military-industrial apparatus of the internet's origins. For all of its ballyhooed connectivity, the web entrenches us within an elaborate matrix of value extraction. Jodi Dean illuminates how participation on the internet, instead of providing a cure, winds up making us sicker. Said another way, the internet hardly treats the addictions peddled by the Institute—in contrast, it becomes a new addiction, a different crutch upon which we must depend. Driven to make commercial/financial exchange speedier, the internet disguises what it truly is (an economic tool) under the façade of a resource for "social improvement." In particular, cyberspace fosters an illusion of unity to bolster financial interactions without genuinely enhancing democratic participation, or attending to demands made by the thoroughly disenfranchised (Dean 532). In other words, the internet has not empowered slaves of History like Jack or Louis; it has instead fostered even more potent delusions of mastery by generating "news silos." Given the veneer of the postmodern interface, Luke's competence in the digital sphere may not look a lot like Jack's scrapbook, or Todd Bowden's jigsaw puzzle in the film adaptation of *Apt Pupil*. But these images can be deceiving. In actuality, hyper-connectivity has kept History with a capital "H" on life support due to its obfuscation of the unsavory mechanisms that propel us forward. Under a spell, swept away by the universal command that we must all become technologically literate in order to survive in the contemporary global sphere, we have not become any less violent, more intimate, or any wiser as a result of our merging into cyber traffic. Quite the opposite is true, since electronic connectivity has ironically made us even more isolated, not less, a result of our heads being eternally bowed in silent supplication to the iPhone gods of social media and the digital universe. The internet has brought us closer to, not further away from, a place that resembles the group think of texts such as *Needful Things, Storm of the Century*, and *Cell*. It serves as a forum where individuals no longer express their individuality so much as they are bombarded by the advertisements of consumer capitalism to craft and manipulate a marketable image of themselves—less a marketplace of ideas than a sophisticated version of television's daily dose of social conformity and mercantile desirability. So why does King's recent work persist in lionizing the internet's democratic potential?

The hodge-podge sensibilities of the dark web extend out into the rest of *The Institute* in a fashion that seemingly champions a historical consciousness driven by dynamic innovation. Early in the novel, Tim admits that the economy is now precarious, and that he and many others are being forced to work multiples jobs "to make ends meet" (18). This recognition does not elicit sympathy or outrage; it encourages us to embrace (or at least, resign ourselves to) a "jack of all trades" mentality. Because Tim drifts freely between jobs, he situates himself to evade the gaze of the ever-watchful Institute; because Luke does not specialize in any single discipline, he alone can outrun the disciplinary clutches of his captors. Are King's Inconstant Readers to believe, then, that a gig economy could resolve their unhappiness? We might picture one of his hypothetical Readers, trying to read a few pages of King's novel before her day job ends and her Uber shift begins. How is King's romanticized precariousness helpful to the precariat, a class that has been blindsided by unstable macroeconomic arrangements? His latest entry into the field of anti-Historicism—replete with characters that blindly accept conditions of volatility and adaptability—cannot be classified as "countercultural" in earnest unless we calcify the text within a 1970s setting (and ignore everything that has happened since).

Today, King's diatribes against American History contribute to a fragile social order by resigning readers to their atomized and exceedingly vulnerable social status. *The Institute* reflects King's rigid reliance on his long-standing hyper-individualism as a cure-all for the oppressive weight of History, as when the novel allows characters to conceive of themselves as "a stock with good growth potential," or when it stumbles upon a "revelation: what you did for yourself was what gave you the power" (50, 390). As a result, the novel dismantles the metanarrative of American History in parallel with its dismantlement of collectivism as a whole (including the collectivism of public bureaucracies as well as private monopolies). Freed from expectations born of History, which is to say, liberated from any debt to the past or any sense of responsibility to the future, King's contemporary nomads experience everything in the short-term. Like an opportunistic investor, the nomad accepts each opportunity as it comes, with little reflection upon how investors used to behave and little energy exerted to forecast the next boom or bust. King's nomad finds efforts at social engineering to be foolish because (the story goes) she could never fully anticipate the consequences of her actions by hunting for historical analogies. That kind of connection is left for the "invisible hand" of the market to sort out because the "small hinges" of history are simply too miniscule for mere mortals to calculate. If readers come to understand history with a lower-case "h" as open-ended and thoroughly privatized, they are habituated into a mode of production as well as consumption that has become all too common. King's fiction and its cinematic adaptations continue, anachronistically, to counter Nixon with Reagan—as though this "choice" is still a pressing one in 2020, as though this black-and-white caricature is anything more than a pantomimed struggle meant to hide the fact that the winners (disciples of Reagan) have been standing at the helm for nearly the duration of King's lengthy literary career.

Channeling the libertarian fervor of Reagan, the final scene of *The Institute* reveals that the Institute obeys the cannibalistic forces of History by harnessing precognitive children as a type of fuel—transforming "our future" (the Child) into petrol to sustain an unpalatable status quo (King explores this theme in *Doctor Sleep* as well). The authoritarian potency of the Overlook and the Micmac cemetery seems to endure as a time-tested trope against which King continues to rally. Managerial to a fault, the Institute looks to control the world of tomorrow by trampling on spontaneity—on happy accidents—to dictate what will come next. Predictably, these ruthless efforts to forecast the future remain futile in King's multiverse, and the Institute collapses after the children successfully revolt against it. The future will not be legislated, King's prisoners insist. "Anything can happen to turn people and the events they're part of in a different direction" (547). Symptomatic of the alternative historical consciousness that manifests in King's post-9/11 work, *The Institute* compels its readers to cave to the logic of unforeseen events and, subsequently, to move in different directions should a particular situation demand it. But what King's text presents as common-sensical—for readers to be flexible instead of recalcitrant—is not quite so easy to accept out of hand, given the precarious nature of American life in the present. Without a shared sense of what came before us, how can we hope to avoid the pitfalls of previous generations? And, with even greater exigency, if we forfeit attempts to plan for the future, which disenfranchised groups will be abandoned and exposed to the vagaries of fortune? (Again, the absence of planning is, in itself, a plan—one designed to benefit a select segment of society.) To understand why these questions are pertinent, we might return to the looming crisis of climate change: the accountability failure for decisions made in the past, and the unyielding rejection of calls to plan for tomorrow, speaks volumes on the dangers of a chorus of anti-Historians that has grown deafening. To respond, King's Inconstant Readers must confront their inconstancy and consider to what extent a relatively coherent notion of American History could prove, in the end, to be vital.

As this book has argued, King's treatment of American History, in parallel with American discourse generally, has evolved over the last sixty years from the dystopian cycles of *The Stand* to the supposedly fluid histories of *The Institute*. Throughout its evolution, King's corpus retains traces of what a monolithic History cannot erase: the bodies of soldiers buried in the name of "progress"; the voices of Vietnamese rebels, muted by an imperial apparatus; a "queerness" that challenges the familiar imperative to reproduce a dying way of life. Although King's preferred model of striking down History fails to generate a genuinely divergent path, and the author succumbs—perhaps inevitably—to the terms and conditions of his unique ideological moment, we might yet train our eyes upon a renewed History in order to approximate common ground as well as a shared purpose. Salvageable from the outermost margins of King's waste lands, this renewed History avoids the errors of days gone by. It could be far more inclusive and more resistant to the corrosion of excessive greed and violence. It could be a History informed by an ethics of the Other: a History shaped by Carol's committed empathy (*Hearts of Atlantis*), by a desire to be worthy of our most innocent admirers (*Dreamcatcher*), and by blind spots—made present to us through our relationships with Others—that invite us to be gracious, humble, and even, on occasion, discrete. These ambitions are all signatures of King's ongoing critique of History, yet they are too infrequent and cryptic to be legible to his mass audience. In sum, we Inconstant Readers of Stephen King should treat American History as something much more than a burdensome weight cast off by atomized individuals. Only with such a shift in perspective might we start the hard work of imagining, in conversation with King's better angels, a better tomorrow.

Notes

1 As Standing writes, "A flexible labour market that makes labour mobility the mainstream way of life, and that creates a web of moral and immoral hazards in the flurry of rules to determine benefit entitlement, forces the precariat into using time in ways that are bound to leave people enervated" (141).
2 For more on this distinction, see Nancy Fraser and Axel Honneth, *Redistribution or Recognition?: A Political-Philosophical Exchange.*
3 Franco "Bifo" Berardi states, "The present does not contain the future as a linear development ... every event is untimely, as the event does not correspond to a chain of causation" (14–5).

Works Cited

Alien. Dir. Ridley Scott. Screenplay by Dan O'Bannon and Ronald Shusett. Twentieth Century Fox, 1979. DVD.
Anderson, Perry. *A Zone of Engagement*. London, UK: Verso, 1992. Print.
Apocalypse Now. Dir. Francis Ford Coppola. Screenplay by John Millus and Francis Ford Coppola. Zoetrope Studios, 1979. DVD.
Apt Pupil. Dir. Bryan Singer. Screenplay by Brandon Boyce. Tristar Pictures, 1998. DVD.
Bachman, Richard. *Thinner*. NY: New American Library, 1984. Print.
Badiou, Alain. *Philosophy and the Event*. Trans. Louise Burchill. Cambridge, UK: Polity Press, 2013. Print.
Barthes, Roland. *The Rustle of Language*. Trans. Richard Howard. NY: Hill and Wang, 1989. Print.
Bartók, Béla. *Music for Strings, Percussion, and Celesta*. 1936. Berlin: Deutsche Grammophon, 2016. CD.
Berardi, Franco "Bifo." *Futurability: The Age of Impotence and the Horizon of Possibility*. NY: Verso, 2017. Print.
Biddle, Arthur W. "The Mythic Journey in *The Body*," in *The Dark Descent: Essays Defining Stephen King's Horrorscape*. Ed. Tony Magistrale. Westport, CT: Greenwood Press, 1992. 83–98. Print.
Blackmore, Bill. "Kubrick's 'Shining' Secret: Film's Hidden Horror is the Murder of the Indian." *Washington Post*, 12 July1987. https://www.washingtonpost.com/archive/lifestyle/style/1987/07/12/kubricks-shining-secret/a7e3433d-e92e-4171-b46f-77817f1743f0/ Web. 11 May 2019.
Blake, Linnie, and Agnieszka Soltysik Monnet. "Introduction: Neoliberal Gothic," in *Neoliberal Gothic: International Gothic in the Neoliberal Age*. Eds. Linnie Blake and Agnieszka Monnet. Manchester, UK: Manchester UP, 2017. 1–18. Print.
Blouin, Michael. *Stephen King and American Politics*. Cardiff, UK: Wales UP, forthcoming.
Bright, Suzie. *Sexwise*. Pittsburgh, PA: Cleis Press, 1995. Print.
Brooke, Rupert. *1914 and Other Poems*. London, UK: Sidgwick and Jackson, 1919. Print.
Brown, Simon. *Screening Stephen King: Adaption and the Horror Genre in Film and Television*. Austin, TX: Texas UP, 2018. Print.
Brown, Wendy. *Politics Out of History*. Princeton, NJ: Princeton UP, 2001. Print.
Browning, Mark. *Stephen King on the Big Screen*. Chicago, IL: Intellect Books, 2009. Print.

Works Cited

Bryant, William Cullen. "Mutation," in *Nineteenth-Century American Poetry*. Ed. William Spengemann. NY: Penguin, 1996. 13–14. Print.

Bryant, William Cullen. "Thanatopsis," in *Nineteenth-Century American Poetry*. Ed. William Spengemann. NY: Penguin, 1996. 10–12. Print.

Buell, Lawrence. *Literary Transcendentalism: Style and Vision in the American Renaissance*. Ithaca, NY: Cornell UP, 1974. Print.

Cabin in the Woods. Dir. Drew Goddard. Screenplay by Joss Whedon and Drew Goddard. Lionsgate, MGM, 2012. DVD.

Callinicos, Alex. *Against Postmodernism: A Marxist Critique*. Cambridge, UK: Polity, 1989. Print.

Campbell, Joseph. *The Hero with a Thousand Faces*. Princeton, NJ: Princeton UP, 1949. Print.

Cat People. Dir. Jacques Tourneur. Screenplay by DeWitt Bodeen. RKO Radio Pictures, 1942. DVD.

Children of Men. Dir. Alfonso Cuarón. Screenplay by Alfonso Cuarón and Timothy Sexton. Universal Pictures, 2006. DVD.

Ciment, Michael. "Interview with Stanley Kubrick," in *The Shining: Studies in the Horror Film*. Ed. Daniel Olson. Lakewood, CO: Centipede Press, 2015. 473–502. Print.

Clark, J.M. "Apt Pupil." *Magill Cinema Annual*. Englewood Cliffs, NJ: Salem, 1989. Print.

A Clockwork Orange. Dir. Stanley Kubrick. Screenplay by Stanley Kubrick. Columbia Pictures/Warner Brothers, 1971. DVD.

Cocks, Geoffrey. *The Wolf at the Door: Stanley Kubrick, History, & the Holocaust*. NY: Peter Lang, 2004. Print.

Collings, Michael. *The Stephen King Phenomenon*. Mercer Island, WA: Starmont House, 1987. Print.

Colombo, John Robert, Ed. *Windigo: An Anthology of Fact and Fantastic Fiction*. Saskatoon, SK: Western Producer Prairie Books, 1982. Print.

Conrad, Joseph. *Heart of Darkness*. 1899. NY: Global Classics, 2014. Print.

Crain, Caleb. "There but for Fortune." Rev. of *Hearts in Atlantis*, by Stephen King. *New York Times*, 12 Sept. 1999. http://movies2.nytimes.com/books/99/09/12/reviews/990912.12craint.html. Web. 16 Sept. 2019.

The Dead Zone. Dir. David Cronenberg. Screenplay by Jeffrey Boam. Dino De Laurentiis Corp., Paramount Pictures, 1983. DVD.

The Dead Zone. Creators Michael Piller and Shawn Piller. Various Directors and Writers. CBS Paramount Network Television, 2002–2007. DVD.

Dean, Jodi. "The Net and Multiple Realities," in *The Cultural Studies Reader*. 3rd ed. Ed. Simon During. NY: Routledge, 2007. 520–535. Print.

DeLamar, John. *The Closet and the Clown: Same-Sex Desire as Contagion in Stephen King's IT*. MS. English MA Thesis. Burlington, VT: University of Vermont, 2013. Print.

Dickerson, Mary Jane. "Stephen King Reading William Faulkner: Memory, Desire, and Time in the Making of IT," in *The Dark Descent: Essays Defining Stephen King's Horrorscape*. Ed. Tony Magistrale. Westport, CT: Greenwood Press, 1992. 171–186. Print.

Dr. Strangelove, or How I Learned to Stop Worrying and Love the Bomb. Dir. Stanley Kubrick. Screenplay by Stanley Kubrick. Hawk Films/Columbia Pictures, 1963. DVD.

Dryden, Edgar. *Melville's Thematics of Form: The Great Art of Telling the Truth.* Baltimore, MD: Johns Hopkins UP, 1968. Print.
Eagleton, Terry. *The Illusions of Postmodernism.* Hoboken, NJ: John Wiley & Sons, 2013. Print.
Edelman, Lee. *No Future: Queer Theory and the Death Drive.* Durham, NC: Duke UP, 2004. Print.
Eigner, Edwin. *The Metaphysical Novel in England and America: Dickens, Bulwer, Melville, and Hawthorne.* Los Angeles, CA: UP of California, 1978. Print.
Fitzgerald, F. Scott. *The Great Gatsby.* 1925. NY: Scribner, 1953. Print.
Foucault, Michel. "Nietzsche, Genealogy, History." *The Foucault Reader.* Ed. Paul Rabinow. NY: Pantheon Books, 1984. 76–100. Print.
Fox-Genovese, Elizabeth. "Literary Criticism and the Politics of the New Historicism," in *The New Historicism.* Ed. Harold Veeser. NY: Routledge, 1989. 213–225. Print.
Fraser, Nancy, and Axel Honneth. *Redistribution or Recognition?: A Political-Philosophical Exchange.* NY: Verso, 2003. Print.
Friedman, Thomas. *The Lexus and the Olive Tree: Understanding Globalization.* NY: Picador, 1999. Print.
Fukuyama, Francis. *The End of History and the Last Man.* NY: Free Press, 1992. Print.
Gallagher, Catherine. "Marxism and the New Historicism," in *The New Historicism.* Ed. Harold Veeser. NY: Routledge, 1989. 37–49. Print.
Gibson, James. *The Perfect War: Technowar in Vietnam.* NY: Atlantic Monthly Press, 1986. Print.
Gorbman, Claudia. "Kubrick's Music," in *Changing Times: The Use of Pre-Existing Music in Film.* Eds. Phil Powrie and Robynn Sitlwell. Farnham, UK: Ashgate Publishing, 2006. 4–18. Print.
The Green Mile. Dir. Frank Darabont. Screenplay by Frank Darabont. Castle Rock Entertainment, 1999. DVD.
Greenblatt, Stephen, and Catherine Gallagher. *Practicing New Historicism.* Chicago, IL: UP of Chicago, 1997. Print.
Haggerty, George. *Queer Gothic.* Champaign, IL: Illinois UP, 2006. 1–9. Print.
Harvey, David. *The Condition of Postmodernity: An Enquiry into the Origins of Cultural Change.* Malden, MA: Blackwell, 1990. Print.
Hawthorne, Nathaniel. *The House of the Seven Gables: Norton Critical Edition.* NY: W. W. Norton & Co., 2005. Print.
Hawthorne, Nathaniel. *Tales and Sketches.* 1835. NY: Viking Penguin, 1987. Print.
Heldreth, Leonard G. "Viewing *The Body*: King's Portrait of the Artist as Survivor," in *The Gothic World of Stephen King: Landscape of Nightmares.* Eds. Gary Hoppenstand and Ray Browne. Bowling Green, OH: Bowling Green State University Popular Press, 1987. 64–74. Print.
Hemingway, Ernest. *The Nick Adams Stories.* 1938. NY: Scribner, 1975. Print.
Hemingway, Ernest. *The Sun Also Rises.* 1926. NY: Scribner, 2006. Print.
Hoppenstand, Gary, with Ray B. Browne. "Introduction: The Horror of It All: Stephen King and the Landscape of the American Nightmare," in *The Gothic World of Stephen King: Landscape of Nightmares.* Eds. Gary Hoppenstand and Ray B. Browne. Bowling Green, OH: Bowling Green State University Popular Press, 1987. 1–19. Print.
Howard, Victor. "On the War." *Journal of American Culture.* 4 (1981): 54–57. Print.
Invasion of the Body Snatchers. Dir. Don Siegel. Republic Pictures, 1955. DVD.

IT Chapter Two. Dir. Andy Muschietti. Screenplay by Gary Dauberman. New Line Cinema, Vertigo Entertainment, 2019. DVD.

Jameson, Fredric. "Historicism in *The Shining.*" *Signatures of the Visible.* NY: Routledge, 1990. 89–98. Print.

Jay, Martin. *Downcast Eyes: The Denigration of Vision in Twentieth-Century French Thought.* Berkeley, CA: UP of California, 1994. Print.

Kaeuper, Richard. *Chivalry and Violence in Medieval Europe.* Oxford, UK: Oxford UP, 1999. Print.

Kaul, A.N. *The American Vision: Actual and Ideal Society in Nineenth-Century Fiction.* Oxford, UK: Oxford UP, 2002. Print.

Keesey, Douglas. "'The Face of Mr. Flip': Homophobia in the Horror of Stephen King," in *The Dark Descent: Essays Defining Stephen King's Horrorscape.* Ed. Tony Magistrale. NY: Greenwood Press, 1992. 187–201. Print.

King, Stephen. *Apt Pupil. Different Seasons.* NY: Simon & Schuster, 1982. 117–335. Print.

King, Stephen. "Author's Note." *Doctor Sleep.* NY: Scribner, 2013. 529–531. Print.

King, Stephen. *Bag of Bones.* NY: Scribner, 1998. Print.

King, Stephen. "Battleground." *Night Shift.* NY: New American Library, 1979. 117–126. Print.

King, Stephen. *The Body. Different Seasons.* NY: Viking, 1982. Print.

King, Stephen. "The Bogeyman." *Night Shift.* NY: New American Library, 1979. 93–104. Print.

King, Stephen. *Carrie.* NY: Doubleday, 1974. Print.

King, Stephen. *Cell.* NY: Simon & Schuster, 2006. Print.

King, Stephen. "Children of the Corn." *Night Shift.* NY: New American Library, 1979. 250–278. Print.

King, Stephen. *Christine.* NY: Viking, 1983.

King, Stephen. *Cujo.* NY: Simon & Schuster, 1981. Print.

King, Stephen. *Danse Macabre.* NY: Berkley, 1981. Print.

King, Stephen. *The Dark Half.* NY: Viking, 1989. Print.

King, Stephen. *The Dark Tower,* Vols. I–VII. Various Publishers, 1982–2004. Print.

King, Stephen. *Doctor Sleep.* NY: Scribner, 2013. Print.

King, Stephen. *Dolores Claiborne.* NY: Viking, 1993. Print.

King, Stephen. *Dreamcatcher.* NY: Charles Scribner's Sons, 2001.

King, Stephen. *Duma Key.* NY: Scribner, 2008. Print.

King, Stephen. *Elevation.* NY: Simon & Schuster, 2019. Print.

King, Stephen. *11/22/63.* NY: Simon & Schuster, 2012. Print.

King, Stephen. "1408." *Everything's Eventual.* NY: Simon & Schuster, 2002. 457–510. Print.

King, Stephen. *End of Watch.* NY: Simon & Schuster, 2016. Print.

King, Stephen. *The Eyes of the Dragon.* NY: New American Library, 1987. Print.

King, Stephen. *Finders Keepers.* NY: Simon & Schuster, 2015. Print.

King, Stephen. *Firestarter.* NY: Viking, 1980. Print.

King, Stephen. "Five to One, One in Five: UMO in the '60s." *Hearts in Suspension.* Orono, ME: Maine UP, 2016. 23–76. Print.

King, Stephen. *From a Buick 8.* NY: Scribner, 2002. Print.

King, Stephen. *Gerald's Game.* NY: Viking, 1992. Print.

King, Stephen. *The Girl Who Loved Tom Gordon.* NY: Scribner, 1999. Print.

King, Stephen. "A Good Marriage." *Full Dark, No Stars.* NY: Simon & Schuster, 2010. 281–364. Print.

King, Stephen. *The Green Mile*. NY: New American Library, 1996. Print.
King, Stephen. *Hearts in Atlantis*. NY: Scribner, 1999. Print.
King, Stephen. *Insomnia*. NY: Simon & Schuster, 1994. Print.
King, Stephen. *The Institute*. NY: Simon & Schuster, 2019. Print.
King, Stephen. *IT*. NY: Viking, 1986. Print.
King, Stephen. *Joyland*. NY: Simon & Schuster, 2013. Print.
King, Stephen. *The Langoliers*. *Four Past Midnight*. NY: Simon & Schuster, 1990. 1–297. Print.
King, Stephen. *Lisey's Story*. NY: Simon & Schuster, 2006. Print.
King, Stephen. *The Long Walk*. *The Bachman Books*. NY: New American Library, 1985. 171–434. Print.
King, Stephen. *Misery*. NY: Viking, 1987. Print.
King, Stephen. *The Mist*. *Skeleton Crew*. NY: New American Library, 1986. 24–154. Print.
King, Stephen. *Mr. Mercedes*. NY: Simon & Schuster, 2014. Print.
King, Stephen. *Needful Things*. NY: Viking, 1991. Print.
King, Stephen. *The Outsider*. NY: Simon & Schuster, 2018. Print.
King, Stephen. *Pet Sematary*. NY: Doubleday, 1983.
King, Stephen. *The Regulators*. NY: Simon & Schuster, 1996. Print.
King, Stephen. *Rita Hayworth and the Shawshank Redemption*. *Different Seasons*. NY: Viking, 1982. 1–102. Print.
King, Stephen. *Roadwork*. *The Bachman Books*. NY: New American Library, 1985. 435–708. Print.
King, Stephen. *Rose Madder*. NY: Viking, 1995. Print.
King, Stephen. *'Salem's Lot*. NY: Anchor, 1975. Print.
King, Stephen. *The Shining*. NY: Doubleday, 1977. Print.
King, Stephen. "Squad D," in *Shivers* VIII. Ed. Richard Chizmar. Baltimore, MD: Cemetery Dance Publications, 2019. 9–21. Print.
King, Stephen. *Storm of the Century*. NY: Simon & Schuster, 1999. Print.
King, Stephen. *The Stand*. NY: Doubleday, 1978; rev. and unexpurg. NY: Doubleday, 1990. Print.
King, Stephen, with Peter Straub. *The Talisman*. NY: Viking and G.P. Putnam & Sons, 1987. Print.
King, Stephen. *The Tommyknockers*. NY: G.P. Putnam & Sons, 1987. Print.
King, Stephen. *Under the Dome*. NY: Simon & Schuster, 2009. Print.
Kipling, Rudyard. *Epitaphs of the War*. The Poetry Foundation. https://www.poetryfoundation.org/poems/57409/epitaphs-of-the-war. Web. 11 August 2019.
Kristeva, Julia. *The Powers of Horror: An Essay in Abjection*. Trans. Leon S. Roudiez. NY: Columbia UP, 1982. Print.
Lauterwasser, David B. "The Red on Yellow: Chiquita's Banana Colonialism in Latin America." medium.com, 4 Sept. 2017. https://medium.com/@FeunFooPermaKra/the-red-on-yellow-chiquitas-banana-colonialism-in-latin-america-1ca178af7616. Web. 25 Sept. 2019.
Longfellow, Henry Wadsworth. "The Fire of Drift-Wood," in *Nineteenth-Century American Poetry*. Ed. William Spengemann. NY: Penguin, 1996. 59–60. Print.
Longfellow, Henry Wadsworth. "Sand of the Desert in an Hour-Glass," in *Nineteenth-Century American Poetry*. Ed. William Spengemann. NY: Penguin, 1996. 57–59. Print.
Magistrale, Tony. *Hollywood's Stephen King*. NY: Palgrave, 2003. Print.

Magistrale, Tony. *Landscape of Fear: Stephen King's American Gothic*. Bowling Green, OH: Bowling Green State University Popular Press, 1988. Print.
Magistrale, Tony. *Stephen King: The Second Decade*. NY: Twayne, 1992. Print.
Mahoney, Dennis. "*Apt Pupil*: The Making of a 'Bogeyboy'," in *The Films of Stephen King: From Carrie to The Mist*. Ed. Tony Magistrale. NY: Palgrave, 2008. 27–41. Print.
Malkin, Marc. "*IT: Chapter Two*: Bill Hader on Richie's Sexuality, His On-Set Injury and Cast B12 Shots." *Variety*, 12 Sept.2019. https://variety.com/2019/film/podcasts/bill-hader-it-chapter-two-richie-sexuality-1203333073/. Web. 19 Oct. 2019.
Marazzi, Christian. *The Violence of Financial Capitalism*. Trans. Kristinia Lebedeva and Jason Francis McGimsey. Los Angeles, CA: Semiotext[e], 2011. Print.
Marx, Leo. *The Machine in the Garden: Technology and the Pastoral Ideal in America*. Oxford, UK: Oxford UP, 1964. Print.
Mathews, Jessica. "America's Indefensible Defense Budget." *New York Review of Books*. 18 July2019: 23–24. Print.
McAleer, Patrick. "The Fallen King(dom): Surviving Ruin and Decay from The Stand to Cell," in *Stephen King's Modern Macabre: Essays on the Later Works*. Eds. Patrick McAleer and Michael A. Perry. Jefferson, NC: McFarland & Company, 2014. 168–184. Print.
Melville, Herman. *The Confidence-Man*. 1857. Oxford, UK: Oxford UP, 2009. Print.
Melville, Herman. *Moby-Dick*. 1851. London, UK: Wordsworth Classics, 1993. Print.
Merton, Thomas. *Faith and Violence: Christian Teaching and Christian Practice*. Notre Dame, IN: Notre Dame UP, 1968. Print.
Miller, Sam J. "Assimilation and the Queer Monster," in *Horror After 9/11: World of Fear, Cinema of Terror*. Eds. Aviva Briefel and Sam J. Miller. Austin, TX: Texas UP, 2011. 220–233. Print.
Nealon, Jeffrey. *Post-Postmodernism: Or, The Cultural Logic of Just-In-Time Capitalism*. Redwood City, CA: Stanford UP, 2012. Print.
Nelson, Thomas Allen. *Kubrick: Inside a Film Artist's Maze*. Bloomington, IN: Indiana UP, 2000. Print.
Nguyen, Viet Thanh. *Nothing Ever Dies: Vietnam and the Memory of War*. Cambridge, MA: Harvard UP, 2016. Print.
Night of the Living Dead. Dir. George Romero. Screenplay by George Romero. Image Ten and Laurel, 1968. DVD.
The Night Porter. Dir. Liliana Cavani. Screenplay by Liliana Cavani and Italo Moscati. Joseph E. Levine Productions, Ital-Noleggio, 1974. DVD.
Norris, Christopher. *Uncritical Theory: Postmodernism, Intellectuals and the Gulf War*. Amherst, MA: UP of Massachusetts, 1992. Print.
Oakeshott, Michael. "Present, Future and Past," in *On History and Other Essays*. Totowa, NJ: Barnes and Noble Books, 1983. 1–45. Print.
Pacolet, Joeri. *Transcendent Writers in Stephen King's Fiction: A Post-Jungian Analysis of the Puer Aeternus*. NY and London: Routledge, 2019. Print.
Pet Sematary. Dir. Mary Lambert. Screenplay by Stephen King. Paramount Pictures, 1990. DVD.
Pet Sematary. Dir. Kevin Kölsch and Dennis Widmyer. Screenplay by Matt Greenberg and Jeff Buhler. Paramount Pictures, 2019. DVD.
Pharr, Mary. "A Dream of New Life: Stephen King's Pet Sematary as a Variant of Frankenstein," in *The Gothic World of Stephen King: Landscape of Nightmares*. Eds.

Gary Hoppenstand and Ray B. Browne. Bowling Green, OH: Bowling Green State University Popular Press, 1987. 115–125. Print.

Picart, Caroline Joan S., and David A. Frank. *Frames of Evil: The Holocaust as Horror in American Film*. Carbondale, IL: Southern Illinois UP, 2006. Print.

Poe, Edgar Allan. "The Masque of the Red Death," in *Poe: Poetry, Tales, and Selected Essays*, 1842. NY: Library of America, 1984. 1996. 485–490. Print.

Poe, Edgar Allan. "The Murders in the Rue Morgue," in *Poe: Poetry, Tales, and Selected Essays*, 1841. NY: Library of America, 1984. 1996. 397–431. Print.

Poe, Edgar Allan. "The Purloined Letter," in *Poe: Poetry, Tales, and Selected Essays*, 1844. NY: Library of America, 1984. 1996. 680–698. Print.

Pollack, William. *Real Boys: Rescuing Our Sons from the Myths of Boyhood*. NY: Holt and Company, 1998. Print.

Popper, Karl. *The Open Society and Its Enemies*. Princeton, NJ: Princeton UP, 1966. Print.

Reesman, Jeanne Campbell. "Riddle Game: Stephen King's Metafictive Dialogue," in *The Dark Descent: Essays Defining Stephen King's Horrorscape*. Ed. Tony Magistrale. Westport, CT: Greenwood Press, 1992. 156–170. Print.

Reino, Joseph. *Stephen King: The First Decade*. NY: Twayne, 1988. Print.

Remarque, Erich Maria. *All Quiet on the Western Front*. 1928. Trans. A.W. Wheen. NY: Fawcett Books, 1958. Print.

Riceour, Paul. *History and Truth*. Trans. Charles Kelby. Evanston, IL: Northwestern UP, 1965. Print.

Richard, Carl. *The Battle for the American Mind: A Brief History of a Nation's Thought*. NY: Rowman & Littlefield, 2004. Print.

Rodgers, Daniel. *Age of Fracture*. Cambridge, MA: Belknap Press, 2012. Print.

Sears, John. *Stephen King's Gothic*. Cardiff, UK: Wales UP, 2011. Print.

Sedgwick, Eve Kosofsky. *Between Men: English Literature and Male Homosocial Desire*. NY: Columbia UP, 1985. Print.

Serinus, Jason Victor. "The Legacy of the Gay Liberation Front." *Bay Area Reporter*, 6 June2009. http://www.ebar.com/pride/article.php?see=pride&article=95. Web. 22 Aug. 2019.

The Shawshank Redemption. Dir. Frank Darabont. Screenplay by Frank Darabont. Castle Rock Entertainment, 1994. DVD.

Shay, Jonathan. *Achilles in Vietnam: Combat Trauma and the Undoing of Character*. NY: Scribner, 1994. Print.

Shirer, William L. *The Rise and Fall of the Third Reich*. NY: Simon & Schuster, 1960. Print.

Slotkin, Richard. "Nostalgia and Progress: Theodore Roosevelt's Myth of the Frontier." *American Quarterly*. 33 (Winter1981): 608–637. Print.

Smith, Andrew, and William Hughes. "Introduction: Queering the Gothic," in *Queering the Gothic*. Eds. Andrew Smith and William Hughes. Manchester, UK: Manchester UP, 2009. 1–10. Print.

Sontag, Susan. *Illness as Metaphor*. NY: Vintage, 1978. Print.

Sperb, Jason. *The Kubrick Façade: Faces and Voices in the Films of Stanley Kubrick*. Lanham, MD: Scarecrow Press, 2006. Print.

Stand by Me. Dir. Rob Reiner. Screenplay by Raymond Gideon and Bruce E. Evans. Columbia Pictures, 1986. DVD.

Standing, Guy. *The Precariat: The New Dangerous Class*. NY: Bloomsbury, 2011. Print.

Stephen King's The Shining. Dir. Mick Garris. Teleplay by Stephen King. Warner Brothers Television/ABC-TV, 1997. DVD.

Stevenson, Robert Louis. *The Strange Case of Dr. Jekyll and Mr. Hyde.* 1886. Ed. Martin A. Danahay. Ontario, Canada: Broadview Press, 1985. Print.

Stoker, Bram. *Dracula.* 1897. NY: Norton, 1997. Print.

Strand, Ginger. *Killer on the Road: Violence and the American Interstate.* Austin, TX: Texas UP, 2012. Print.

Strengell, Heidi. *Dissecting Stephen King: From the Gothic to Literary Naturalism.* Madison, WI: Popular Press, 2005. Print.

Strengell, Heidi. *Stephen King: Monsters Live in Ordinary People.* London, UK: Duckworth, 2007. Print.

Thinner. Dir. Tom Holland. Screenplay by Michael McDowell and Tom Holland. Spelling Films, Paramount Pictures, 1996. DVD.

Thoreau, Henry David. "Walden." *The Works of Thoreau.* 1854. Ed. Henry S. Canby. Boston, MA: Houghton Mifflin Company, 1937. Print.

Turner, Fred. *Echoes of Combat: The Vietnam War in American Memory.* NY: Doubleday, 1996. Print.

Twain, Mark. *The Adventures of Huckleberry Finn.* 1877. NY: Penguin, 2003. Print.

28 Days Later. Dir. Danny Boyle. Screenplay by Alex Garland. Twentieth Century Fox, 2002. DVD.

2001: A Space Odyssey. Dir. Stanley Kubrick. Screenplay by Stanley Kubrick and Arthur C. Clark. Metro-Goldwyn-Mayer, 1968. DVD.

Underwood, Tim, and Chuck Miller, Eds. *Bare Bones: Conversations on Terror with Stephen King.* NY: McGraw-Hill, 1988. Print.

Unearthed and Untold: The Path to Pet Sematary. Dir. John Campopiano and Justin White. Screenplay by John Campopiano and Justin White. Ocean's Light, 2017. DVD.

Webster, Patrick. *Love and Death in Kubrick: A Critical Study of the Films from Lolita to Eyes Wide Shut.* Jefferson, NC: McFarland, 2011. Print.

Weinstock, Jeffrey A. "Maybe It Shouldn't be a Party: Kids, Keds, and Death in King's *Stand by Me* and *Pet Sematary*," in *The Films of Stephen King: From Carrie to The Mist.* Ed. Tony Magistrale. NY: Palgrave Macmillan, 2012. 41–51. Print.

Wetmore, Kevin J. *Post-9/11 Horror in American Cinema.* NY: Continuum, 2012. Print.

White, Hayden. *Figural Realism: Studies in the Mimesis Effect.* Baltimore, MD: Johns Hopkins UP, 1999. Print.

Whitman, Walt. "Drum-Taps." 1865. *The Complete Poems.* NY: Penguin Classics. 1975. 1996.

Whittington, Paul. *The Shining Explored.* Self-published MS. 2015. Print.

Zapf, Hubert. "Literature as Cultural Ecology: The Example of Herman Melville's *Moby-Dick*," in *Living by the Golden Rule: A Festschrift for Wolfgang Mieder's 75th Birthday.* Eds. Andreas Nolte and Dennis F. Mahoney. NY: Peter Lang, 2019. 201–208. Print.

Žižek, Slavoj. *Event: A Philosophical Journey Through a Concept.* NY: Penguin, 2014. Print.

Žižek, Slavoj. *Violence.* NY: Picador, 2008. Print.

Index

Alien 100
All Quiet on the Western Front 53
American History 1–4, 38, 69, 71, 109, 112, 115–18, 121–22, 134, 152, 156–7; and American wars 40; in *IT* 31–4; nineteenth-century 6–7; in *Pet Sematary* 6, 38, 40–3; September 11, 2001 9; in *The Shining* 2, 7, 56–87; small town 1; and Vietnam 2, 8, 89–109; warfare in 1, 40, 43, 48, 50, 59–62, 73, 92–3, 98–100, 102, 106; *see Hearts in Atlantis, Dreamcatcher*
American imperialism 58n10, 99, 103, 105, 109n6
American Romanticism 4–7, 11–14, 22–3, 28–30
Anderson, Perry 54
Apocalypse Now 109n3
Apt Pupil 6, 62, 111–19, 122–3, 128–30, 131n1,155; homosexuality in 110–11, 113, 115, 117, 128–31
audience, King's 35
automobiles 47

Bachman, Richard 22, 35, 109n6, 127, 127, 144, 148–9, 150
Barthes, Roland 67, 7
Bartók, Béla 76–9
"Battleground" 91
Benjamin, Walter 49
Berardi, Franco 158n3
Biddle, Arthur W. 12
Blackmore, Bill 65
Blake, Linnie 47
Blouin, Michael 58n7
"The Boogeyman" 91
Bright, Susie 125
Brooke, Rupert 43
Brown, Simon 10n5, 35n2, 89, 159

Brown, Wendy 5, 9n2, 135
Browne, Ray 58n6
Browning, Mark 12
Bryant, William Cullen 35
Buell, Lawrence 24, 35n7, 160

Callinicos, Alex 72
Campbell, Joseph 12
cancer 39, 105, 106, 109n6, 149
capitalism 7, 11, 44, 54–5, 80–1, 84–7, 133, 155, 164
Castle Rock 15, 17, 19, 21–2, 132
Cat People 100
Cell 6, 8, 27, 137, 140, 142, 144–5, 150, 155
Chiquita Brand Fruit Company 58n10
Ciment, Michael 79, 87n3
Clark, J.M. 132n6
A Clockwork Orange 77
Cocks, Geoffrey 63
Collings, Michael 126
The Confidence Man 22
Crain, Caleb 89

The Dark Tower 1–2, 79, 111
Darwin, Charles 135
The Dead Zone 6, 20–1, 89
DeLamar, John 123
Derry 27, 29–33, 120, 122
detective fiction 9, 112, 133–4, 142–7
Dickinson, Mary Jane 35
Doctor Sleep 68, 76, 121–3, 127
Dolores Claiborne 125, 132n7, 144
Dracula 57n1
Dreamcatcher 24, 60, 89, 99–107, 152, 157
Dr. Strangelove or: How I learned to Stop Worrying and Love the Bomb 100

Dryden, Edgar 23, 33
Duma Key 35n8

Eagleton, Terry 74
Edelman, Lee 118, 122, 126–9, 152
Eigner, Edwin 23
Einstein, Albert 79
Elevation 132n8
11/22/63 1–2, 5–6, 140–3, 152
evil: defined in King's fiction and films, 27, 45–6
Eyes of the Dragon 132n9

Faulkner, William 35n6
Firestarter 109n2, 152
"Five to One, One in Five: UMO in the 60s" 90–1
Foucault, Michel 134, 136
"1408" 35
Fox-Genovese, Elizabeth 4
Frank, David 118, 132n6
Frankenstein 54, 58n6, 71; see *Pet Sematary*
Fraser, Nancy 158n2
Friedman, Thomas 48, 58n8
Fukuyama, Francis 9n1

Gacy, John Wayne 120
Gallagher, Catherine 2, 4
Gerald's Game 11, 123, 125, 132n7
Gibson, James 100, 109n4
The Girl Who Loved Tom Gordon 14–15
A Good Marriage 125
Gorbman, Claudia 77
Gothic: architecture 77; elements and tropes 7, 12, 27, 45, 53, 57, 84, 106, 110, 121, 127, 133, 144, 148
The Great Gatsby 18; compared to *The Shining* 82–3, 86–7
Greenblatt, Stephen 2–3
The Green Mile 109n6, 111; homosexuality in 123–4
"group think" 21, 26–7, 32, 109, 122, 138, 155

Haggerty, George 110
Hawthorne, Nathaniel 14, 26
Heart of Darkness 109n3
Hearts in Atlantis 6, 60, 89, 92–9, 133, 152, 157
Heldreth, Leonard 12
Hemingway, Ernest 14, 93–4, 109n3

hero/ines: in King's fiction and film 21–2, 27–8, 68, 103, 109, 127, 132, 139, 144, 152–3
heterosexuality 8, 110, 119–20, 121–3, 125–31, 132n7; see *Apt Pupil*
homophobia 11, 117, 119, 132n8; see *Apt Pupil; IT; The Green Mile*
homosexuality 8, 110–1, 113, 115, 117–18, 119–131, 132n7, 132n8; see *Apt Pupil; IT; The Green Mile*
Honneth, Axel 158n2
Hoppenstand, Gary 58n6
Hughes, William 110

The Institute 9, 151–7
Invasion of the Body Snatchers 100
Irigary, Luce 115
IT 6, 13, 22–34, 35n6, 45–6, 79, 94, 111, 123, 153; compared to *Moby-Dick* 22–34; homosexuality in 119–24, 127–8
IT: Chapter Two 128, 132

Jameson, Fredric 74, 80–1, 85
Jay, Martin 130

Kaeuper, Ricchard 58n4
Kaul, A.N. 25
Keesey, Douglas 123
Kipling, Rudyard 98
Kojève, Alexandre 40
Kristeva, Julia 120

"The Langoliers" 147n1
Lisey's Story 6, 126, 141–4
Longfellow, Henry Wadsworth 35n3
Lyotard, Jean-Francois 71, 74

McAleer, Patrick 137
McNamara, Robert 101
Magistrale, Tony 12, 57n1, 91, 136
Mahoney, Dennis 117, 131n1
male-bonding 121
Malkin, Mark 132n10
Marazzi, Christian 49
Marx, Leo 5, 16–7
Mathews, Jessica 98
Merton, Thomas 9n3
military, U.S. 67, 89–90, 98, 104
Miller, Chuck 92, 122, 124, 149
Miller, Sam 125
Misery 36n8
The Mist 12, 27, 133, 153
Moby-Dick 6, 13, 23–34, 35n5; see *IT*

Monnet, Agnieszka Soltysik 47
monsters 8, 30, 35, 64, 110–1, 120, 124–5, 130
Mr. Mercedes 6, 8, 145–6
Mulvey, Laura 115

Native Americans: see *Pet Sematary*, *The Shining*
Nazism 63, 74, 111–18, 127, 131, 152; see *Apt Pupil*
Nealon, Jeffrey 73
Needful Things 27, 138, 144–5, 153, 155
Nelson, Thomas Allen 77
New Historicism 2–5, 61–2, 70, 74, 87n1, 112, 134–5, 151, 161; post-Historicism 40, 48
Nguyen, Thanh Viet 92, 98
Night of the Living Dead 138
The Night Porter 116
Norris, Christopher 87n2

Oakeshott, Michael 134

Pacolet, Joeri 12
pastoralism 12–18, 29–30, 34–5, 44, 52, 149–50, 164
Pet Sematary 5–7, 37–58, 99, 131n2–3, 143, 155; borders and barriers in 46, 56–8; the cemeteries 51–4; *Frankenstein* influence on 44, 46, 54; and Native Americans 37–9, 43, 45, 51; oil and oil companies in 39, 41, 50–2, 57n1; and *The Shining* 59, 64, 71, 74; toxic masculinity in 43–4, 48; wars, American 37–49, 50–5, 58n4; Wendigo mythology in 38, 52, 54; women in 43–4, 48, 58
Pharr, Mary 58n6
Picart, Joan 117–18, 132n6
Playboy interview (King's) 121, 124
Poe, Edgar Allan 70, 133–4
Pollack, William
pollution: moral and environmental 39, 51–2, 57n1; see *Pet Sematary*
Popper, Karl 46, 61, 135
postmodernism 74, 87, 160–1, 164

Reagan, Ronald 20, 40, 65, 85–6, 156
Reesman, Jeanne Campbell 35n6
reproductive futurism 3, 118–19, 121–2, 128–9, 131, 152, 154
Richard, Carl 108
Ricoeur, Paul 1–2

Rodgers, Carl 141
Roosevelt, Teddy 41–2, 55, 59, 165

'Salem's Lot 12, 138
Sears, John 23
Sedgwick, Eve Kosofsky 119
September 11, 2001: 9, 103, 130, 136–7, 140–1, 147n3, 153
Serinus, Jason Victor 126
sexuality: in King's fiction, 121–4
The Shawshank Redemption 6, 111, 121; homosexuality in 123–4
Shay, Jonathan 100–2
The Shining (King's novel): 2, 5–7, 59–87, 99, 111, 121–2, 131, 155; and homosexuality 121; and Native Americans 59–65; and Nazism 63, 74; New Historicism 65–70, 74; and postmodernism 61; and World War II 61, 71–4
The Shining (Kubrick's film): 7, 6, 74–87; Bartók's music in 76–9; compared to *The Great Gatsby* 82–3, 86–7; Hallorann's death in 65–6; Modernism in 76–80; Native American genocide 63–5; time frames in 69–87; and the Twenties 71, 75, 77–87
Shirer, William 131n4
Slotkin, Richard 41
Smith, Andrew 110
Sontag, Susan 109n6
Sperb, Jason 83
"Squad D" 92
The Stand 6, 109n1, 111, 123–6, 128, 133, 138, 144, 149
Stand by Me 6, 12, 14–22, 35n4; and machines 16–17, 22; and *Walden* 13–9, 22
Standing, Guy 158n1
Storm of the Century 12, 27, 138, 144–5
The Strange Case of Dr. Jekyll and Mr. Hyde 113
Strengell, Heidi 34n1, 46

The Talisman 12, 111, 123
Thinner 35n5, 122
The Tommyknockers 2–4, 23, 27, 46, 138, 152
toxic masculinity 19, 43–4, 48, 84, 131, 133
Trump, Donald 124
Turner, Fred 109n5
Twain, Mark 14

Under the Dome 6, 109n1, 136–7
Underwood, Tim 92, 122, 124, 149
Unearthed and Untold: The Path to Pet Sematary 53

Vietnam vii, 3, 7–8, 39–42, 61, 87, 89, 90–109, 150, 152, 154, 157, 161, 164–5; anti-war movement 8, 95–6, 109n7; Students for a Democratic Society (SDS) 90, 92; *see also* *Dreamcatcher; Hearts in Atlantis*

Walden 6, 13, 15–7, 20, 22
Webster, Patrick 87n4
Weinstock, Jeffrey A. 13
Wetmore, Kevin 139
White, Hayden 69
Whitman, Walt 35n6, 60, 166
Whittington, Paul 65
Williams, William Carlos 35n6

Yeats, William Butler 43, 62, 64, 149

Zapf, Hubert 30
Žižek, Slavoj 5, 9n4–10, 139, 147n2